About the author

Akhtar Badshah trained as an architect at the Centre for Environmental Planning and Technology, Ahmedabad, India. He subsequently did his doctorate in Architecture, Art and Environmental Studies at the Massachusetts Institute of Technology. After lecturing at MIT and the Roger Williams University for several years, he started his own consultancy firm in 1992, doing work for, *inter alia*, UNDP's Regional Bureau for Asia and the Pacific and UNESCAP, the United Nations Economic and Social Commission for Asia and the Pacific. His research has concentrated on a wide range of urban issues, particularly in Asia, including urban management strategies, the role of design for housing in the South, and how to transfer and adapt urban innovations from one city to another. Over the years, he has contributed to a number of publications and scholarly journals. He is currently Director of Programmes at the Mega-Cities Project, based in New York City.

This is a fascinating study. Illuminating for those interested in new attitudes to public sponsored housing. South and South East Asia are leading the world in experimenting with innovative approaches to housing. The author has handled the complexities of a difficult subject in a clear and straightforward way which should appeal to a wide readership.

Ronald Lewcock, Professor of Architecture, Georgia Tech

A remarkable work. It does not conclude with the conventional call for new approaches to the problems created by rapid urbanization, but tells us what those new approaches should be. It is based on the real-life experiences of an author with a keen eye for what works in communities and a wonderful talent for telling us about it.

Richard A. Ludwig AICP, University of Washington, Seattle

An outstanding contribution to the literature on people-centred urban development. Through his detailed case studies of local initiatives, he has demonstrated the need to empower people to find solutions to their own problems and to create an enabling environment which promotes their initiatives ... This book will be highly valuable for urban development planners and practitioners in developing countries, programme management staff of bilateral donors and multilateral agencies, and students and faculty members interested in urban development in developing countries.

Dr Shabbir Cheema, Acting Director, Management Development and Governance Division, UNDP

OUR URBAN FUTURE

New Paradigms for Equity and Sustainability

AKHTAR A. BADSHAH

Zed Books Ltd
LONDON & NEW JERSEY

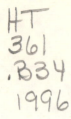

Our Urban Future: New Paradigms for Equity and Sustainability
was first published in 1996

South Asia
Oxford University Press, 5-Bangalore Town, Sharae Faisal,
PO Box 13033, Karachi-75350

Rest of the World
Zed Books Ltd, 7 Cynthia Street, London N1 9JF, UK, and
165 First Avenue, Atlantic Highlands, New Jersey 07716,
USA

Cover designed by Andrew Corbett
Set in Monotype Garamond by Ewan Smith
Printed and bound in the United Kingdom
by Biddles Ltd, Guildford and King's Lynn

A catalogue record for this book is available from the
British Library

US CIP data is available from the Library of Congress

ISBN 1 85649 405 5 hb
ISBN 1 85649 406 3 pb
South Asia ISBN 0 19577688 7

Contents

Preface   ix

1 The Challenges of a Changing Urban World   1

Global urbanization trends /1   The challenges of
urban growth /2   Obstacles to urban transformation /5
Conventional approaches to managing urban growth /6
Approaches to developing urban settlements /7
Conventional housing approaches – have they worked? /9
Self-help in squatter settlements – does it work? /11
Site-and-services /12   Problems with self-help and site-
and-services /13   Present policies and programmes for
housing and urban services /14   Towards an equitable
and sustainable urban future /15

2 Responding to Changing Needs   18

A new vision for sustainable and equitable
development /19   Equality and human development/ 20
The marginal, the silent, the forgotten /22
Decentralization and partnership programmes /26
The role of local institutions in urban development
programmes /27   The advantages and risks of private
sector involvement /28   Opportunities and constraints
of community involvement /30   Maximizing choices /34
Changing family life-styles /35   Implications for new
development programmes /38

3 NGO and Community Partnerships for Integrated
Area Development   40

Development of *katchi abadis* in Karachi /41
The Orangi Pilot Project (OPP) /41   The Orangi Pilot
Project's development and history /43   The Orangi Pilot
Project's Low-cost Sanitation Programme /43
Health and family planning programme for low-income

housewives /48   Programmes for women's employment /50
The Orangi Pilot Project's housing programme /51
The solution /53   Elements of success /59
Perceived problems /60   Potential for transfer
and adaptation /61   Lessons learned /62

4   Multi-Sectoral Partnerships for Environmental
    Micro-Enterprise Development   65

History of solid waste management in Cairo /66
The problem /67   The solution: the Zabbaleen
Environmental and Development Project /68
Programme components /70   Elements of project
success /77   Perceived problems /80   Potential for
transfer and adaptation /84   Lessons learned /84

5   Local Government and Private Sector Partnerships
    for Land-Sharing and Incremental Development   87

Land-sharing /88   Citra Niaga Urban Development
Project /91   The project /93   Lessons from Citra
Niaga /96   Potential for transfer and adaptation /98
Incremental development /99   Khuda-ki-basti
Incremental Development Scheme /100   Conditions
in Khuda-ki-Basti /104   Potential for transfer and
adaptation /107   Future directions for incremental
development schemes /109   Lessons from Citra Niaga
and Khuda-ki-basti /110

6   Local Government and Private Sector Partnerships
    for Low-Cost Housing Design   112

Project history /112   Project financing /113
Site context /114   Planning and design /114
The planning and design process /122
Project analyses /129   Potential for transfer
and adaptation /136   Lessons learned /137

7   A New Agenda for Urban Equity and Sustainability   140

Reducing inequity /141   Principles for equitable and
sustainable developments /142   Urban development
through consensus /142   Conditions for private sector

involvement /145   The role of intermediaries /150
Increasing community accountability and decision-making
responsibilities /153   Introducing external and internal
components to urban development programmes /156
Optimizing the range of choice available to the
community /159   An equitable allocation system /161
Supporting egalitarian housing developments /163
Integrating site design for urban development /165
Conclusion /167

8   Our Urban Future: Opportunities and Challenges   169

The importance of international cooperation /170
Sharing approaches that work /171   A catalyst for
change /172   The transfer of urban innovations and
lessons learned /173   Increasing local control /176
Training urban professionals /177   Improving interagency
and inter-city cooperation /178   Improving local
dialogue /179   Can reducing inequity and increasing
choice lead to sustainable and equitable environments? /179
Problems that arise with private sector, community and
NGO involvement /180   A new vision for equity and
sustainability /181

Notes   184

Bibliography   199

Index   214

To Alka, Anish, Aseem and Akash

Preface

This book is an attempt to outline a vision that sees development nurtured by empowering the people so that they can create their own identities and their own institutions. This vision is people-centred, gender-conscious and seeks equity for all. It is based on my experience that people and communities all over the world struggle against civic decay and constantly develop new ways of solving their urban problems. Amidst all of the gloom that one sees in cities there are also rays of hope, most visibly through an outpouring of promising new community development programmes. Underlying the majority of these programmes is the conviction that no amount of government or private money will make much of a difference unless the people who now live in squatter settlements and other blighted areas take the lead in improving the living conditions in their settlements. A few examples of community, NGO, government and private enterprise partnership approaches show that these initiatives are not singular: their success lies in their comprehensive and inclusive approach. If these solutions are supported and multiplied then there is the potential to have equity and sustainability in our urban neighbourhoods.

The book began as a journey that I embarked on several years ago, as a student and lecturer at the Massachusetts Institute of Technology, and has come to fruition in my work as the Director of Programs at the Mega-Cities Project. I learned during this exploration, talking to residents, community leaders and local organizations, that a vast resource of human vitality and creativity exists that is largely untapped. I also observed how, with a little help, civic life regenerates itself and the community is revitalized. However, the conventional solutions that most urbanists develop are missing two vital elements: creativity and energy. This is because the most prevalent approach taken to address the local concerns is a 'problem-solving' approach. This approach has its limitations, because by the time the problem is identified, the causes analysed, the plan of action formulated and implemented, the original problem is often no longer the problem, and the community needs have often changed.

New models have begun to emerge particularly in the organizational development field that can allow us to re-evaluate the 'problem-solving' approach with an 'appreciative inquiry' approach. Appreciative inquiry focuses on building capacity, valuing the strongest features of the community under consideration, envisioning what 'might be', discussing what 'should be' and achieving innovative solutions.

I have evaluated five programmes and projects which I believe come close to following the 'appreciative inquiry' approach rather than 'problem-solving' approach. Using them as examples I have identified nine factors and conditions that encourage the development of sustainable and equitable urban communities.

The book is divided into three parts. The first part, written in two chapters, is introductory and context setting. In the first chapter, I describe some of the major challenges facing our changing urban world and show the shifts that have taken place in the development paradigm. I also highlight some of the important urban policies that have evolved over the recent decades that have combined the role of government agencies, private sector investment and community involvement. Projects undertaken in developing countries are often supported by international development agencies seeking to promote cooperative ventures through pilot or demonstration projects. I suggest that it is time to move on and to incorporate the lessons learned from these demonstrations into full-scale local and national urban-management strategies.

Developing criteria for sustainable and equitable housing and urban services is the focus of the second chapter. Here I argue for the need to reduce inequity in housing and urban services planning and implementation. To do this, two interrelated approaches are suggested: to increase choices that the community is given and create conditions that promote community decision-making; and to optimize the role played by government agencies, private sector organizations, community groups, non-government agencies and other local groups.

The second part of the book consists of five detailed case-studies: the Orangi Pilot Project in Karachi, Pakistan; the Zabbaleen Environmental and Development Project in Cairo, Egypt; the Citra Niaga Land-Sharing Project in Samarinda, Indonesia; the Khuda-ki-basti Incremental Development Scheme in Hyderabad, Pakistan; and the Aranya Township Site-and-Services Project in Indore, India. Each project is evaluated to determine the process by which the programme was planned and implemented, and to identify the driving ideas, the kinds of decisions taken, the roles played by the various participating groups, the problems encountered and the lessons learned. The role of non-government organizations and community organizations in settlement upgrading programmes is also evaluated, considering the advantages and risks of private sector involvement and the potential role of community groups, non-government organizations, private developers, government agencies and housing finance institutions in urban development projects.

The third part concludes in two chapters with recommendations that urban development services programmes have a better chance of becoming sustainable and equitable if they are developed through the following: consensus rather than confrontation; encouraging and promoting private sector involvement under conditions that are clearly understood and instituted; and when NGOs and other intermediary organizations play a vital role in community empowerment and management. The study also concludes that community accountability and decision-making must be increased, local management promoted and programme components in which the community has a larger implementing role introduced. Similarly, the role of small-scale building contractors must be enhanced and the needs of the broadened client groups understood and reflected in planning and design. Finally, site design for urban developments has to be integrated into the larger community and to respect the needs of its immediate surroundings. In the last chapter, I discuss the importance of sharing successful approaches and the steps needed to accelerate the process of sharing the lessons learned.

Many of the suggestions and proposals offered here are not broad strategies, but suggestions for feasible ways of improving society's chances of solving its urban development problems. They are not blueprints, but simply ideas for generating new approaches that will deal more adequately with the immediate and increasingly severe housing shortages, and they recommend actions for preventing difficulties that may otherwise arise in the future. Finally, the recommendations in this study are strategic, not project-oriented. In their implementation the locus of responsibility rests with the cities themselves.

My critique and evaluations are largely intuitive convictions based on personal experience corroborated by my field research – sometimes modified, sometimes qualified, and always supplemented by friends and colleagues whom I have encountered along the way in academia and in practice. I am indebted to all these people who, in different ways, have shaped my career thus far.

I would particularly like to acknowledge Ronald Lewcock for his encouragement, support, ideas and guidance over the last ten years of my work. He has been my mentor, tutor and guide and has taught me to view people and the environment with humility, care and with an eye toward genuine discovery. My gratitude is extended to William Porter, for his valuable guidance and encouragement and for helping me appreciate what was new or different about what I was saying. Thanks go to Bishwapriya Sanyal for his invaluable comments, for expanding my vision and for providing constructive criticism.

I am also grateful to Janice Perlman, who has been championing the cause of identifying successful approaches that work, and transferring and adapting them in other cities and contexts. Her work, and my association with her over the last two years, have shaped my thoughts and the direction of my research.

The financial support of the Aga Khan Programme for Islamic Architecture, which enabled me to undertake most of the travel for this research, is greatly appreciated, as is the friendship of numerous colleagues and students with whom I worked at the Massachusetts Institute of Technology and the help given by colleagues at the Mega-Cities Project. No study is complete without valuable assistance from those whose task it is to make sense of random thoughts and sentences that make up the text. Margaret Sevcenko undertook this task with her usual enthusiastic dedication and with much sacrifice of her free time to meet my deadlines; I am extremely grateful for this much-needed help.

Finally, and most importantly, my special gratitude to my wife Alka. Her strong support for my work is evidenced by her ability to cope with my endless absences, carrying the load of raising our three sons, and continuing her own professional career at the same time. Her patience and steadfastness have provided me with the personal reinforcement needed to complete this work. I dedicate this book to her and to my three sons, Anish, Aseem and Akash.

CHAPTER I

The Challenges of a Changing Urban World

Cities are a testimonial to human civilization and a well spring of opportunities. The city will also be the place where compelling social issues such as poverty, homelessness, crime and unemployment will take on a dimension far bigger and more complex than ever seen before; where most of the world's population will live and work; where most of the economic activity will take place; where the most pollution will be generated; and where the most natural resources will be consumed. Sustainable development will thus be the most pressing challenge facing humanity in the twenty-first century.[1]

The rapid increase in the number and seriousness of environmental problems threatens all societies. Exploding population, the depletion of energy sources and the wanton destruction of nature in the name of development are posing real and present threats to the globe and have already taken a severe toll on our cities. In particular, the migration of rural populations into already overcrowded cities is putting immense pressure on the urban infrastructure and resulting in uncontrolled growth. The relationship between man, culture, environment and technology is extremely complex, but it none the less needs to be addressed when one sets out to discuss future policies.

Urban planning in developing countries must assume that population growth will continue for the foreseeable future. Instead of rejecting or resisting expansion, development strategies, planning and design must allow for it. They must also take into consideration the aspirations and changing life-styles of populations. Their strategies must be oriented towards improving the quality of life while still reaching the condition of 'environmental equilibrium' that Watt and his colleagues call the 'dynamic steady state'.[2] The ramifications of all these problems extend beyond the scope of this book, but they are the whole, of which sustainable development is a part.

Global urbanization trends

United Nations estimates indicate that by mid-1990 43 per cent (2.3 billion) of the world's population lived in urban areas. With the urban population growing two and a half times faster than its rural counterpart, the level of urbanization is projected to cross the 50 per cent mark in 2005. UN projections further show that by 2025, more than three-fifths of the world's population will live in urban areas. The urban population in that year will be approximately 5.2 billion, of whom 77 per cent will live in developing countries.[3]

Just over 20 years ago, more than half the world's urban population lived in developed countries. This balance had shifted by 1975 largely as a result of rapid population growth in developing countries, along with the movement of migrants from farms to cities. By 1990, far more of the world's population – 61 per cent – lived in developing countries. In 2025, it is projected that developing countries will have nearly four times as many urban dwellers as developed countries.[4]

It is also important to note that the pattern of migration identified in many developed countries, that is, growth in large metropolitan areas, has now become the norm in developing countries. World-wide, the number of cities comprising 5 to 10 million inhabitants grew from 18 cities in 1970 to 22 cities in 1990. It is expected that, by 2010, there will be 33 megacities – cities with more than 5 million inhabitants – and 21 of them will be in developing countries. Of the 26 urban agglomerations expected to have 10 million or more inhabitants by 2010, 21 will be in developing countries: Asia will be home to 14 of the very large cities; 5 will be in Latin America and 2 in Africa.[5]

The challenges of urban growth

Demographic trends around the world show that the distribution of people among settlements is neither random nor precisely planned. Historically, people clustered together in locations that were favourable for making a living. The urban structure of a country is shaped by a number of factors; among them are history, topography, natural resources and climate. Economic forces, however, probably contribute the most to urban growth. Unfortunately, these forces have not been able to solve problems associated with urban poverty, a deteriorating urban environment and inadequate infrastructure. With limited budgets, cities in developing countries also face urgent crises in land management, municipal finance and administration, and the centralization of power.

Higher urban wages reflect the higher productivity of labour in cities, where economies of scale and agglomeration have made households and enterprises more productive. This productivity growth, although beneficial, has not solved the massive urban problems of the developing world. The creation of jobs in new urban industries brings migrants from surrounding rural areas. Even after most jobs in the city are filled, the influx of migrants persists. Newcomers without skills or experience have little choice in the labour market. If they stay in the city they tend to fill in the niches of the informal sector with part-time or low-level jobs while they search for more permanent work. Many households have found no employment and income-generating activities at all, and many people have no choice but to live in squatter areas unserved by essential infrastructure.

Urbanization has brought an alarming rise in the incidence of urban poverty. According to UNDP estimates, more than half the poor will be concentrated in urban areas by the end of the 1990s. About 90 per cent of poor households in Latin America, 40 per cent in Africa and 45 per cent in Asia will be in urban areas.[6] Although urban incomes are generally higher and urban services and facilities more accessible than in rural areas, the urban poor generally live in overcrowded slums or squatter settlements and often have to contend with bad sanitation and contaminated water. These people usually suffer rates of disease and death comparable to or even higher than their rural counterparts.[7]

Urban activity depends heavily on infrastructure such as power, roads and water supply. Similarly, the health of urban population living in high densities is dependent on sanitation and clean water supplies. Some activities, such as urban transport, are particularly complex because of their effect on settlement patterns and congestion and the high cost often involved. Failures of public management and scarcity of financial and technical capacity have resulted in widespread deficiencies in water supply, electricity, transportation, communication and solid waste management. These deficiencies impose heavy burdens on the productive activity of urban households and enterprises.[8]

Economic activities in large cities use natural resources and discharge wastes in ways not conducive to environmental quality. Policy-makers usually undervalue the long-term effects on environmental resources in favour of immediate gains, thus encouraging rapid depletion of resources. One of the major sources of urban pollution and environmental degradation is the extensive use of fossil fuels. The strong dependence of developing countries on oil and coal has been economically costly and contributes to worsening air pollution, since these fuels release substantial amounts of carbon into the atmosphere. Automobiles and other motor vehicles that increasingly clog the streets release toxic emissions that contribute to human health problems. Attempts by developing countries to introduce alternative transport systems have been largely unsuccessful. The close proximity of large numbers of people, in an environment which provides no protection from the pollution caused by their own and other city wastes, creates conditions very favourable to the rapid spread of a variety of infectious diseases, often in disastrous epidemics.[9]

National and local government in most countries own the largest percentage of urban land and also control the biggest parcels. However, they have yet to consider seriously urban land as a resource that has inherent value and therefore has to be managed. When planning norms are introduced they have most often made matters worse; for example, low-density rules for newly developed planned areas have encouraged dispersed development, and perversely expanded vehicle use and energy consumption. Several governments have spent considerable effort in regulating land ownership and controlling its transfer (a process that is difficult to enforce) rather than managing it as a resource. The challenge is to develop policies that promote sustainable development through appropriate development and density standards, that will lead to the reduction in the use of motorized vehicles, in the lowering of energy consumption, recycling of waste and in an environmentally sustainable disposal of sewage and other waste.[10]

The performance of government is critical to the effective management of urban growth. While access to basic infrastructure, shelter and employment depends as much on private initiatives and enterprises, these are critically affected by public sector policies and functions that only government can perform. Growth in prices, population and economic activity in rapidly urbanizing countries imposes demands for public expenditure that can only be met by both substantial and buoyant resources. The challenge is to identify sources that combine these characteristics with an equitable incidence and the encouragement of efficient use.[11]

In most countries many essential services in cities are managed by local governments. Public sector management is commonly a concern at all levels of government, but the financial and technical weakness of municipal institutions can place severe constraints on important urban-based economic activities as well as on public health. The dominant role of national governments in the planning and financing of urban infrastructure in the post-independence period in Asia and Africa has starved local government of financial resources. In no developing country have municipalities had the ability to bid for credit at market rates on a sustainable basis. Yet some municipalities are expected to finance long-term assets without access to finance.[12]

The massive number of people 'waiting in the wings of urbanization' will need to be properly fed, housed, clothed and provided with other basic urban services and amenities. Thus, a major challenge for urban planners and programme implementors at the threshold of the twenty-first century is to create and sustain processes and structures which will focus on alleviating poverty, on strengthening local government and decentralizing power and resources to cities, on providing housing, infrastructure and essential services for the poor, on improving the urban environment and on promoting the private sector, non-governmental organizations and gender concerns.

Obstacles to urban transformation

Underlying the need for altered resource allocation priorities, ecological sustainability and accelerated innovation processes is the need for a new vision of urban life. This vision, however, will inevitably generate winners and losers. In this book I argue that this new concept for development is one that provides fairness and opportunity for all of the world's people and not just a privileged few, without destroying the world's finite natural resources and carrying capacity. To achieve this vision we have to overcome not only major political, economic and structural barriers (including the international flow of capital and labour, the debt crisis and structural adjustment and elite-dominated political systems), but also internal mind-set obstacles that block any creative leap towards urban transformation.

However, the tremendous growth of urban centres projected by 2025 will be one of those profound shifts in history in which a quantitative change actually necessitates a qualitative leap to a new order. Some of the underlying obstacles are as follows.[13]

1. *Hopelessness and despair.* A prevailing sense of hopelessness and despair, which paralyses policy-makers and the general public alike. Policy-makers are so overwhelmed by day-to-day crises that they can hardly envision an alternative. Innovative solutions that do arise and become successfully implemented gain little recognition and are frequently written off as insignificant anomalies in the face of overwhelming odds.

2. *Outmoded assumptions of policy-makers.* In the present mind-set of many policy-makers and urbanists there are several basic assumptions that need to shift dramatically if high-yield urban strategies are to be devised for the future.

3. *Isolation among sectors, disciplines and cities.* Public, private and voluntary sectors, the academic community and the media tend to operate in isolation from each other rather than to cooperate in grappling with joint problem-solving.

4. *Counter-productive incentives.* In terms of investment, there is little incentive to encourage private sector research and development work or investment in collective urban services. What is needed is to aggregate the massive needs in the big cities into market demand in such a way as to make private investment in the area more attractive.

5. *Resistance to change.* Every system has a built-in inertia and resistance to change, especially when change implies major shifts of power and resources. The innovations sought are not politically neutral changes, but rather imply a shift in priorities. It is often not the lack of ideas or even of proven successes that block the policy transformation, but lack of political will.

6. *Entrenched bureaucracy.* In almost every country red tape and bureaucracy at the local and national government level is endless and at times mind-boggling. This leads to endless delays causing gross inefficiencies. Such an environment stifles creativity and leads to general apathy.

7. *Corruption.* Along with entrenched bureaucracy there exists corruption at all levels in most countries. This leads to an increased cost of undertaking any project. This obstacle in most cases is not explicitly recognized. However, if we are to move beyond the rhetoric and undertake meaningful projects we have to deal with it.

8. *Selfishness.* People in general, and politicians in particular, do not like to implement other people's ideas. They tend to prefer to argue that they have their own solutions and that each situation has its own unique solution.

Conventional approaches to managing urban growth

The 'trickle-down' theories of the 1950s and the 1960s, and the planning processes associated with them, brought about new opportunities for many people, but for a larger number of people living standards were not improved. By the 1970s, it was recognized that poverty had to be tackled directly alongside the economic growth model. This approach, however, avoided the questions of whether the development process itself (in the form that it had taken in many countries) created poverty and deprivation and how the process could be reformed and even transformed. The 1980s was a decade of debt crises in many countries followed by structural adjustment in those countries classified as 'free-market economies'. The end of the decade and the beginning of the 1990s saw the breakdown of many centrally planned economies. We are now at a crossroad, in a situation of uncertainty. Such a situation signals danger as well as opportunity.

Past urban operations focused on neighbourhood interventions such as site-and-services and slum upgrading during the 1970s and municipal development and housing finance during the 1980s. Assessments of this assistance conclude that city-wide impacts have been rare and that the pace of urban growth far exceeded the scale of the urban programme.

Since 1972, government efforts, particularly those supported by bilateral donors, have addressed urban growth and urban poverty through low-cost investment projects in shelter, water supply, sanitation and urban transport. For example, site-and-services and slum-upgrading projects were intended to demonstrate replicable approaches that could provide benefits to the poor while recovering costs and reducing the financial burdens on the public sector. Many of these projects were successful in meeting their physical project objectives, but were less successful in sustaining policy change and strengthening institutions. As a result, they have not had a major impact on the policies of national and local governments and on the broader issues of managing the urban economy. In only a few cases, such as the Kampung Improvement Programme in Jakarta, have city-wide impacts been achieved. Government and donor programmes tended to divide a city into projects, improving specific neighbourhoods without the urban policy and institutional framework such as the functioning of city-wide markets for land and housing. Government efforts have not mobilized the private sector and community initiatives, but in many cases have increased the cost of private solutions through overregulation and the rationing of scarce capital for investment.[14]

Approaches to developing urban settlements

Urban growth has given rise to a variety of models for producing the housing needed to shelter the population, but they all fall into two general categories. The first, usually labelled 'formal', refers to housing built by an organized system of institutions, and governed by regulations and legal contracts. The second, usually referred to as 'informal', produces housing on land where ownership or tenure is not officially recognized. The settlements that result are at least initially outside the system of rules and laws imposed by the government. For that reason the tenants are usually without services and amenities as well.[15]

Another way of describing housing delivery is to distinguish between the 'provider' approach – the most common approach in housing – built by government agencies or by private developers, and the 'self-help' approach, which promotes the building of housing stock by the people themselves. When done effectively the self-help approach uses locally available resources, including labour skills, services, utilities, materials and money. These two approaches are often seen as incompatible, and they do present significantly different intellectual, physical, political and economic fields of action for architects and planners.[16] In the 'provider' approach the key actors are government agencies, consultants, financiers, large contractors and developers. In the 'self-help' approach the key actors are the families, local developers, community groups, non-government organizations, small contractors, money-lenders and local government agencies.

In both approaches, the government, the private sector and community-based organizations all play a role. In the 'provider' approach, however, the dominant institutions are government and the private sector: there is little opportunity for collaboration between the government and the community. The inability of the government to provide housing for the poor, combined with the hope seen in self-help-produced squatter settlements led some to argue that government should stop building housing for the poor and let the poor build their own. However, over the last decade, attitudes have shifted again, and the idea that partnerships between the people, private investment and the government can produce housing for poor people as well as for the rich in developing countries is taking hold and is bringing the state back into the equation through partnerships between the public and the private sectors.[17] Government support under this most recent system includes assessing existing stock and managing land, and providing labour, services, utilities, material and money. This approach assumes that the state does have a role to play in housing poor communities.[18] The 'support' approach has been manifested in solutions ranging from 'site-and-services' (which is the government's way of in-volving the community) to 'settlement upgrading' projects undertaken by the community itself with approval from the government and extensive assistance from non-governmental agencies.

The argument promoting 'self-help' was, in essence, anti-state: it assumed that self-help constituted a threat to the government and therefore the government was unable and unwilling to do its part of the job.[19] But, although there are obvious differences between how a state, private invest-ment and ordinary people function, these differences need not be in constant tension. The government and non-governmental organizations are not always in conflict; state intervention in housing is not always detrimental; and people's own initiatives need not necessarily circumvent the market forces at every turn.[20] A non-governmental effort has only to establish close connections with the government and elicit the support of government officials to be effective.

In the rural areas of the developing world, 90 per cent of all houses are built by the dwellers themselves; in the urban areas, the proportion is about 50 per cent. In both cases the proportion of houses that are designed by architects and built by developers and development agencies is small, mainly because they are unaffordable by the low and low-middle-income groups who make up the vast majority of the population. But that does not mean that the designer cannot play a greater role than formerly in the develop-ment of housing, whatever the approach. The widespread disillusionment with the 'good-houses-make-good-people' notion that led to 'slum-clearance' projects through the 1960s and ended in crime-ridden public housing, particularly in the United States, shows what happens when public housing is badly designed and the community has no say in what is being built. Housing where bedrooms and living and dining spaces were placed with no regard for how people live or might wish to live; where there were too many unprotected areas; where parks between towers became battle-grounds for gangs; and where parents found it impossible to supervise children from apartments high off the ground are familiar products of the slum-clearance approach. The reaction, however, has been to disregard altogether the need for design and to become project- and process-oriented. Housing authorities have planned either too much or not at all.[21]

Saad Eddin Ibrahim, a leading Egyptian sociologist, thinks that it is possible to upgrade mass housing but that, with a few exceptions, architects, bureaucrats and politicians are not likely to do so. They are unconcerned with cultural authenticity; they only want to win commissions and complete projects. The challenge, therefore, is how to influence the people in power into improving and stressing the importance of design.[22] In spite of Ibrahim's pessimism the process has already begun. Over the last decade governments, development agencies and designers have examined design in housing and have recognized that satisfactory housing is not just a luxury for the affluent, but is essential for the future stability and well-being of the low and middle-income groups. Some neighbourhoods built over the last decade have already begun to reflect this new attitude.[23]

Thus, a major challenge for urban planners and implementers is to help create and sustain processes and structures that can bring about a development that provides healthy environments and decent and secure livelihoods, and at the same time gives people greater control over their own lives. Attempts to address what can and needs to be done in this area must re-examine the macro-planning process itself as well as anti-poverty programmes in the context of a rapidly changing world.

Conventional housing approaches – have they worked?

It is now clear that, barring a few successful examples, government agencies in developing countries have been unable to cope with the demand for housing. Singapore, Hong Kong and to some extent the Republic of Korea are the exceptions: they have increased the supply of multi-storey buildings so substantially that the living standards of the entire population have been greatly improved.[24]

Hong Kong and Singapore were successful for particular reasons: affordability, a scale of operation that affected the general level of rents throughout these two cities and thus created a successful trickle-down effect, relatively high per capita incomes, the necessary management and technical resources and strong governments capable of implementing housing programmes and enforcing the rules.[25] Most public housing construction programmes elsewhere do not have these capabilities and, unless significant changes are adopted, increasing government spending is not going to increase the housing stock or improve housing for the poor.

The total expenditure by most governments in the developing world is small compared to that of Hong Kong and Singapore and the outlay outside the government system. For example in India, total funds from budgetary outlays, government agencies and financial institutions were about Rs 2,200 crores (approximately US $1 billion) in 1987–8. The private sector in the same period had an outlay of about Rs 8,900 crores (approximately US $4 billion).[26]

In Singapore success was partly due to a managed housing finance programme. Household savings were mobilized, capital flow increased and interest rates held in check. Housing finance in most developing countries has been perceived in terms of budget outlays of the government rather than in terms of housing finance in the country from available household savings.[27]

Significant advances have been made in India, South Korea and Indonesia with recently developed housing finance systems. In India over the last decade more significant changes have taken place in the housing finance sector. The promotion of the Housing Development Finance Corporation (HDFC) 13 years ago as the primary finance institution in the private sector has given a tremendous impetus to housing finance. The HDFC provides loans to individuals and charges them 14.5 per cent interest and requires the deed to the house or apartment as collateral. It was developed with little or no initial government support. Today it is a premier housing finance institution in India and touted as a model of success. However, its growth has been predicated on institutional support from government-owned banks and financial institutions.[28] In 1989–90 the HDFC's cumulative loan approvals grossed Rs 20 billion and loan disbursements Rs 15 billion for nearly 400,000 units all over India. Outstanding housing loans amounted to over Rs 12 billion.[29]

In the 1980s the annual gross capital formation in housing was about one-third of what it was in 1990 (about Rs 31.3 billion compared with Rs 110.6 billion).[30] In just over a decade, housing finance has become a major component of the total formal-sector finance. In 1990, the flow of net credit to housing has increased to nearly Rs 20 billion a year.[31] This exceeds, in one year alone, the cumulative institutional contributions to housing in 1980.

Ten years after the promotion of the HDFC, the government set up the National Housing Bank (NHB) to develop a network of specialized housing finance institutions in the country. In fact the NHB came into existence at a time when local and regional finance institutions were yet to be developed. The NHB also acts as a regulatory body. It has been conceived as a multi-functional bank for the housing sector operating the housing finance system at non-subsidized rates of interest with full cost recovery. At the same time it is supposed to induce cross-subsidization – low interest rates being charged for the poorest households – but to keep in view the fiscal concessions enjoyed by the high-income households.[32]

As long as there remains an excess demand from the middle and upper-income groups in virtually all major cities, there is going to be a constant struggle for the poor to find housing, and, once they find it, a constant struggle to retain it. Therefore there is a need generally to improve the urban land assembly and development process and improve the capabilities of the building industry, the building materials industries and housing finance systems. Although the primary responsibility of the public sector is to shelter low-income groups, their need for shelter cannot be reasonably satisfied as long as the demands from middle-income groups go unmet.

Self-help in squatter settlements – does it work?

For a long time governments in the developing countries saw squatter settlements as a problem that had to be eradicated. They were viewed as the physical manifestations of social ills. Some urbanists and researchers saw hope in them, however. Charles Abrams, and, latterly, Mangin, Turner, Peattie and Perlman, all of whom studied these settlements, found that the squatters had managed to build shelters for themselves: however modest, they were still housing. Turner established that people had produced 50,000 dwelling units in Lima, Peru, in a seven-year period (1949–56), while in this same period the government had built only 5,476 units, none of them affordable even by an average family.

Seeing squatter settlements as part of the solution rather than as part of the problem led to the approach that came to be known as 'self-help'.[33] It turned the focus of mass housing from 'central provision' towards what Turner called 'local enablement', whereby the financial and other resources of the future dwellers were channelled into housing construction.

The self-help approach identified by Turner took advantage of the self-sufficiency, autonomy and decentralization that the squatter settlements represented. Self-help assumed that small communities could be sustained independent of larger economic and political institutions and might eventually join together in a self-governing network that would transform society from the bottom up.[34] Turner therefore argued that governments should cease building and managing houses, which it does badly, and let the users develop their own. 'Self-help' became the new buzzword.

More recently, the user, or 'grassroots', or 'development from below' approach has been promoted. This is distinctly different from 'self-help'. The 'grassroots' or 'development from below' approach is based on people empowerment and on increasing the community's role in decision-making. Self-help has been limited to using people's own labour in urban development. As Bishwapriya Sanyal points out, 'grassroots' or 'development from below' meant that many inequalities could be rectified through new initiatives generated at the bottom of the social hierarchy, rather than, as previously executed, by the bureaucracy.[35] 'The assumption was', says Sanyal, 'that these activities would generate profit, savings and investment at the bottom, thereby eliminating the need for income to trickle down the social and spatial hierarchy.'[36]

The revised approach is in favour of a participatory planning process where the future beneficiaries of the project are involved from the very beginning. According to Arif Hasan, the development from below process is sending a message to governments: 'we always tell [the government], to ask people to participate in your programs ... but maybe it is time for you to participate in the peoples' programs.'[37]

The user approach regarded the non-governmental organizations (NGOs) and private voluntary organizations as appropriate agents for fostering development projects. Sanyal puts forward five reasons to support this. First, the NGOs and private voluntary organizations were supported because they were small and therefore considered to be bureaucratically less unwieldy. Second, they were thought to be free of corruption and truly committed. Third, they were thought to be locally based and therefore appropriate institutions to foster decentralized developments. Fourth, they were perceived as being more innovative than governments. Finally, they were viewed as particularly capable of fostering participation by the poor through the creation of community groups.[38] However, NGOs have also acted as bridges between the low-income communities and the government. It was often in the interest of community groups to work with NGOs who were capable of dealing with government agencies and were able to understand often arcane government regulations.

Site-and-services

The model that was eventually developed to achieve participation was not exactly a synthesis of the two earlier approaches, but at least it advocated a partnership of sorts. Under the site-and-services system, the state provided serviced land and the actual house was constructed by or through the occupants. Variations on this theme were introduced, among them 'core' or 'shell' housing, which provided a serviced plot and a core, or serviced land and a room, to which other rooms could be added later by the owners as and when they could afford it. Horacio Caminos and Reinhard Goethert, in their pioneering work, developed elaborate models and tools for these site-and-services projects, to help communities and local organizations to craft programmes and housing projects themselves.[39] They reduced housing to a set of quantifiable and comparable data and developed an elaborate and precise system of site evaluations in order to figure out the best and cheapest possible way in which to provide urban infrastructure and other services. Their objectives were clear: to subdivide land and provide services for the neediest. Techniques were provided for making decisions affecting policies as well as for designs. Politicians and administrators were given a method for analysing what level of services was needed. Designers were given techniques and indicators to ensure optimal use of land and to provide guidelines for design.

The site-and-services approach was eventually adopted by the World Bank and promoted in developing countries as a means of providing an appropriate level of services and reducing costs. Alain and Marie-Agnes

Bertaud developed the Bertaud Model, a computational tool that makes it possible to identify very quickly and cost effectively the key physical and financial cost characteristics of a wide variety of physical design alternatives for low-income settlement projects. It also correlates expected costs to household incomes and expenditure patterns, making it possible to identify the socio-economic groups for which a particular alternative will be affordable using specific assumptions about cost-recovery policies and financing terms.[40]

Problems with self-help and site-and-services

Questions about the effectiveness of self-help were soon raised by those who believed that, on its own, it was not going to solve the urban housing problem. Though it reduced construction costs, created employment and skills training, and strengthened the community and individual identity, it also had pitfalls. For one thing, reducing construction costs by doing the work oneself proved not to be sufficient to bridge the rent–income gap. Sites-and-services and self-help projects remained dependent on heavy subsidies – albeit less heavy than other forms of housing – which are not forthcoming.[41] Conceptually there is nothing wrong with the site-and-services theory that people will build what they can afford. However, the central concept of the serviced lot implies a monthly charge and frequently a down payment, which themselves are sufficient to raise the project cost above the economic threshold of a substantial proportion of the urban poor.[42]

Secondly, the question of location is for the very poor much more critical than shelter itself. For those with no regular source of employment, each day means a new search for one's daily bread. A prime requisite for survival is easy and continual access to the central pools of economic activity (i.e., the job market), which are normally located in the middle of the city. Due to the scale of site-and-services projects, peripheral locations are favoured, but they also make life more costly and difficult for their lowest income participants.[43] In the way projects are planned and designed, the relationship to the rest of the city and linkages with other amenities in the city are never adequately established, and in most cases are completely ignored.

Studies show the link between settlements and areas of employment and the importance of proximity of housing to sources of work. Old settlements evolved over time and urban services grew around them, but new ones cannot wait for that to happen. Low-income settlements must be located in areas near employment, or at the least provided with heavily subsidized public transport or scattered along with dispersed employment locations throughout the city.[44]

It is important to understand the link between economic opportunities and settlement patterns. In site-and-services projects land is costly. That means that plots are small, making it difficult to undertake any small manufacturing or light industry on them. Upper-floor expansion for rental or use as a workshop is only possible after the owner has accumulated sufficient capital to build an upper floor.[45]

Thirdly, the community was never seen as being able to contribute anything; they were intended to occupy the site once the services were installed. No role involving the community in the development of the project itself or in the maintenance and management of it was envisaged. All aspects of the project were controlled by the development agencies and the international financing agencies that funded the project. Access for poor groups to decision-making and the implementation process was largely curtailed. Large, highly centralized organizations, especially development authorities, were counter-productive in that they tended to restrict the influence of local associations and did not mobilize the settling groups.

Present policies and programmes for housing and urban services

More than a decade and a half ago the Habitat I Conference identified the provision of housing as one of the key issues facing developing countries' urban settlements. The overriding objectives of settlements policies should be to make shelter, infrastructure and services available to those who need them, in the sequence in which they are needed and at a monetary or social cost they can afford. Social justice depends on the way in which these facilities are distributed among the population and the extent to which they are made available.[46]

Since that time the general shelter conditions of the world's poor have worsened, particularly during the 1980s when world economic recession hit governments and resulted in a decline in investment in housing. It has also become increasingly clear that the vast majority of governments do not have the means or capacity to provide affordable housing for everyone who needs it.

Nevertheless, there is reason for optimism for future decades in the widespread change in attitudes and approaches to housing which has taken place. By now nearly everyone is conscious of the evolution of government positions toward slums and squatter settlements from one of unconcern, to one of hostility and eviction, to one in which attempts to provide low-cost public housing were constructed, to one where slums and squatter settlements became tolerated and even accepted, and aided self-help housing schemes were supported, and finally to one in which assisted sites-and-service or slum upgrading projects were adopted.[47]

Habitat II, 'The World City Summit', to be held in 1996, has mobilized the urban community to model new paradigms of development, particularly as it relates to poor people and their communities. The creation of communities through development is the key concept of sustainability. Therefore, participation of people throughout the development process is what will generate new development processes and control of change. It is the inclusion of community participation in the creation of communities that ensures sustainability.

Planning for sustainable and equitable communities is no longer a choice but a necessity. Ismail Serageldin issued the challenge to urbanists that 'the fundamental issue is not whether cities are sustainable, but how to make them so'. He went on to suggest that 'human behavior determines the quality of the urban environment, and the quality of the urban environment determines the quality of life in cities'.[48] Implementing sustainable and equitable policies, however, presents us with a paradox; i.e., the world markets and institutions, which link global actions with local development, must work to empower nations so that they can become self-sufficient, yet the world economy often works in ways that thwart positive development. Thus it is important to understand how the behaviour of world markets undermines self-sufficiency, and how global institutions influence trade patterns and the transfer of technology.

The development model, which equated growth to export, was unsuccessful. The export of natural resources from developing countries was not a viable way to achieve economic development in the long run because natural resources are finite. Exporting countries found themselves at the mercy of the world economy.

Another model, based on international aid, has not fared any better. As a rule, most donor countries give technical assistance and emergency relief rather than the technologies for sustainable development. And financial crisis and political conflicts often prevent national governments from providing aid to their poorer citizens. As a result, the focus of policy debate is shifting from the notion of government-provided aid to the concept of sustainable development; in other words, from a policy of dependency to a policy that fosters communities supporting themselves with local resources.

Towards an equitable and sustainable urban future

It is time to reflect on what has worked and what has not and to share these lessons with one another in order to create a secure common future. Many of the issues that once were handled within national boundaries have become globalized and the urban areas are the setting of many of them. Financial markets, information systems, technological development, environmental problems and diseases such as AIDS cannot be controlled by solely national decision-making structures. New arrangements and relationships have to be developed to deal with a rapidly changing world that has created two different tracks – high growth and low growth among countries and within the countries themselves. It is against this background that the book reviews the approaches in various cities that have worked and have the possibility of being adapted and replicated in other cities. The projects range in scale, complexity and the number of people that they have positively affected; they cover issue areas ranging from infra-structure upgrading, solid waste recycling, land-sharing, incremental development and the design of site-and-services projects. The objective is to provide a general evaluation of the high level of approaches that are being developed by community organizations, local governments, NGOs and the private sector and the lessons from these practices so that major issues can be highlighted for action by governments, intergovernmental organizations, NGOs and private enterprises.

Despite the current urban trends in developing countries, in every city there are rays of hope, most visibly in an outpouring of promising new development programmes. The majority of these programmes have been initiated by the people who live in the most severe conditions, as they take the lead in making significant improvements to their physical, economic and social environment. In these times of severe resource constraints, citizens need to discover new ways to learn from each other's successes and to multiply the impact of policies, programmes and projects that work. It is through cross-cultural learning, replication and adaptation that effective urban practices can have a significant and sustainable impact on our cities. But first it is important to define what is meant by an effective practice for urban management.

Simply put, an effective practice is one that can be recommended for further application, whether in a similar or adapted form. It is an initiative or project which has resulted in clear improvements on the quality of life and the living environments of people in a sustainable way. The initiative itself must successfully solve an urban problem, without creating or promoting other unintended problems. In order to screen out policies and projects that benefit the elite only, that pollute the environment, that are too costly to be replicated on a mass scale or that are too situationally or culturally specific to be useful in another context, effective practices must be socially equitable, ecologically sustainable, economically viable and culturally adaptable.

In order to define what success means in each case, the solution must be evaluated in its contextual framework and settle the aims of the proposition in the perspective of sustainable human development. In order to make this evaluation, we should answer the crucial question: who has benefited from this initiative? Some initiatives provoke structural changes, others bring immediate results in some people's daily lives and others start a transformation process that takes years to mature. Thus, in evaluating the implementation of an innovation we should consider its aims and expectations in order to evaluate it properly.

There is a need to reduce many kinds of inequity that exist at the interpersonal, community, urban and national scales while promoting efficient economic growth. I argue that it also necessary that we develop sound principles for government devolution and community empowerment. There can be no community empowerment without greater trust and cooperation between communities and local government and between different levels of government. The major challenge for governments and people of the developing world is to ensure human-centred sustainable developments.

Human-centred development recognizes the fundamental duality in that people are both a 'means' and an 'end' of development. People are ultimate beneficiaries of development, while they are also the most critical contributing element in the development process. Where the emphasis is on the 'means', development activities will be associated with the strengthening of the economic dimensions of human resource – implying a manpower productivity or human capital approach to urban development. Where, on the other hand, the emphasis is on the 'end', development activities will be associated with the strengthening of the social dimension of human resources, implying a human needs approach. The challenge is to develop policies that emphasize both.

CHAPTER 2

Responding to Changing Needs

Over the last two decades, policies, position papers and approaches for urban development programmes have all tried to reduce the role of central planning in urban development programmes. For a long time central planning and administration were considered necessary to guide and control the economy and to integrate and unify nations that were emerging from long periods of colonial rule. They were also required by the international assistance agencies that were providing large amounts of capital in the 1950s and 1960s, through their insistence that borrowers had comprehensive and long-term plans for the investment of external capital.[1] Since the 1970s, however, it has become evident that centralized government, with a few exceptions, has neither brought prosperity nor alleviated poverty. Given the present state of the urban environment it is clear that central planning and administration have not worked in the cities either.

Decentralization of government control or no government control at all are now seen as part of the solution, and development theorists have set about finding ways to minimize the role of central government. Greater equity in the distribution of income and wealth, many development theorists argue, requires wider participation in the economic, social and political processes through which wealth is generated and distributed.[2] To reduce the emphasis on national planning and devise an administrative structure that would permit decentralization and local autonomy in planning, designing and implementing development programmes requires changes, particularly a transfer of power from groups who dominate the centre to those who have local control.[3] Local empowerment is not, however, a solution in itself; it is only one way to achieve sustainable and equitable development. Poor people in the developing countries have not been able to house themselves with support from non-governmental organizations (NGOs), partly because NGOs, to be successful, require strategic linkages to institutions at the top – that is, they need the same contacts with government bureaucrats that any interest group needs, whether central or local. Survival and self-interest also discourage cooperation among NGOs, because more often than not they are competing for funds from the same organizations. To attract funding each NGO must show that it alone has been generating and implementing innovative ideas, although in fact successful projects usually result from cooperative efforts between NGOs, private investors and the government.[4] That is why recent efforts have concentrated on getting communities to work together through NGOs and community-based organizations. The rate of success of projects organized in this way is increasing, even though the number of partnerships between the state, private investment and the people fluctuates because they are subject to the ups and downs of economic, political and social trends.

These partnerships are very different from earlier strategies. Site-and-services were essentially government projects, which gained popularity because they were promoted by international lending agencies. These new approaches develop programmes that link several institutions together.

Owning a house represents savings and investment; it has symbolic value; it has cultural significance; and it is thought to affect family relationships. A single approach to producing it cannot fulfil all of these considerations for everyone. Now self-help and community participation are in danger precisely because of becoming the only housing policy, in part because they provide an excuse for governments to abdicate their responsibility to provide housing for their people. But the relationship between the state, private investment and ordinary people seems to hold promise as it can accommodate changing economic, political and social circumstances in situations where vested interests are always in conflict.

A number of projects have already experimented with these partnerships. In some places, squatter land has been divided between the owners and the squatters. In others, private land is provided with services and infrastructure by the state in return for part of the land, which is then used for low-income housing. In incremental development schemes the state provides unserviced land to beneficiaries for a very low entry cost, and services are installed by the state as soon as the community can afford to pay for them. In all these projects emphasis is on providing land and services through cooperation between the state, the private sector and the community affected.

A new vision for sustainable and equitable development

For the first time in human history, the world is close to creating a single, unified global system. The Preparatory Committee of the United Nations Conference on Environment and Development (UNCED) developed 'Agenda 21', which includes sections on human settlements, and calls for protection of the interests of the world's poor in the face of rapid economic globalization.

How are the interests of the world's poor protected and what policy instruments need to be developed, so that protecting their interests is not another prescriptive solution where planners and policy formulators tell the poor what is good for them? The real challenge is to develop programmes by which the poor themselves are able to make choices regarding their well-being and are also able to change these choices when the need arises. This does not preclude other participants in the urban development process, but defines new partnerships between the various actors.

What does become clear is that this new vision calls for the widening of choices not only for the current generation but also for future generations.[5] It implies a new concept for development – one that provides fairness and opportunity for all of the world's people and not a privileged few, without destroying the world's finite natural resources and carrying capacity.

Arguing for sustainable and equitable development means that there has to be some potential for societies to improve their quality of life. The task before contemporary societies, therefore, is to identify those components that constitute an improved quality of life for the people of their own societies without jeopardizing the interests of other societies or pre-empting the choice of options for future generations. Once the relative importance of the components of the quality of life is determined, then policies aimed at providing and sustaining these components can be developed. Thus an optimum sustainable quality of life is when growth is organic. Kenneth Watt and his colleagues in their analyses of the environmental problems, growth and culture, conclude that organic growth is achieved when the ecosystem is maintained and the economic system is in balance, the basic physical needs for human development are met, and basic social needs for human development are also satisfied.[6]

Equity and human development

Reducing inequity and increasing the ability of all segments of society to participate and make decisions for themselves is the focus of this study. The problems of equity are closely linked with basic need satisfaction. On a planet of finite resources where the power to obtain, develop and distribute these resources is monopolized by a relatively small minority of people and institutions, gross inequity can spell starvation, depletion, dependence and in general an intolerably low quality of life for the overwhelming majority of the population.

Thus equity becomes a priority component of the quality of life. A conceptualization of equity suggested by Dudley Weeks sheds light on the global dimension of this complex phenomenon:

> In contemporary human society equity can be defined as a condition in which the dominant patterns of interaction not only promote justice and fairness, but also (1) facilitate for all people a condition of life beyond that of bare survival

(a 'survival-plus' condition), (2) limit the unequal distribution of power, resources and benefits to a differential too low to facilitate monopolization and exploitation, (3) promote a sufficient degree of autonomy so that each society's sustenance and development is not merely a dependent consequence of another society's activity, but rather the result of its own decisions. The key component of equity, then, is equal *access* to the benefits of existence, and to the tools essential to self-development.[7]

To develop equitable development strategies we must recognize that inequities exist at both interspatial and interpersonal levels. At the regional or interregional level this new strategy aims at reducing disparity, increasing per capita income, reducing urban poverty and understanding how coordination and integration in policies for the development of urban areas need to be undertaken. However, the principle of reducing inequity is often in conflict with the goals of economic growth and development, and nowhere has this been more evident than in the urban policies of many developing countries.[8] Today, however, within cities themselves the issue of equitable distribution of wealth is being addressed more seriously. The major reason is that the urban poor are gradually becoming more cohesive as a political force.

At the second, more specific level, problems still exist in developing policies that will encourage all sectors of civil society to participate in the decision-making process that affects their lives and livelihood. How to reduce inequity at this level is one subject of this study. Some of the mechanisms are: (a) optimizing the contribution of groups and subgroups in society who do, can, or might contribute to housing and urban services programmes; and (b) maximizing people's choices in how, where and what kind of housing and urban services are developed and implemented.

One major step that has to be taken before any of the other measures can be successful is to recognize that the needs of various subgroups that have traditionally been viewed as 'disadvantaged' are different from the rest of us and that they too have a role to play in urban development programmes. Among the poor, the disadvantaged are even worse off and they include women, the aged, children, physically and mentally challenged and other specially disadvantaged persons. Once this has been recognized, two conclusions follow:

1. The role of each organization that is involved and those that may be involved in urban development programmes have to be optimized. These include central planning agencies, local institutions, private sector organizations, community groups and special subgroups. The relationships that are formed between the private sector, government and the community before programmes are initiated also need to be evaluated in terms of their advantages and drawbacks.
2. How local municipalities, NGOs and community organizations can best

assume control over decision-making in urban development programmes needs to be determined: are they to improve or build housing and infrastructure, or are they to undertake city level improvement programmes? The nature of the relationships that need to be formed and whether such partnerships are always advantageous need also to be determined. At the local level decisions might include choice of location, type of construction, level of self-help and types of houses. These choices would be influenced by wealth, religious affiliation, social standing and family composition, and will change over time.

Choices should ensure that all sectors of society contribute something, and, to facilitate their contribution, that local communities have control over their own resources. Unless local communities participate in urban development, the models available will be limited. Eventually they will simply become project-oriented, and will languish, without any possibility of replicability or continuity.

The marginal, the silent, the forgotten

Women, children, the elderly and the disabled, and other specially disadvantaged persons, require special attention when we discuss new paradigms for equity and sustainability. Women, the elderly and children have often been relegated to the shadows in development activities. But of late, women are playing a major role in the improvement and maintenance of the residential environment. Still missing, however, are programmes aimed at the young, the elderly, the physically or mentally impaired and others whose poverty is equally enduring, equally pervasive and equally oppressive.

The marginal: women

In most developing countries women are usually the decision-makers in family as well as societal matters, and this allows them to play an important role in improving their family's welfare.[9] Studies done on existing settlements show that the female labour force has been increasing steadily for over two decades in every country in Asia and has been accompanied by higher proportions of women in the rural-to-urban migration stream. Defining an equitable economic role for women is clearly an urban-management issue of major importance.[10]

Very few poor women can afford to sit at home. They supplement the household income as maids, vendors, daily-wage labourers, artisans and casual labourers such as rag-pickers.[11] Some economic programmes to help women start their own businesses and promote development projects for women have already been initiated. For example, in Ahmedabad, the

Self-Employed Women's Association assists women in small-scale enterprise. In Bangladesh, the Grameen Bank gives low-interest loans to women and provides assistance in building shelters for them. In Jamaica, the Women's Construction Collective is an example of a skills and employment project for women.[12] Another area in which women can contribute is general environmental upkeep, which they usually do, even in a limited manner, already. However, these jobs have to be created as part of a community cleaning programme which encourages their participation and provides income as well.

Family hygiene is one obvious area where women can and do play a role, and if given the opportunity can effectively contribute even more. Saving energy is an area that is not so obvious. Most cooking is done by women, and in poor houses it is usually done on a wood-burning or kerosene stove. Both are potential fire hazards and cause pollution. With education about energy uses and their consequences, improvement can be achieved.

Landscaping and kitchen gardening are other areas where women can function effectively. Community tree planting can be started in settlements to combat the high rate of deforestation, and can improve life in cities. Women can also help control noise pollution made by home industries and refuse pollution caused by their own habits of garbage disposal.

As most other involvement programmes, these functions have potential but are not a panacea. Illiteracy and social pressures against women participating in such activities are barriers. Men's attitude towards women's role in society and existing social norms also mitigate against their participation. It will help if their roles are fully integrated into other community involvement programmes and not limited to female participation only.

The silent: children

Few aspects of poverty are more disturbing than the persistence and conditions of child labour. Children are malnourished, illiterate, sick, overworked and underpaid – often working and living in dangerous conditions. Children who earn incomes for themselves and their families are found in the highest- as well as the lowest- income countries. The most abominable practice is children being sold into bondage and as chattels to the wealthiest of urbanites and to other wealthy countries. These children are incarcerated in a life of misery and abuse without any hope of improvement. The denial of basic human rights and the active suppression of efforts of the weakest segment of society to organize for their own betterment or to contest the abuse of power has to stop.

In so far as poverty persists in rapidly growing cities, children will continue to be compelled to enter the labour force at extremely young ages, but this practice must undergo changes. The future betterment of society depends on what society and its representatives – the government – do about improving the life and conditions of children and thereby determining the role they will play in society. Education, access to basic hygiene and health, and nutrition are their fundamental needs.

In 1989 UNICEF conceded that although it may be difficult to make a case against child work in many societies that have long depended on household labour, the conditions of work should be a concern everywhere, and governments have direct responsibility for ensuring that legal frameworks to redress substandard conditions are in place and laws protecting working children are implemented. The protection of working children is the first step, but much more needs to be done if the welfare of the child is to be improved. At the family level, much can be done through health and nutrition programmes targeted at low-income families and children. Improving the health and welfare of mothers also has a direct and positive correlation with the child's health and welfare. At the community level, basic improvements in housing and infrastructure can also improve the 'work sites' of children who earn incomes in the lanes and open areas of poor communities.

Planners and NGOs must seek alternative income-generating activities for children – activities that are not detrimental to their well-being but make a positive contribution to their overall growth. Furthermore, children and young people can play an important role in protecting and safeguarding the urban environment. The 'Magic Eyes' campaign organized by the Thai Environmental and Community Development Association in Bangkok, where an anti-litter environmental education campaign for children has been successful in drawing attention to the pollution in the Chao Praya River, is a successful example

The Magic Eyes campaign is directed at children 10–16 years of age, and is based on the theory that lifetime habits are formed during this period, and that children can influence their parents' behaviour if offered a face-saving way to do so. Using the campaign's specially created symbol of frowning 'magic' eyes and the light-hearted jingle, 'Ah, ah, Magic Eyes are watching you!', children can remind themselves and adults not to litter the environment while still showing the required respect. The campaign has reduced litter in the streets of Bangkok by 90 per cent.[13]

Another programme is the Child-to-Child Health Programme, where schoolchildren in low-income areas of Bombay are educated in basic health, hygiene and nutrition. The children are then taught to act as basic health-care workers for their families and communities. The programme builds on the cultural practice of older children caring for younger siblings, and taps the energy and ability of children to provide an invaluable health service to themselves and their communities. A variety of non-traditional activities are used to educate the children and community at the classroom, school and community level. Between 1989 and 1995, a total of 186 schools followed the programme, educating approximately 20,000 children. If each child adopted its own family and five others, 120,000 families or approximately 600,000 people in slum communities of Bombay would have their health monitored by 'mini-doctors'.[14]

Several such examples from around the world show the positive benefit of children's participation in urban environment programmes; however, the challenge is to find roles that also provide income-generating opportunities for them. No matter what course of action is taken, the plight of the poorest and most vulnerable citizens of the world is such that it will require more than creating work for them: it will require advocacy from all sections of society, including the government.

The forgotten: the elderly and the disabled

The elderly and the disabled have been largely ignored by advocacy groups and governments, yet their condition deserves additional attention. Their plight was highlighted in a leading Indian magazine: 'A silent revolution, a coup of sorts, is taking place. The patriarch, the matriarch, the eldest son, the aging boss, the village elder are being elbowed aside. The youth are moving in.'[15] The elderly are being forced out by their children; they have no place to go; their earning capacities are minimal. Because of improved health conditions, they are living longer, but they are spending considerable amounts of extra time looking for a decent place to live or, having no choice, living on streets.

The elderly can play a positive role in urban development projects and planners must envisage these roles for them before the problems reach such proportions that elders become a burden on society. They can play a role in community-based projects, help manage some aspects of it, look after the children while mothers are out working, or assist in the education of children. Besides helping the elderly to play a productive role in development projects, they also need assistance to start economic activities, so that they do not have to depend on the continuing largesse of their family for their livelihood.

The needs of the disabled are similar to those of the elderly, except that in most developing societies governments do not yet know how to respond to their needs. Their plight is often hidden and their needs relegated to the shadows of most development programmes. Their misery is further compounded because few advocacy groups speak out on their behalf. More needs to be done; governments and advocacy groups must increase the attention paid to their requirements. Besides treating them as equal members of society and providing them with an equal chance, governments must institute specific disabled access codes to make the environment accessible for their use. In most countries the building codes do not take the special needs of the disabled into consideration. Governments can at least start by providing ramps and entry and egress areas fit for their use in public buildings.

The magnitude of urban problems facing governments are such that issues dealing with the elderly and the disabled receive less attention. Prioritization becomes the justification for inaction; however, governments must view these groups positively and use the available resources judiciously to provide an urban environment that is capable of serving the needs of all members of society. Unless there is a change in perception, and society stops viewing the elderly and the disabled as liabilities, it will be very difficult for the elderly and the disabled to participate productively in urban development programmes.

Decentralization and partnership programmes

Although 'decentralization' and 'partnership' are currently touted as the solution by donor and development agencies, studies on decentralization show that in most cases they falter in implementation. Local administrative organizations have been given broad powers in some countries to plan and manage development, but often not the financial resources and qualified personnel to carry those plans out.[16] Decentralization needs the involvement of groups other than the central government and local development agencies. The groups who need to be involved include, in addition to the central government, local institutions, private sector investment, the community and specific subgroups such as women, children and the elderly.

The government's approach to urban services lacks balance and adaptability. National development plans prescribe standard urban investment priorities for all cities. In Indonesia, for example, providing piped water was emphasized even where drainage or solid waste management required more urgent attention. The result was problems with financing and maintaining unnecessary services, and difficulties in financing necessary ones.[17]

Local government agencies have rarely been much more effective. Studies of towns in the region surrounding New Delhi, India, for example, show that water, sewerage and other basic services are minimal. They also show that government agencies recover as little as one-fourth of the costs of providing and distributing water because 30 to 40 per cent of the revenues is lost in leakage, theft and waste. Cost recovery rates for public transportation services in many Indian cities are as low as 40 per cent.[18]

Central government agencies in many countries also give little priority to new construction and low priority to maintenance. Other problems arise because people regard services and infrastructure as 'free' and something to which they are entitled rather than as local resources they should provide for themselves and for which they should pay. Scarce central government resources are drained off from other uses to support services that could be provided and paid for locally.[19]

Some researchers have argued, based on the track record of various governments in providing shelter and urban services, that central governments should withdraw from municipal services and allow the communities to do what they do best, i.e., provide housing and services for themselves. However, in most countries any involvement of the private sector, community organizations, non-government organizations and local municipalities depends on the central government's being allowed to play some key role. Political ideology, resource constraints, socio-cultural traditions and most voluntary organizations, at least in Asia, were created by the central government, and ministry officials often hold dominant positions in them, making central government participation or approval a requirement in most partnership programmes.[20]

The case-studies that follow show how relationships with the central government can be developed. Most successful projects which involve community, NGO and private participation do not run parallel to government efforts, but rather are linked to the central government at key junctures. These linkages can change from project to project and from country to country, but some sort of government connection is necessary for success.

The role of local institutions in urban development programmes

Urban management and development policies are today enabling the poor to do more towards providing their own improved housing and urban services than they once did. But if residents of slums and squatter settlements and those in need of shelter are expected to deliver and maintain their own facilities, then policies are required that will help them to decide when, where, how and at what level services are needed. There are still powerful political forces in place that seek to prevent the direct involvement of the poor, not the least of them the barriers posed by bureaucracies. Many small and insulated decision-making structures must be opened up one by one. Until that happens, the true involvement of NGOs and community groups in urban management and development decisions will remain minimal, although a number of countries have pronounced a policy of official cooperation with NGOs.[21]

Local governments were set up to manage and maintain an urban system, not to develop a new one. They apply existing laws and regulations to the routine maintenance, operation and incremental extension of urban services, and control and regulate certain activities within the city.[22] Hierarchical bureaucratic systems work quite well for these purposes. Urban development programmes need to resolve problems on the spot, to reduce inequity and to increase participation. This calls for an organization that is non-hierarchical, open to a variety of participants and not burdened by regulations. It also calls for different technical and managerial skills than one normally finds in bureaucracies.[23]

How to allow for two different kinds of local government organizations – one to manage and maintain services and the other to undertake new programmes – to co-exist, how to coordinate their activities, how to develop a clear understanding of their roles and responsibilities and how to identify and train a new kind of manager remain to be seen.

The advantages and risks of private sector involvement

During the past decade, privatization policies have been adopted by governments in most developing countries. Evidence suggests that under proper conditions private enterprises and NGOs can – and indeed, in many countries already do – play a crucial role in improving and expanding urban services, infrastructure and shelter.[24] Governments in developing countries have been experimenting with privatization for a variety of reasons. Leading lending institutions such as the World Bank and the Asian Development Bank have been pressuring governments to privatize as part of the overall structural adjustment reforms.[25] But these pressures have also been reinforced by domestic economic, demographic and social changes.

In India, for example, various federal and state government agencies are encouraging private companies to become more heavily involved in land development and low-cost housing construction. In Ahmedabad, for example, the Parshwanath Group, a private construction and housing finance company, plays an active role in providing low-cost housing with support from local regulatory authorities. This private company assembles land for housing projects, obtains approvals from the Ahmedabad Urban Development Authority, helps organize cooperative societies that hold title to land and perform maintenance functions after the project is completed, and obtains mortgage financing for beneficiaries from the Housing and Urban Development Corporation (HUDCO). With government assistance and encouragement, the company has been able to construct more than 17,000 low-cost housing units in and around the city of Ahmedabad.[26] The Parshwanath Group is able to make profits by efficiently integrating its supply systems, constructing the projects quickly to minimize the adverse impact of price increases for building materials and investing efficiently in large tracts of land on the periphery of the city.[27]

Governments in some countries are transferring service delivery functions to NGOs or simply leaving the provision of some types of urban development to private enterprise. In Asia, cooperative organizations, trade unions, women's and youth clubs and religious groups are all involved in some aspects of urban service provision.[28]

Government agencies in developing countries are also offering guarantees or fiscal incentives to induce private organizations to provide shelter and services and loans or subsidies to individuals or groups to purchase services or housing from the private sector. In India, for example, the National Housing Bank has provided equity capital to some private housing finance companies that offer mortgages to individuals buying privately constructed houses. The Housing and Urban Development Corporation in India has used government funds to re-lend to private organizations providing low-cost shelter.[29] Although many countries are experimenting with these and other forms of privatization, the proper role of the private sector in providing what has traditionally been considered 'public services' is still being debated.

Experience thus far with private corporations, NGOs and even informal sector enterprises indicates that all of them have advantages over government agencies in providing some types of service. These include the ability of private companies operating in competitive markets to offer lower production and delivery costs; to increase efficiency in service delivery; to improve access to the latest technology; and to provide greater capacity to obtain and maintain capital equipment, choice and flexibility in service provision; and they are efficient in decision-making. They can also reduce the financial burdens on government for wages, operating costs, debt servicing and investment and lower restrictions in work and hiring practices. Finally they are more flexible in adjusting types and levels of services to changing needs.[30]

In Asia, minibus services are now provided in a number of cities by private contractors. The service is convenient and flexible and serves the slums and squatter settlements that the public bus systems do not cater to. In some cities public parking lots are operated by private companies. In others, the inter-city rail lines which were operating at a loss when run by government agencies turned a profit under private operators.[31] Housing construction is another function best done privately. Despite the fact that many governments have had large public housing programmes, most of the shelters built in developing countries are still constructed by small informal sector enterprises and individual builders.[32]

Opposition to privatization nevertheless remains strong. Among the most frequent obstacles to privatization are: inadequate organization within government for eliciting the participation of the private sector; political opposition from civil service unions or powerful interest groups; the fears of political leaders that control over public enterprises will be lost to unpopular ethnic, religious, political or regional groups; opposition by leaders of NGOs who fear that the poor will be excluded from services or will not have the income to pay for adequate services at market prices;

inability of private companies to provide needed services and infrastructure at affordable prices; insufficient private sector management skills to provide services efficiently and effectively; opposition from those who fear that privatization will allow governments to ignore serious social problems that cannot be addressed adequately by private organizations; and public suspicion of or hostility to private sector participation in service provision.[33]

These obstacles nevertheless are surmountable and the case-studies show how some of these have been overcome. What is important is that private sector involvement be encouraged, for the contribution of shelter to the gross national product, savings, investment and income, turns out to be much greater than most economists and central government planners have realized.[34] Economists are beginning to recognize that investment in housing with private sector investment makes particular sense in developing countries, because it reduces the drain on scarce items such as skilled labour, capital and foreign exchange, and replaces them with relatively low-technology production.[35] Finally the evaluation also shows that private sector participation is not an isolated attempt but has to become an integral part of a larger system, otherwise it is bound to fail.

Opportunities and constraints of community involvement

'Community participation' is defined for the purposes of housing and urban services programmes as the residents' involvement in collective activities aimed at improving their standards of living, including houses in which they dwell.[36] This definition can be further elaborated to include those activities that the community involves itself in to produce housing and urban services, and they include establishing community development committees, fulfilling demands on behalf of the community, identifying and implementing local development projects, mobilizing community resources and disseminating information concerning improved hygiene and nutritional practices.[37]

Three views on the nature and the possible role of the community in the provision of housing and basic urban services have been put forth in the recent literature. According to the first, deficiencies in shelter and basic urban services and subsequently the need for community participation and local action are the symptoms of the exploitation of the poor by the rich.[38] According to the second, community participation is shaped more by governmental constraints and needs than by local needs or settlement conditions.[39] According to the third, held in particular by John Turner, active participation of communities in collective actions furthers the provision of shelter and basic urban services and should thus be promoted and strengthened.[40]

Each of these favours different approaches and is based on different assumptions. When people assume the burden of providing shelter for themselves, they reduce pressure on the government to make up through policies or subsidies the failures of the private market. It has been argued by O'Connor that in a capitalist system the state is caught between two basic and often mutually contradictory functions – trying to maintain or create the conditions in which profitable capital accumulation is possible, and trying to maintain or create conditions of social harmony by looking after the interests of the poor.[41]

One of the strongest critics of community participation as advocated by Turner is Rod Burgess. In Turner's view, a viable housing policy would be based on the principle of self-government in housing and the use of small-scale technological and managerial tools. The principle of self-government implies the replacement of centrally administrative systems with a 'multiplicity of locally self-governing sub-systems'.

Burgess examined Turner's conception of the nature of housing, the relationship between popular government and the private sector, the role of the state and the planner, and his policy recommendations, and argues that the housing problems in the developing countries can be best understood as products of the general conditions of capitalist development rather than the product of particular technological or organizational systems, as Turner suggests.[42] He goes on to argue that, with the exception of a few token schemes, the self-help housing policies suggested by Turner are unlikely to be implemented; the establishment of a 'department of self-help' in each government housing agency would not significantly increase the access of the poor to low-income housing; and that the suggested measures 'can be seen as a technical attempt to level out the symptoms of a structural malaise and to maintain the status quo'.[43] He adds that, even if policies proposed by Turner were implemented, it would lead to a massive diversion of investments away from the middle class, an increase in prices of basic building materials, a dramatic effect on land values and an increased burden for providing infrastructure.[44] The positions advocated by both Turner and Burgess are extreme, however.

It may be much more useful to review the importance of community involvement by examining several interrelated 'myths' that were pointed out by Angel and Benjamin.[45] They argue that middle-class and 'elite' attitudes towards the poor are impediments to squatter settlement improvement and that without considerable change in these attitudes, the squatter problem cannot be solved. They go on to argue that contrary to common belief housing built through community involvement tends to be better kept and enables traditional family structures to be maintained. They add that the urban poor build their dwellings incrementally and therefore require different financing systems, and that squatters usually occupy unused or underutilized land held by private speculators or by government agencies; and that decisions about land use are made to favour landowning interests that dominate local and national politics.[46] Several additional reasons could be advanced in favour of and against community involvement. Some of these are summarized below.[47]

Reduction of cost. One of the main reasons why some government development agencies and international funding agencies promote community participation in urban projects is because it can save money. The argument is that the government's financial and human resources contribution can be reduced if the community undertakes some of the tasks otherwise performed by government agents. Furthermore, the organizational or technical solutions adopted by local participants are usually both cheaper and more appropriate than those that might be imposed from above by the government. This is substantiated by experiences in developing countries discussed in the case-studies in Chapters 3, 4, 5 and 6.

Extensions of services to all communities. Community participation facilitates the dissemination of needed services to more recipients, often faster than it is possible through conventional government services agencies. However, communities have differences among them which can lead to factionalism and conflict.

Mobilization of community resources. Communities are more likely to contribute funds, labour or management in situations where the people are actively involved in decisions concerning project locations, the choice of implementing agencies and individuals, the choice of community leaders for the project, the selection of beneficiaries and the allocation of project resources within the community. However, many cannot or will not want to participate due to lack of motivation, time and technical knowledge. Also, many will not be able to raise funds either from their own members or from government agencies.

The community's identification with the project. Where the community has been actively involved in the development activities, it feels more responsible for the project and is more inclined to maintain and preserve community services and facilities. However, the sense of community responsibility is a necessary but not sufficient condition to sustain interest. In addition, not all will have the ability to manage and sustain the community's interest over the long period of time that may be necessary to achieve results.

Identification of community needs. Community participation ensures an accurate assessment of needs and requirements. Without it the community's response to government initiatives is that of a passive recipient. Local expertise in building and construction can be used, making the results easier to maintain and repair and less dependent on outside skilled manpower. There are, however, limits to the use of indigenous knowledge and expertise. Depending on scale and complexity, design, planning or management might be better undertaken by professionals. The community's involvement also increases its ability to undertake programmes affecting its physical and social well-being, which reduces dependency on government agencies.

Constraints to community involvement. There are some fundamental contradictions inherent in the incorporation of community participation in housing. Governments are wary of community participation, even though they may support it for political expediency, and they have a real fear that grassroots organization will allow too much power to fall into the hands of local communities. Funding agencies want to support and are increasingly supporting community participation, but because they have to control costs and maintain schedules, they are unable to do so extensively, nor do they incorporate community participation into the decision-making and design stages of projects.[48] There is a lack of adequate experience and a paternalistic attitude on the part of government officials and professionals that stems from their training in conventional housing techniques. Evaluations that overemphasize completion of tasks and targets set by government officials or international donor agencies can impede success, as can the rigidity of bureaucratic structures and procedures, since flexibility is needed for community participation. Government officials will often not even wish to encourage it, because the will to instruct the bureaucracy in how to work with the community is lacking. NGO experience in community participation often tends to be limited to the local, rather than the national, level for both economic and political reasons. Therefore such projects tend to remain modest in scale. Finally, communities are not homogeneous in composition, and the gap between the degree of community homogeneity required to develop effective local organization and the economic, political and social heterogeneity that actually exists in communities is fairly wide.[49]

Community participation is time-consuming; it requires the formation of an organization which will be responsible for negotiating an agreement with either the government or the private developer and for carrying out the various tasks involved, such as the allocation of plots, the determination of plot sizes, the subdivision of the site, the implementation of site development and individual house building, the financing of both land purchase and house building, and the management and maintenance of the project. It is not necessary for the community to be responsible for all of these things. Depending on the organization's strength and commitment, it can assume responsibility for all or only a few of them.

The identification of clear aims and gains has to be undertaken and understood by all involved if participation is to be successfully initiated and sustained. Yet with all its pitfalls, community involvement holds promise if government development agencies, NGOs and private developers are willing to embrace it.

Maximizing choices

Increasing people's choices in urban development programmes can be addressed at two levels. At the general policy level, choices can be increased by decentralizing central government and promoting partnerships between the state, private sector investment and community-based organizations. Second, choice can also be maximized at the local implementation level where its effects are immediate and affect a much larger group. This includes maximizing specific choices that deal with location, construction, level of participation, neighbourhood organization, house type, changing family values, social and religious affiliations and individual or familial preferences.

Can maximizing choice through design participation work?

Interesting and successful examples of housing built with community participation already exist in Western countries. Yet even in the West scholars and professionals are still trying to formulate a design process which would allow the community to be involved in an equitable and sustainable manner. The complexity of community involvement planning and design is even greater in less-developed countries, where diversity in social and cultural background often makes participation a fairly difficult process. The issues related to design and community involvement and the boundaries in terms of what should be designed by professionals and what should be left for the community to undertake needs to be explored.

In developing countries, a question that becomes important is how does the planner, designer and implementor determine who the members of the community are that will participate in the design and planning process? Can all parties participate in all aspects of the design and development process? If not, what kinds of design decisions can be left open for discussion, and how will the input affect the overall design? When one talks of about 5,000 or 10,000 housing units, the process of information that needs to pass from the constituency that one wishes to house to the people who are responsible for the project is fairly substantial. The process becomes complicated and time-consuming. When the choice is between staying within budget, getting the project completed in a timely fashion and providing the people with an opportunity to express their opinions, the community invariably loses. This gets back to the larger question of how one organizes communities so that their needs are articulated in an organic and structured manner in a language which people can respond to. That is perhaps one of the most delicate issues in housing programmes in developing countries because communities are not necessarily organized and they are not necessarily articulate.[50]

In the industrialized world, the process of community involvement has to be structured within the overall political decision-making process. Towns and communities are independent of central authority and have the flexibility to make their own decisions. People are also aware of how town participatory processes work, and there is a continuing tradition of activism that helps others become aware of issues relating to their problems. In developing countries, the enormity of economic and social problems mitigate against participation. In many societies there is a tradition of deference to elders and those in power; therefore people may be intimidated or uneasy about voicing their true opinion and will allow either the elders or the community leaders to make decisions for them. Community involvement in developing countries may require innovative approaches that are flexible in the way they allow people to voice their opinions and less deterministic about the kinds of involvement envisaged.

It may not be possible for all housing or urban services programmes to allow the community maximum choice, or even participation in the process. Where that is the case, how can their needs be better served? Designers, developers and housing agencies usually know the income of the target group for whom the housing is being developed, but not its socio-cultural background. They therefore tend to base their design decisions solely on factors thought to be related to income and tied to the ability of the person to afford that particular type of house or apartment. To get a better understanding of community structure and preferences the selection process of beneficiaries may have to be revised from the present random selection of plot or house type to one which is inclusive, where the people can have a say in selecting where they want to live and the type of house that is best suited for their requirement, based on family size, need, work and affordability. The present process of housing programmes, which is to plan, design, implement, select and allocate, may also need to be re-evaluated and revised to allow maximization of choices and community involvement.

Changing family life-styles

The role of changing life-styles in housing, particularly the changing position of women, has been under debate for over a century in the West, and several models have been proposed to address these changes. Since female-headed households, including single mothers, widows and the elderly, are disproportionately represented among the poorest people – in the developing world as in the West – this is an important consideration in project planning. The literature which surveys these changes is limited, but in some of the low-income site-and-services and self-help projects it is apparent that they are taking place. Working women are on the increase and so are their childcare needs. In a number of developing countries, childcare facilities for women working on construction sites are provided by mobile crèches. However, affordable childcare facilities in housing projects need to be developed so that they are accessible to poor working women who require them in other spheres as well.

In developing countries, the fastest growing age groups in society are those over 60 and those under 15. By the turn of the century, for example, there will be 76 million people in India over the age of 60. In the past decade alone, the increase in the oldest population was a little over 38 per cent; the rest went up by only 19 per cent.[51] Until now approaches to institutional housing were based on the assumption that men would do the work and earn the money, but amongst the poor, women and children work too. The physical and space requirements of women, youth and the elderly need to be understood and their energies harnessed if a comprehensive housing programme with individualized approaches is to be developed.

Physical implications related to changing family life-styles

In the West a number of innovative housing projects have been proposed that take into account changing household dynamics. The Danish collective housing model is one such innovation which is being adapted in the United States and other European countries. These communities of about 30 or 40 families supplement complete individual dwellings with a 'common house' that contains a common kitchen, a dining/living area, and various other shared spaces and facilities. The common space in clustered housing is not in itself so unusual; several condominium-type developments have a club house or community centre. A common house differs from a club house, however, in the way the space is used and in its extensiveness. In the Danish 'co-housing' the common house is perceived as an extension of the private residences and is used by the residents on a daily basis and considered as an essential part of community life.[52] The common house concept is based on sharing household responsibilities, where meals, childcare and household duties are shared among family members. Significantly these communities are planned and designed with the residents, and they are also managed by residents themselves. One of the main objectives of 'co-housing' has been to design 'child-friendly environments' that give children many different opportunities for playing and interacting.

In developing countries, small communities where some common facilities are shared could be developed for those families who otherwise may have no social ties: migrant families, the elderly who have been disowned by their children and young single parents who are shunned by the community at large. In 'co-housing' it could now be shared among people who have come together because of specific needs. Rather than housing the elderly in old people's homes and forcing single parents to move from relative to relative in search of temporary shelter or housing them in transitional homes, co-houses would integrate them into the community and provide for their needs at the same time. 'Co-housing' may not be a commune or a religiously motivated community, but it has ideological implications, as it does presuppose that people want to live in a prescribed manner. Therefore such a solution may not be applicable in all cases. However, it does present an alternative which considers changing family life-styles and needs.

Ideological and religiously motivated developments also influence what is planned, designed and built. The standards used, the community involvement achieved and management of the development undertaken may be very different and in such cases may not be replicable for other projects. Communes based on religious or ideological beliefs operate under a different set of rules. Here community involvement can be more effective because the community is already formed, their belief systems clearly articulated and the community leadership is in place. Secondly, the design can be more particularly focused as community preferences can be more readily translated into built form. The rules of living and day-to-day conduct are structured and therefore can be translated into design. Such developments are quite prevalent in India, and they have been based on traditional residential patterns. However, it may not be possible to apply the plans and design for these developments to other developments where religious or ethnic backgrounds are not considered as a prerequisite for participation.

Finally, the recognition of changing family life-styles has implications in the way housing for the poor is designed and planned. Those involved in advocacy, management and community development work find that process, advocacy and management are important but equally important are planning and design. Without planning and design, a comprehensive framework that incorporates changing family needs and requirements as well as locational needs and preferences may not get sufficient consideration. People tend to prefer houses that are pre-built because they assume that finished homes are better designed and built to a much higher standard than that which they could hope to build by themselves, though they might wish to have a say in what is built and some control over its production.[53] Pre-built homes are not necessarily better, as we have learned. Yet there is a large segment of the population that may not be able to design and build houses and certainly is unable to plan and design for the total community. Their needs also have to be met.

Implications for new development programmes

The focus of our housing policies for the poor are shifting from housing construction and site-and-services alone to one of active participation in community development. Local governments and NGOs are beginning to understand the importance of land development processes and are recognizing the economic potential of land. Over-reliance on 'do-gooder' attitudes prevents governments from looking for solutions based on managing the land as effectively as possible and participating in the land market as effectively as developers do. Most land is owned by governments in most countries; yet government cannot effectively manage and maintain it.[54] An effective and equitable method of increasing land for housing and for the homeless is to make it a condition of negotiation between governments and developers in major projects, along the lines of plans now used in San Francisco and Boston, where permission to build in the most profitable areas of the city is tied to providing either low-cost housing elsewhere or providing public space in the project itself.[55] Housing community groups have entered joint-venture agreements with private investors. The Massachusetts Housing Partnership, State Housing Assistance for Rental Production Program and the Home Ownership Opportunity Program provide state support to promote joint ventures between the community and private developers, a strategy that should be investigated for its applicability in the developing world.[56]

One kind of joint venture, called 'land readjustment', permits the recovery of costs for the installation of infrastructure through an exchange of land rather than cash. It is used in Japan, South Korea and Taiwan, and it may be worth experimenting with in other countries. It converts outlying undeveloped land to urban land in return for creating a consortium of owners and the servicing of the land. Government or development agencies take a proportion of the land, usually about 30 per cent, as payment.[57] The payment is offset by the increased value that serviced land commands and often results in full cost recovery. Land gained by the development agency can then be released at below market rates as a direct subsidy or used for cross-subsidies. Since land readjustment adds to the stock of urban land it can also reduce its overall price.

Land-sharing and incremental development are two approaches that try to incorporate private investment, government actions and community involvement. In land-sharing, land occupied by squatters is negotiated between the original owner and the squatters. In incremental development, unserviced land is provided to the poor. Services are brought in incrementally when the community can afford it with the help of local developers. Both options offer benefits and pitfalls that need to be explored in individual circumstances to understand how, where and why they could be used. The Citra Niaga project in Samarinda, Indonesia, and the Khuda-ki-basti project in Hyderabad, Pakistan, have been evaluated to highlight the potentials and risks of such undertakings.

Some of the newer approaches and projects seem to point to a heightened appreciation of the subtle differences in the way people live. The interdependency of community, private and public sector institutions and the increasingly pluralistic character of the political climate in most countries point to new government, community and private partnerships that simply did not exist earlier. Three projects evaluated in this study – the Orangi Pilot Project in Karachi, the Zabbaleen Environmental and Development Project and Khuda-ki-basti in Hyderabad, both in Pakistan – show how such projects have been undertaken and where the problems lie.

Planners of housing projects, however, still need to develop a better understanding of the roles which each of the various actors, including project designers, planners, implementors, financiers and beneficiaries, need to play in order to create communities that offer an environment of reasonable quality to all their occupants. The Aranya township in Indore, India, a mixed-use site-and-services project, and Khuda-ki-basti highlight the complexity of new housing projects, and the issues of planning and design in them.

Increasing choices for people and extending their participation also have their pitfalls. Private interests can manipulate community interest in the guise of improvement and development opportunities. Excessive community involvement can impede and hamper the development process by imposing undue restrictions and controls. Specific communities or other special interest groups can get together and block projects that do not specifically contribute to their well-being even though these programmes may benefit the larger community. The key question remains whether maximizing people's choices and optimizing participation will be used as a control mechanism or as a tool for efficient planning. The danger in any such efforts is that they may become prescriptive, with key development agency officials, planners and designers patronizing the poor and providing them with a controlled opportunity for participation, instead of maximizing their choices and optimizing their involvement.

To claim a direct link between physical space and patterns of behaviour is difficult. In spite of considerable research into the subject, it is not easy to establish the exact connections between environments and behaviour and impute causal relationships to them. There is a wide degree of flexibility in the way people use space. They either adapt their life-styles to the environments, change the environment, or do a little of both. The case-studies described here illustrate some of the issues that need to be addressed. By providing a wide range of choices and, where possible, involving the community in urban development projects, it is hoped that positive attitudes will themselves result in improved living conditions.

CHAPTER 3

NGO and Community Partnerships for Integrated Area Development

Over the last decade, a successful experiment to create an equitable and sustainable community environment has been evolving in Orangi, a *katchi abadi* (illegal subdivision or ISD) on the north-west periphery of Karachi. This 15–year project was initiated by an NGO in response to the problems the residents of *katchi abadis* face getting access to basic urban services.

Karachi has been, and continues to be, one of the fastest growing cities in the world. It has a compound annual growth rate of 4.7 per cent per year. In 1994, the population of Karachi was over 10 million people spread over an area of 2400 sq. km., and it is estimated that it will grow to 13.5 million by the year 2000.[1] This population growth has been the result of the large influx of people to Karachi in 1971 after the creation of Bangladesh, due to rural-to-urban migration and internal growth.

As the city grows, the pressures on Karachi's housing and land markets have also increased and the city clearly faces a severe housing crisis, with fewer and fewer households able to afford formal housing. This has forced a large segment of the poor to seek housing in the informal sector. *Katchi abadi* housing, therefore, has proliferated at about twice the rate of formal sector housing. Over the past ten years, the *katchi abadi* population has increased from 25 per cent to 40 per cent of the total population of Karachi.[2]

Living conditions in low-income areas and *katchi abadis* vary enormously. Over the years, many of these settlements have developed into decent places with fairly good houses and reasonable level of services. In others, practically all services are absent and some have huts made of reed matting, second-hand tin sheets and similar low-quality building material. These settlements have no piped water or sewerage, limited electricity and the health of residents is very poor.

Against this background, the Orangi Pilot Project in 1980 undertook a low-cost sanitation project in Orangi. Since 1980 several other projects have been developed in Orangi in partnership with the community, local service providers and entrepreneurs to improve the living, health and economic conditions of the residents.

Development of *katchi abadis* in Karachi

Karachi's immense size and explosive growth means that most people do not have the means nor the possibility to settle legally. They cannot get a piece of land in planned government or private housing projects, so they encroach upon land with the assistance of middlemen and build their houses in any open place that is convenient to them, without permission of the authorities. Today, Karachi has about 650 *katchi abadis* accommodating about 41 per cent of the population and growing at the rate of 9 per cent against a total urban growth rate of 4.7 per cent.[3] These *katchi abadis* are mainly located on government land without any regard to 'legal property rights'. Over the years the residents of these *katchi abadis* have developed themselves largely through their own efforts and acquired electricity, gas and other facilities. Their housing units have evolved from *katcha* (makeshift) to *pukka* or concrete units.[4]

The most frequent government response to squatter settlements was bulldozing, eviction and resettlement. In the early 1970s a change of policy was announced and the clusters of shacks comprising at least 40 dwellings were called *katchi abadis*. In 1978, the Katchi Abadi Improvement and Regularization Programme (KAIRP) was started by the government with support from the World Bank and Asian Development Bank. Since its inception only 1,210,963 *katchi abadi* residents out of 5,504,380 have benefited from the programme.[5] This programme has been overwhelmed by problems and has not met its target, forcing a large segment of the *katchi abadi* residents to rely on their own ingenuity, or on middlemen and other entrepreneurs to improve their living conditions.

The Orangi Pilot Project (OPP)

Orangi is the largest *katchi abadi* in Karachi.[6] It was first developed in 1963 as a government township of 500 hectares, but migrants flooded the settlement after the 1971 war and the creation of Bangladesh, swelling the settlement to more than 3,200 planned and unplanned hectares. The population is ethnically diverse, consisting of Mohajirs (immigrants from India after partition), Biharis (immigrants from Bangladesh), Pathan immigrants from the northern regions, immigrants from Punjab and local Sindhis and Balochis. This population of about 800,000 living in 94,000 houses[7] include labourers, skilled workers, artisans, shopkeepers, pedlars, clerks and a few white-collar workers. The average family income is estimated to be 1,500 rupees per month (about $59),[8] a number which includes incomes from under 500 rupees ($18) a month to more than 25,000 rupees ($980) a month.[9]

The Orangi Pilot Project (OPP) is an NGO which has been working in Orangi since April 1980. According to its director, Dr Akhter Hameed

Khan, the OPP has adopted a research and extension approach to community development. Dr Khan's work in Orangi is based on his conviction that people organized in small groups can help themselves: 'if social and economic organizations grow and become strong, services and material conditions, sanitation, schools, clinics, training, employment, will also begin to improve'.[10] This kind of community development depends on small units of organization; in the Orangi community, these building blocks are lanes of 20–40 families. At this level, organizers and implementers often have little technical knowledge,[11] so that technical assistance must be geared to maximize local resources and knowledge.[12] These principles of small-scale organization, community research and appropriate technology have determined the OPP's development strategy.

The programmes

The OPP started its work in Orangi in 1980 with a low-cost sanitation programme and spent the next four years working with all members of the community (housewives, middlemen, teachers, health service providers and building material providers) to build community trust and confidence that the OPP was going to be part of the community and stay for the long haul. Once the sanitation programme had gained momentum, in 1994, the OPP started introducing the following programmes: (1) a basic health and family planning programme; (2) a programme for supervised credit for small family enterprise units; (3) a low-cost housing upgrading programme; (4) a school programme to assist in the upgrading of physical and academic conditions of schools established by private enterprise; (5) a women's work centre programme; and (6) a rural development programme. Each programme was introduced after a thorough analysis of the community needs and who the most important actors were in each case. After its inception each programme has been constantly re-evaluated and changed to respond to the evolving community needs. This chapter describes the sanitation and the housing upgrading programme in detail, and outlines the basic health and women's work centre programme.

The innovation in Orangi is Dr Akhter Hameed Khan's approach to sustainable and equitable community development. Through an examination and critique of how illegal settlements are developed, he took the idea of self-help and extended it beyond its definition of houses constructed by individuals who will live in them and applied it to the community as a whole. According to Arif Hasan, who is a consultant to the project:

> Most of Orangi is a squatter colony developed by local developers and private entrepreneurs (*dalals*). The people here have built their houses with the advice and assistance of local building material manufacturers and suppliers (*thallawalas*). A housing program in Orangi could not be successful if it aimed at anything more than helping people to continue doing in a better way what they were

already involved in doing. To achieve this it was necessary to understand what was happening in Orangi in the housing area and the roles of the various actors in the housing drama and their relationships with each other, on the one hand, and with materials, technology and culture, on the other.[13]

From this, the OPP has developed for Orangi a comprehensive programme of 'community help'.

The Orangi Pilot Project's development and history

The Orangi Pilot Project was organized in 1980 after Aga Hasan Abidi, the founder of the Bank of Credit and Commerce International (BCCI), invited Dr Akhter Hameed Khan to undertake social work in Orangi.[14]

The OPP, officially established as the Orangi Pilot Project Society and Orangi Trust, gets its funds from other sources besides the BCCI Foundation; other supporters are UNICEF, the Aga Khan Rural Support Programme, the Aga Khan Foundation, the Swiss Development Corporation and other international donor agencies. In the year 1990–1 it was granted Rs 2,200,000 from BCCI and Rs 6,930,381 from other agencies for a total budget of Rs 9,130,381. Of this it spent Rs 4,918,560 on both OPP societies and Rs 4,155,000 on the Orangi Trust, which gave out loans for family enterprise work, for a total of Rs 9,073,560.[15]

Dr Khan's approach in Orangi is based on his conviction that people organized in small groups can help themselves; 'if social and economic organizations grow and become strong, services and material conditions, sanitation, schools, clinics, training, employment, will also begin to improve.'[16] Dr Khan believes that community participation on a large scale without the existence of smaller organizations is impossible. These small organization units should begin with a lane, and then expand to the community. Engineering technology and implementation procedures, the product of the traditional client, engineer, contractor relationship, have to be constantly modified to suit the new system, where the users, organizers and implementors often have little or no technical knowledge or artisanal skill.[17] Expert assistance is provided to maximize the use of local resources – personal savings and initiative, manual and managerial skills.[18] These principles lay behind the OPP's approach in developing the Orangi Pilot Project.[19]

The Orangi Pilot Project's Low-Cost Sanitation Programme

In 1981, the OPP began to implement a community-based sewerage system in Orangi. Originally Orangi had primitive forms of excreta disposal, poorly laid drains and no rainwater drainage, creating a dangerously unsanitary environment that led to disease, death and damage to housing stock. For that reason sanitation was considered to be a more urgent problem than housing. Water-logged lanes and soakpits were destroying the health of the inhabitants and the value of their property.

Before the OPP's sanitation programme, most residents used the bucket latrine, where a shell of a truck or car battery would be used for collecting excreta. The sweeper would remove this shell and throw out the excreta into a natural creek (*nullah*). The waste water usually flowed out into the street. The cost of the sweeper service was about Rs 15 per month (60 cents). The more affluent residents dug soakpits. The cost varied from Rs 1,800 to Rs 3,000 ($72–120). Here too the waste water flowed out into the streets, and the soakpits filled up in two to three years. The cost of having the soakpit emptied by the municipal truck was about Rs 75 ($3). In most cases after the first cleaning the soakpit filled up every three to six months as it fell further into disrepair. Some residents of Orangi also laid sewerage lines from their houses to the nearest natural drain. However, this was not common and in most cases the work suffered from technical shortcomings.[20]

The OPP concluded that Orangi's population should have modern sanitation (flush latrines and underground sewerage lines) in place of the disastrous medieval sanitation that existed there. Dr Khan was convinced that it was possible for low-income people to install their own systems at an affordable cost. Using simple technologies the OPP started using the organizational capabilities of the local leadership in each lane. To do this the modern sanitation system was broken down into its various components: (1) the sanitary latrine inside the house; (2) underground sewerage lines with manholes and house connections in the lane; (3) secondary or collector drains; (4) main drains and treatment plants.

Through surveys the OPP found that the house owners in Orangi were willing and able to assume responsibility for funding, constructing and maintaining the first three levels, which made up 80 to 90 per cent of the system. The main drains and the treatment plants, like the main roads and water lines, would remain the responsibility of the central authority.

Through research the OPP was able to reduce the cost of construction drastically and to persuade the house owners to accept full responsibility for it. To do this they simplified designs and standardized steel shuttering for the manholes that could be installed by the home-owners themselves. They then surveyed and mapped the site, prepared models, slides and visual aids showing how the sewerage lines were laid out, and prepared instruction sheets, posters, etc.

The Orangi Pilot Project's approach to community involvement

Removing the mistaken belief that people in *katchi abadis* would be supplied with sewerage and sanitation without charge by the government was the difficult part. When Dr Khan asked people in the community, it was clear that they wanted a conventional sewerage system, but it was also clear that they were unwilling to pay for it – they wanted Dr Khan to persuade the Karachi Development Authority (KDA) to provide it free, as it did (or so the poor perceived) to the richer areas of the city.

Dr Khan spent months, accompanying representatives of the community to petition the KDA to provide the service. When it was clear that this would never happen, Dr Khan set to work with the community to find alternatives. He would later describe this first step as the most important thing he did in Orangi – liberating, as he put it, the people from the immobilizing myths of government promises.

Once it was clear that the people would have to finance the sewerage system themselves, actually getting them to pay for it was not difficult. The people living in Orangi were not destitute. They were poor, but they had built their houses with their own savings. Their houses represented an average investment of RS 20,000–25,000 ($800–1,000),[21] and the desire to improve them was a powerful motivation for constructing sanitary lines and underground sewerage.[22]

Motivating the community

As part of their extension approach the OPP next looked for individuals in each lane willing to act as leaders and trained lane managers and masons; provided and explained maps and estimates; loaned out tools and shuttering; and provided social and technical guidance and supervision.

Motivating the residents in Orangi was achieved by the OPP's 'social motivators', that is, local residents who had been involved with the development of Orangi. One was a *thallawala*, another had assisted a land-subdivider, another had been a building contractor and yet another a plumber. They were responsible for communicating with the people, organizing meetings and helping settle sociological and organizational problems. With the help of slides, posters and leaflets, the benefits of the OPP's low-cost sanitation was explained. In these meetings the importance of lane organizations was stressed; no technical assistance was possible without such an organization.[23]

Another motivating factor was health, especially of children. Mothers saw most clearly the connection between filth and disease, and realized that sanitary lines and dry lanes would reduce disease and the price paid for it. Installing the underground sewerage system would also stop the expense of cleaning overflowing soakpits and solve the problem of not getting timely help at cleaning the soakpits.[24]

The lane as a unit for organization

The most important decision made by the OPP was making the lane, which consisted of 20 to 40 houses, as the unit around which community involvement was planned. The lane was a small unit where all people knew each other, so problems of mistrust would not arise. This also meant that the OPP did not have to involve the existing political leadership in Orangi, which functioned at the neighbourhood or sector level. The selection of the lane as a working unit, however, caused technological problems in developing an underground sewerage system, but they were eventually solved quite ingeniously.

Each lane selected its own lane manager, who on behalf of the lane formally applied to the OPP for assistance. There was no standard structure for the organization; it varied from lane to lane. The lane managers collected the money, received tools and organized the work.[25]

The OPP's simplified design and method of construction reduced the cost of sanitary latrines and manholes to less than a quarter of the contractor rates. The system also eliminated kickbacks and profiteering, and this further reduced the cost to an investment of Rs 1,000 (an average month's income). The residents were asked to consider the lane as an extension of their house and to manage and finance it as they had financed and managed their own house. Initially, the OPP staff met with resistance and grumbling. However, slowly and over a period of two years, the message got across, and after the first couple of lanes accepted the idea and started the work, the others followed.

To convince the residents of the need to participate, the OPP staff had to redesign the proposed sewerage system to allow individual lanes flexibility to decide and organize how they would work. Concentrating on lanes as the unit for involvement was important, as it gave the OPP time to assist lane managers in organizing the other lanes. Residents were also able to see the results in the lanes that had already implemented the OPP's proposal, which helped convince both those residents and international development agencies that were questioning the OPP's approach that the system worked – physical conditions were improving and there was less pollution.

The sewerage system and the technology used

Physical planning was done for one lane at a time. Invariably in the beginning only those lanes which were located near a creek (*nullah*) or could easily discharge into it participated in the programme. However

after four years, by 1986, the unit of operation increased to entire neighbourhoods.[26] This also came about because of a change in design for the
sewerage system used.

The design of the original sewerage system was that sewage be dis-
charged into the *nullah* running through the settlement. However, this
meant that the problems of the lanes was simply being shifted to the
creeks. Initially only those lanes located near the creeks benefited from
the programme. The lanes far away from the creeks had to come together
first to lay secondary drains to reach the creeks. This would be difficult
and would also take much longer. It was felt that many sewerage lines
would clog up occasionally and would have to be cleaned out. However,
due to the lack of water, proper flow of sewerage was not possible.

To overcome these problems it was decided to place a one-chamber
septic tank, or *haudi* as it is known locally, between every connection. This
mini-septic tank prevents solid matter from flowing directly into the drains.
A T-joint at its outlet is designed to prevent scum from entering into the
sewers. The size and design of the *haudi* were determined by its cost to
the user and not by any engineering standard. The *haudi* was to be emptied
when full by the respective households. To popularize it and educate the
people in maintaining it, meetings were held and posters prepared and
pasted on the walls in each lane. The building of the *haudi* has added to
the cost but this had to be done in order to provide a better and disease-
free environment.[27] The *haudi* is connected to a square manhole which has
a 6- or 9-inch diameter reinforced concrete pipe laid along each lane.
Connections to household squatting pans are through a 4-inch diameter
reinforced concrete pipe.

The manhole was also changed from the circular manhole design
specified by the municipal corporation. This manhole required skilled
labour and cost more; it was also too light. People could easily lift it and
throw in garbage. To stop this from happening the manhole cover was
changed into a *in situ* concrete slab, which was too heavy to lift and
projected beyond the manhole chamber, reducing the need for highly
skilled labour. The cost of the manhole was also reduced to Rs 120 from
Rs 400 per manhole. The OPP supplied the reusable steel shutters for this
type of manhole construction. The pipe diameter, of 6–9 inches, was
oversized in order to give the advantage of more tolerance for errors in
slope when working with unskilled labourers.[28]

Secondary drains were eventually introduced. The design and implementation of secondary drains is more complex than the lane drains. Technically it involved calculating the location of lane drains and their slope
without a master plan. This has caused problems initially where, because
the calculation was incorrect, the connections did not meet. At this stage
locally elected councillors were involved, as they were seen to be most
effective in persuading neighbourhoods to join in. They were also used to

pressure the municipality into financing the people's scheme. Councillors get money from the municipality for specific development works in the areas they represent. The number of neighbourhoods that are now forcing councillors to spend funds on laying underground secondary drains is increasing as they are now aware of the advantages of having the whole system functioning effectively. More recently, water supply has increased, and with the laying of most lane drainage and secondary lines, the *haudi* has been eliminated from the design.

Between 1981 and 1993, Orangi residents, under OPP coordination, installed sewers serving 72,070 out of 94,122 houses.[29] As of November 1993, the total investment by the people was Rs 57.2 million ($2.28 million); OPP investment in research and extension of new technologies was Rs 3.78 million ($151,200) – a ratio of 1:15.11.[30] In areas where the OPP provided services, 87 per cent of lanes have underground sewerage and 88.9 per cent of houses have latrines. In non-OPP areas, 38 per cent of lanes have sewerage and 42.5 per cent of houses have latrines.[31] The OPP was able to provide these sewerage lines at one-fifth of the cost of the service provided by KMC – Rs 15.28 (60 cents) as opposed to Rs 90 ($3.60) per linear foot.[32] The cost of a sanitary latrine inside the house and the underground sewerage line in the lane was Rs 1,000 ($90) per household.[33]

Lessons from the sanitation project

The lessons learnt from the sanitation programme gave the OPP the expertise needed to solve other problems and improve the quality of health, the houses the residents live in and their economic conditions. They showed that *katchi abadis* in Karachi can build their sewerage on their own without international aid, without waiting for the local bodies to take decisions, without resorting to large-scale technological changes and without catering to a system of development where corruption is an integral part. Furthermore, in the process of acquiring these services the OPP has brought about a change in the unequal political relationship that people have had with their governments and has developed their trust in the OPP. The Orangi Pilot Project no longer needs to motivate the people into organizing for the sanitation programme. The people organize themselves, and it is their representatives who approach the project. Instead of one lane at a time, now whole neighbourhoods represented by their councillors are approaching the OPP for technical know-how.

Health and family planning programme for low-income housewives

OPP research showed that Orangi had a very high incidence of typhoid, malaria, dysentery, diarrhoea and scabies, as well as very high infant and mother mortality. A survey showed that a substantial portion of income was spent on curative health care, and yet little attention was paid to preventative measures. In June of 1984, the OPP started a pilot programme to impart health education and family planning information to poor women.

Once again, the OPP programme depended on the coordination of very small-scale organizations. Conventional clinics were ineffective because traditional gender segregation made it difficult to reach women through a public facility. In place of a fixed centre or clinic, the OPP introduced mobile training teams which approached groups of women through selected activist families in their neighbourhood. A neighbourhood consisted of 10 to 20 lanes. The mobile teams consisted of female doctors, health educators and social organizers. This discreet intervention proved to be a more effective educational strategy.

To complement the education programme, the OPP arranged a decentralized system of delivering medical and family planning supplies, in which the neighbourhood health activist became the distributing agent. The health activist was a permanent and confidential source of supply for the members of her group. She also arranged for IUD fittings and sterilizations by the mobile health team.

Originally, the OPP's health and family planning education and services were limited to 3,000 families. The effectiveness of this programme is evident in a survey undertaken by the Aga Khan Medical University, which found that over 95 per cent of the children are immunized, 44 per cent of families practise birth control, epidemic diseases are controlled and personal hygiene and nutrition have improved.[34] The Aga Khan Medical University study also showed that infant mortality per thousand fell from 130 in 1982 to 37 in 1991. Morbidity also fell from 18.94 to 8.29 per cent during the same period.[35] Housewives were taught the value of personal cleanliness (the improved physical conditions in the settlement has made a big difference), and they have been shown the different food groups that constitute a balanced diet. In 1991, the OPP revised its model to reach out to a larger number of families. A three-month health curriculum was introduced on the prevention of common Orangi diseases, methods of family planning and improved nutrition and hygiene.

The OPP's Health and Family Planning Programme had identified a large demand for immunization and family planning services among Orangi women. Now that this demand had been revealed, many private clinics were suddenly able to provide the services in conventional clinic settings. In the light of this development, in November 1993, the OPP revised its health programme, shifting emphasis from the neighbourhood health activists to more formal programmes in schools, private clinics and family enterprise units. It is too early to evaluate the success of the programme, but the OPP's health section continues to manage the health centre training and provides support to existing clinics. The annual budget for the health programme is only Rs 476,388 ($19,000). The average annual cost of teaching prevention disease and birth control to one low-income family is Rs 100 ($9).[36]

Programmes for women's employment

A programme of Women Work Centres (WCC) was started by the OPP in March 1984, beginning with a survey of employment patterns in Orangi. The survey revealed that the traditional patriarchal pattern of exclusive dependence on the father's earnings was being undermined by the rising costs of living and uncertain employment; in Orangi, wives and daughters were being forced to work to supplement family income.[37]

The OPP chose to address the largest category of women's employment in Orangi: 'stitchers' completing piecework for contractors in Karachi. Women stitchers in Orangi complete piecework bound for export to international markets. The system of contracting that employs the women was exploitative financially and socially; male contractors paid women unfair wages, often mistreating and sexually harassing them. Domestic gender segregation made it difficult for Orangi women to organize as a labour force.

The OPP set up Women Work Centres to fill the role of the contractor, dealing directly with suppliers and customers, and paying fair wages to individual workers. The WCCs, located in family homes in the neighbourhood, were lent machinery and supplies by the OPP and were assisted in contacting clients. Families running WCCs in their homes were allowed to charge minimal overheads, and were required to earn a majority of their income through their own piecework. This eliminated rent and cut out the profit which had formerly gone to the middleman contractor; reduced costs allowed the WCC to pay a fair wage to the workers. The WCC daily wage was Rs 20 (80 cents), compared with the standard daily wage of Rs 15 (60 cents). WCC managers tended to be women, and to treat the women workers, who were also neighbours and friends, fairly.

Initially, the WCCs required substantial financial and managerial support from the OPP. Because they were inexperienced in dealing with suppliers and customers, and because they had difficulty disciplining their labour force, WCCs tended to lose money. Over time, however, WCC managers learned to weed out untrustworthy suppliers and customers, to motivate their workers and to increase quality control. WCCs, operating as supportive community organizations rather than exploitative contractors, have proved more efficient and reliable than traditional contractors. Clients in Karachi actually prefer to use WCCs because of their greater productivity, and individual workers prefer to work for WCCs because of their higher wages.[38]

By the sixth year of the programme, productivity in the WCCs had risen to the point that they had become self-sustaining. All subsidies from the OPP were discontinued. The OPP continues to provide loans for the creation of new WCCs, but these are paid back with interest.[39] As of August 1993, there were 168 stitching centres to whom Rs 2,189,580 ($87,580) have been given in loans, of which Rs 1,207,980 ($48,320) had already been recovered. The WCCs perform the functions of contractors in a friendly manner without cheating the women workers. The presence of women managers and the location of the centres in family residences has made the profession of stitching quite respectable.

The Orangi Pilot Project's housing programme

In 1986, the OPP started a housing programme following the same research and extension approach. Most building materials and construction in Orangi depended on *thallawalas*, the local building material manufacturers and suppliers. Technically, construction was substandard due to the builder's lack of technical knowledge and the lack of adequate supervision by the owner. Faulty construction resulted in dangerous and unsanitary conditions, and in wasted time and resources.

The OPP recognized that improving housing depended on the participation of the *thallas* in upgrading building materials and construction norms. Research into the operations of *thallas* was undertaken to learn how the OPP could improve their technology without disrupting their operation.[40] The OPP set about improving material fabrication on site, in direct contrast with the conventional approach of conducting research at either educational institutions or national building centres.

Whenever land was subdivided in Orangi, a building contractor moved in and established a manufacturing yard for blocks, lintels, pipes and slabs. Asbestos sheets and other industrial roofing material are also stocked by them. In Urdu the building material yard is called a *thalla* and the yard owner *thallawala*. The thallawala has been responsible for the building of Orangi houses. He supplies not only materials and labour on credit to the new plot owner, but also cash credit at times. His profit margins are low and most do not use physical force to recover dues – social pressure is far more effective. Most people want to live in that area and do not want a bad name. The thallawala is indispensable to the community, and his advice and intervention is sought in most public and personal matters. Besides the production and supply of building components and the extension of credit, the thallawala also plays other complementary roles; he coordinates skilled labour for construction, imparts technical advice, supplies tools and accessories on rent, coordinates the sale and purchase of plots and houses and also serves as a social worker for the area.[41]

In the earlier part of the subdivision, most plots were 80 square yards;

in the recent subdivisions further to the north and west it is 120 square yards. The quality of houses and their construction have improved substantially since the 1970s when most houses were *jhuggis* (shacks made of reed mats and bamboo). Today most of the houses are block masonry with asbestos or tin-sheet roofing. A small but increasing number are being built in reinforced concrete, the ultimate in affordability and social status. The permanent nature of this construction is a function of security; structures in these areas have been legalized and owners have property rights. The cost of an 80-square yard serviced plot sells for anywhere between Rs 60,000 ($2,400) and Rs 100,000 ($4,000), far beyond the reach of any poor person. In the 1970s when the subdivision was taking place, plots were being sold for Rs 1 (4 cents) a square yard.

House construction

House construction in Orangi has been incremental, the quality and extent of construction depending on the availability of resources at any given time. By now the settlement is old enough for most areas in Orangi to have essential services. With the emergence of the thallawalas as a strong local service centre, building materials and other components and tools are also readily available on credit. The result is the permanent (concrete and block masonry) construction that we see today.[42]

In Orangi, studies carried out by the OPP show that: 5–7 per cent of the houses were built by the people themselves without any help; 55–60 per cent of houses were constructed with the help of skilled masons and unskilled labour hired on a daily-wage basis; 15–20 per cent of the houses were built on labour rates by contractors hired by the owner; and 4–5 per cent of the houses are classified as permanent structures as they have *in situ* concrete plinths, plastered walls and reinforced concrete roofs.

Faults and problems in house construction

This process of house construction is full of problems and wastage. Technically, construction is substandard due to the lack of technical knowledge of the mason and lack of adequate supervision by the owner. Substandard workmanship, lack of curing of concrete and faulty details are common. The galvanized iron roofs leak because of incorrect transversal and longitudinal overlapping and insufficient slopes; roof supports sag, and the unplastered walls absorb water when it rains. The most serious defect, however, is the erosion of plinth walls and foundations from sulphate in the soil and the consequent rising damp in the walls.[43] Another source of weakness is the use of substandard hand-made blocks, the main building component for walls and foundations. They are usually not dried long enough and the concrete is not cured long enough, causing cracks in the buildings that lead to eventual collapse. Most houses have faulty ventilation and sanitation systems (though the latter has since been addressed by the sanitation programme); the ventilation in most houses is non-existent. The use of galvanized iron or tin for the roof makes the interior of the house unbearably hot in summer.

When houses are extended and new reinforced concrete roofs put on them, the walls usually have to be rebuilt, wasting the previous construction, and consequently both material and money. This is also true when floors are added – foundations and walls have to be rebuilt and the investment made at phases two and three is wasted. In phase four when the upper floor is added, construction is affected to such an extent that nearly the whole house has to be reconstructed.

The solution

The OPP research introduced standards for the construction and design of buildings elements such as improving hand-made blocks to machine-made blocks, improving the production of a pre-cast lintel and a pre-cast staircase and introducing a new batten-and-tile roofing system. In addition the OPP also designed foundations for load-bearing walls, developed standard house plans and designed new windows and wind-catchers for ventilation. As part of their extension programme they developed the thalla as a research and extension base, offered training to masons for using the new building components, provided plans and estimates, lent tools and shuttering and provided supervision and technical guidance.

Machine-made blocks

There are about 200 thallas making concrete blocks by hand. The most popular sizes produced are blocks of $3\frac{3}{4}" \times 5\frac{3}{4}" \times 9\frac{3}{4}"$, known as cut size, and $4" \times 6" \times 10"$ (full size), which together constitute about 95 per cent of production. The cut size is both more profitable and most produced. Technical problems in the blocks result from poor compaction, curing and improper mixing of cement and concrete. These make the blocks brittle and prone to weathering and sulphate attack. These sub-standard blocks are capable of bearing a load of only 100 pounds per square inch (psi), one-eighth of what is required for good construction.

Improving the quality of the blocks made in the thallas was therefore essential. To ensure uniform mixing, firm compaction and curing, block-making was mechanized. After extensive research the OPP perfected a block-making machine in 1987, which would work on a miniature scale, so that each thalla would be able to purchase its own mechanized block-making machine, a concrete mixer, vibrator, pump and moulds. A local supplier was found, and after suitable modifications the machine was made available to thallas at Rs 75,000 ($3,000) each. The OPP loaned the money to buy the machine. In all 29 thallas are now producing machine-made blocks, four of which are working under OPP supervision. Each has received a loan which they are paying back at the rate of Rs 2,000 ($80) a month.

The machine-made blocks are four times as strong as the hand-made blocks, and cost 30 per cent more. They were initially sold at the same price as the old blocks to ensure that people would buy them. The OPP demonstrated that the thallas could recover the cost because mechanization had tripled the daily production from 700–800 blocks to 2,000–3,000. Machine-made blocks are also larger, 6" × 8" × 12", so the total number of blocks needed is reduced. Therefore, even if a new block costs more than an old block the total cost remains more or less the same and the new ones have the advantage of a load-bearing capacity of 800–1,000 psi, allowing an additional storey when desired without rebuilding. They also eliminate the need for reinforced concrete columns in two-storey structures and they support reinforced concrete roofs.

Lintel and staircase design

The design and production of the lintel were also improved by demonstrating to the thallawalas the importance of mixing cement and *bajri* (sand) in the correct ratio, of proper placement of reinforcement bars for optimum strength and of building simple hangers to keep a half to one inch of space between the bottom of the lintel and the bars to achieve the right strength. Misplacement of reinforced bars not only causes the lintel and slabs to flake, but throws load distribution off balance, leading to a weakening in strength of both the slab and beams used.

The OPP has also introduced the design of a staircase built with pre-cast slabs. Its components cost Rs 2,000 ($80) compared to Rs 4,000 ($160) for a reinforced concrete staircase. The pre-cast slab staircase takes up less space and can be constructed in 3 days compared to 15 days for the reinforced concrete staircase.[44]

Foundations and ventilation

The OPP has developed simplified foundation design, where plain concrete footings have a load-bearing capacity of 2,500 psi and are strong enough to support a ground-plus-one-storey house. Two alternatives, one for soil-bearing capacity of one ton per square foot, which has a wider footing of 3' × 3" and another with a shorter footing of 1' × 9" for soil-bearing capacity of two tons per square foot were developed.

Ventilation in existing houses was improved through window design and location. In the case of using the new roof, the ceiling was made 10 feet high and fanlights were designed to improve air circulation. Air circulation was also improved by locating a 1' × 4' window on the windward side and a 4' × 4' window on the leeward side, installed at 2-foot height from the floor level. Also the traditional concrete or brick *jali* (grille) was replaced by a new flat iron grille which covered three-quarters of the length of the room and was 1' × 6" in height. The new grille cut down the dust accumulation and was easier to clean and maintain.

On the roof, vents were designed as openings in the ceiling covered with a grille to allow light and ventilation. However, they have run into problems as chickens are raised on the roof here, and chicken and other bird droppings tend to fall into the house.

Batten-and-tile roofing

After having established a working relationship with some of the thallawalas in Orangi, the OPP turned to providing an alternative roofing design using batten and tiles. People with low incomes build houses first with tin or asbestos roofs, and eventually remove the roof and replace it with a permanent one. To do this the old walls have to be demolished entirely. The cost of reinforced concrete used for the new roof is also unaffordable to most, so in fact roofing improvements to houses are rarely undertaken. Most of the urban poor continue to live under roofs that are too hot in summer and leak when it rains. The batten-and-tile roof design is an innovation based on a pre-cast roofing design. The technology of producing pre-cast beams and slabs was modified so that they could be manufactured by the thallas.

The new slab is 2' × 3' in dimension, more like a large tile, and is 2 inches thick. It has reinforcement bars of ¼ inch diameter, 3 of them in each direction. The screeding on top of the slab is about 1½ to 2 inches. It also includes a layer of waterproofing and is evenly finished to form an impermeable surface. The new slab, being smaller in size, is lighter and can be lifted in place with a small pulley. Most pre-cast slabs are much larger and need a sophisticated lifting system to be put in place. Being smaller it can also be thinner, making it lighter. The required thickness is then gained by screeding. The batten is 8" × 4" × 3" which supports the slabs, with a ring beam of 3" × 6" that goes around the wall.

The thallas pay Rs 60,000 ($2,400) for the purchase of moulds, vibrators and curing tanks to produce the slabs and battens. This investment adds another product for the block-making thalla. The cost of a batten-and-tile roof works out at Rs 21 (84 cents) per square foot. The 1½-inch screeding costs Rs 4 per square foot; the ring beam Rs 3 per square foot; and labour costs are Rs 7 per square foot, for a total cost of Rs 35 ($1.4) per square foot. An asbestos roof costs about Rs 25 ($1) per square foot.[45]

The batten-and-tile roof has significant advantages over asbestos, tin or reinforced concrete. It allows for a double-storey extension; it has the same strength as reinforced concrete roofing; it allows the house to be rebuilt incrementally, room-by-room; allows for expansion and has flexibility of growth. It is quick: using this technology a room can be built in a day. It is cheaper: reinforced concrete costs Rs 60 ($2.4) per square foot, about 40 per cent more than batten-and-tile. But it also allows no flexibility; the whole house has to be built at the same time.

Reinforced concrete columns can be added to existing 4-inch walls by cutting wall corners and adding a ring beam; the structure is then strong enough to carry an upper storey. Using this technique it is not necessary to demolish all the walls; 40–50 per cent of the existing wall is saved. This means that houses with old walls can be provided with new roofs incrementally and, if needed, an additional storey could be added without much cost.

As of now, only one thalla is producing and supplying batten and tiles. A second thalla will join it, but has not yet started regular production because its moulds proved defective. Two more thallas have shown interest in batten-and-tile manufacturing.

Role of the thalla

These simple improvements in technology and quality have been important and have avoided the necessity of the OPP having to set up its own thallas to compete with the existing ones. The OPP realized that the thalla was an institution that played both major and complementary roles in Orangi. The thallawala's relation to his customers is both social and commercial. The credit he provides is flexible and informal, and repayment depends on the social pressure the thallawala can exert on his clients.[46]

On average a thalla employs 4 or 5 people. In 50 per cent of the cases the thallawala is illiterate and has to employ a *munshi* (accountant). Labourers hired for the production of blocks, lintels and slabs are paid by the block or by the square foot in the case of slabs and lintels. The average wage is Rs 0.50 Rs per square foot and Rs 0.15–0.25 per block, depending on size. Wages are paid monthly, but the workers are given a daily allowance (*bhatta*) of Rs 10–15 (40–60 cents), about 20 per cent of their daily wage.[47]

Besides employing labour and an accountant, the thallawala also employs a cart driver, either on contract or on wages, to deliver the finished product. Cartage is a source of profit; 66 per cent of thallas own donkey carts. The drivers' monthly pay ranges from Rs 900–1,200 ($36–48) and the expense of maintaining the donkey is about Rs 300 ($12).[48]

The OPP's recognition of the thalla's role in the community was important; it encouraged the thallawala to accept the OPP's recommendations and purchase the mechanized block-making equipment. Even so, however, the number of thallawalas that are manufacturing mechanized blocks is not sufficient to meet the local demand, partly because OPP studies found that those thallawalas who make mechanized blocks sell 70 per cent of them to customers outside Orangi. By March 1991 thallas in Orangi had sold 5.5 million machine-made blocks of which only 1.6 million stayed in Orangi.[49] Although the use in Orangi of machine-made blocks is slowly increasing, the demand from outside is still much greater and thallawalas sell to whoever comes to them first.

When a house owner goes to a thalla to get machine-made blocks, in most cases they have to wait a month or so for delivery. Time set aside for construction of home improvement is very limited and work generally has to be done in 15–30 days, so delaying work because blocks are not available causes great inconvenience to the family. In addition there might not be another thalla close enough for the house owner to go to. The house owner is unwilling to wait, and buys hand-made blocks instead.

Another reason for thallas selling so many machine-made blocks outside Orangi is that they do so through dealers. Consequently orders are much larger than those placed by individual home-owners. Selling to dealers assures thallas of future and long-term orders and a constant source of income. Therefore, even if local demand increases, the demand from outside will continue to be much more lucrative.

Mason training

A mason training programme was introduced in 1987 as part of the OPP's effort to improve the skills of masons working in Orangi. They receive training in construction techniques, the proper use of equipment, the importance of waterproofing, proper earth compaction, curing, the proper ratio for mortar used in jointing, the batten-and-tile roofing system, the building of correct foundations for walls and the installation of pre-cast staircases.

An important aspect of their training is to learn to provide adequate ventilation using skylights, vent cowls and the courtyard. Training is given through class lectures, meetings, instruction sheets, leaflets and manuals and on-site supervision. Ninety-six masons have been trained thus far.

Analyses of the Orangi Pilot Project's housing programme

The OPP, through its research and extension programme, acts as a consulting agency to the home-owner when extensions or new houses are built. When the home-owner decides to build an extension, add a new roof, build an upper storey, or build a new house, he has usually had two options: he can ask the thallawala for building material, consult with him on how to build and have a mason referred to him, or he can approach a mason for the construction and through the mason approach the thallawala. With the introduction of the OPP's housing programme, the home-owner now has the third option of approaching the OPP for these services. Unfortunately many are not aware of this housing programme, as it is not well advertised. A lack of trained masons and not enough thallas manufacturing the required building materials have also slowed down the effort.

Since 1986 the OPP has provided 50 households with services ranging from structural redesign and ventilation improvements, to new reinforced concrete structures, machine-made block walls, and batten-and-tile roofing. For this study, 20 of these houses and 20 houses where the OPP did not provide its expertise were surveyed. They included houses with no recent changes and those that had undergone substantial changes, some that pre-dated the batten-and-tile roofing system and some using machine-made blocks. The survey showed that in both OPP and non-OPP houses 95 per cent were owners of their property and 5 per cent were renting the premises.

Of the houses surveyed, over 60 per cent of occupants were introduced to the OPP through the thallawala; 35 per cent had become aware of its housing programme in other ways, or were employed by the OPP; 5 per cent had been advised by masons who had received training from the OPP. Once the occupant decided to use OPP services, which are provided free of cost, the OPP prepared a plan, worked out the quantities required and gave an estimate of construction and material costs. It also suggested design modifications, particularly to improve the stability of the structure and the ventilation. After the plan was prepared and estimates made, a work schedule was drawn up, materials ordered, and work commenced. During construction the OPP provided supervision to ensure quality of construction. It also loaned equipment for lifting the batten and slabs when new roofing was being done. Other equipment is loaned to masons during construction.

The survey showed that, in general, the overall condition of houses where the OPP has intervened is much better than those without OPP intervention. Houses without any improvements in the sample were generally at the second stage of development, that is, they had walls of hand-made blocks covered by galvanized iron roofs. The condition of the houses reflected their income: the poor lived in structures with unplastered walls with cracks in them, the roof had leaks and holes, slopes for draining rainwater away from the house were not adequate, flooring was cracked and uneven and ventilation in most cases was non-existent. In houses where the occupants earned combined incomes of around Rs 5,000 ($ 200) per month, the houses were in better condition, the walls were plastered and maintained, the roof had no holes, but the ventilation was still insufficient and improvements were needed.

Where additions or improvements had been made, 95 per cent of them used RCC construction. In only two houses, did people use batten-and-tile roofing without OPP assistance.[50] In these houses the condition of the structure and quality of construction were fairly good, but ventilation had still not improved.

In houses where the OPP had provided services, the conditions of those rooms where improvements had been made were good. Where new batten-and-tiles roofs had been added the ceiling height had been increased to 10 feet, improving ventilation. However, in rooms where no improvements had been made, the conditions were similar to those of unimproved houses. OPP technology has definitely improved conditions, even in older interventions where only guidance to improve ventilation by introducing vent windows under roofs had been given.

The survey showed that in over 60 per cent of cases, OPP suggestions for design improvement and ventilation had not been followed. In some cases they were too expensive; in others, the home-owner had been convinced by the mason that these changes were not required and that the slab openings for wind would leak. The design of the OPP's wind-catchers was not accepted because it was felt that it would lead to problems in upper storey expansion or cause dirt to fall into the room.

Elements of success

The success of the OPP's work in Orangi is clearly visible and is unquestionable. Most residents in the community of 800,000 have access to drinking water and underground sewerage. The streets are no longer flooded with waste water and raw sewage. The conditions of houses have also improved. Houses are being upgraded from mud-brick temporary construction to permanent construction using either the OPP's batten-and-tile or other construction systems. A large percentage of homes are now owner occupied and Orangi is developing into a mixed-income community with incomes ranging from 500 rupees ($18) per month to more than 25,000 rupees ($980) a month.

Infant mortality rates are dramatically down, having fallen from 130 per thousand in 1982 to 37 in 1991, and compare favourably with other low and middle-income settlements where the rates are much higher, i.e., ranging from 95–110 per thousand. Programmes for women's economic empowerment also have had a measured success.

The housing programme has also had measured success. By November 1993, 130 demonstration units had been constructed; this statistic hides the fact that a significant number of OPP residents are making changes to their houses using OPP technology, but without formal OPP assistance.

These simple improvements in technology and quality have built upon the traditional roles of the thallas in Orangi. With the emergence of the thallas as a strong local service centre, building materials have become readily available on credit, enabling most houses to be built with permanent (concrete and block masonry) construction materials. The thallawalas have retained their traditional social and commercial relationships, providing flexible informal credit to their friends and neighbours who are also their customers.[51]

The success of the OPP's approach can be measured by the replication of its approach in other cities and the failure of the government-sponsored Katchi Abadi Improvement and Regularization Program (KAIRP).

Using its internal-external concept, the OPP has now replicated the Orangi sanitation project in several *katchi abadis* in Karachi and other cities in Pakistan.

In contrast the KAIRP, started in 1978 by the government with support from the World Bank and Asian Development Bank, has been overwhelmed by problems and has not met its target. Since its inception only 1,210,963 *katchi abadi* residents out of 5,504,380 have benefited from the programme.[52] To keep pace with the increasing backlog, the programme will have to service 100,00 households per year over the next decade. The recovery rate of the programme is very poor; for example, the Lahore Development Authority (LDA) has spent 200 million rupees ($8 million) and recovered only 10 million ($400,00) in the last seven years. The project design makes it inoperable if there is more than a 20 per cent default in payment.[53] According to Arif Hasan, 'OPP's Low-Cost Sanitation Program points a way out of this dilemma.'

Perceived problems

Despite considerable success, the Orangi Pilot Project faces problems that constantly need to be addressed.

The *nullahs*, which carry the sewerage to the sea, are silting up and with heavy rain they are prone to flooding. Untreated sewage, to which not only Orangi, but also the whole of Karachi is contributing, is being taken to the sea. The housing programme has had limited success and has to grow to make a major impact on the physical conditions of the homes in Orangi. Also the Womens Work Centers and the Family Planning Program are constantly under threat from religious fundamentalists.

Since the OPP has expanded the role it is playing in Orangi it runs the risk of assuming the *de facto* responsibilities of all problems that arise in the community. Therefore it must draw up a clear statement outlining its responsibilities and identifying the stages at which it will be involved. This will make the community aware of the OPP's role and responsibility and that of the other local service providers. As it stands, everyone assumes that since the OPP has developed the project, it is responsible for all problems associated with it.

This is particularly important, given the current socio-political climate and increasing ethnic strife. Orangi is an ethnically diverse community and is particularly vulnerable to ethnic and racial conflict. Also, the OPP has diversified its work from a more neutral role of technical solution provider to that of a social, economic and educational service promoter. This change of roles is being viewed by some as conflicting with traditional social and cultural values. The OPP has to be very careful about its role because, within the current tensions in the city, its work, so painstakingly built up over the last 14 years, could easily be undermined.

Potential for transfer and adaptation

Urbanists around the world are re-evaluating the traditional model of government-sponsored urban infrastructure to the poor communities. The OPP's research and extension approach fundamentally questions conventional service delivery systems, taking a new look at how communities can assume responsibility for services formerly considered the responsibility of government. The effectiveness of the OPP's flexible research and extension methodology, and the division of the sanitation project into external and internal components, can be reapplied to a number of projects.

To transfer this innovative approach to community upgrading, attention must be given to the needs, abilities and desires of the community. Communities involved in such projects must have the technical guidance of a supporting organization to manage and finance such efforts and to identify the potential and capacity for community organization. The success of the OPP continues to be used to promote community-managed development projects.

Since 1983, community organizations, activists and NGOs from other *katchi abadis* and informal settlements in Karachi and other cities of Pakistan have requested OPP assistance in replicating its Low-Cost Sanitation Programme in their areas. The OPP is involved in several transfers and adaptations of its approach.[54]

In Karachi, social and technical guidance is being provided to other NGOs and CBOs working in: (1) Manzoor Colony; (2) Malir Cantonment; (3) Islamia Colony; and (4) Welfare Colony. In Bhitai Colony, assistance and guidance is being provided to the officials and engineers of the Cantonment Board on the design, estimate and implementation of external sanitation as well as on coordination for internal development.

In Sukkur, through a UNICEF Urban Basic Services Programme, external development work has been completed in three *katchi abadis* (Gole Tikri, Kaan 18–19 and Pind Bhusa lane).[55] A 28-acre cesspool has been drained and a plan for converting it into playgrounds has been prepared. A pumping station has been built, and a low-cost treatment plant near a river bed designed. Also, a trunk sewer from the cesspool to the pumping station has been laid. Work on internal development is also in progress.[56]

In Hyderabad, through the World Bank Shelter Project, work has started in three *katchi abadis* (Gujrati Pura, American Barracks and American Quarters). Assistance, guidance and training has been provided to Hyderabad Municipal Corporation engineers for design, and an estimate been prepared for the implementation of the external project. Training is being provided to local NGOs for the implementation of the internal component.[57] The lessons learned from the OPP's replication efforts are:[58]

1. Given the right support and motivation, the capacity of communities to work together in most informal settlements can be enhanced.
2. There are four levels of sanitation: the latrine in the house; the primary drain in the lane; the secondary collector drains that link the primary drains; and the trunk sewers and treatment plants. In all settlements that the OPP has worked in, the communities were in a position to invest in and manage the construction of the first three levels.
3. The external and internal components have to be carefully planned, sequenced and managed. The project can only be undertaken if there is a plan to undertake the external development in a short period of time, or if there is another alternative available for the discharge of the raw sewage. The community cannot be asked to wait for ever for the trunk lines to be completed. Also for the successful implementation of the internal component, an NGO or another intermediary has to fulfil the function of motivating, organizing and training the community. Government agencies cannot fulfil this function.
4. The role of the government agency has to change. It must provide funds for the NGO to set up and operate an office on site, and appoint and fund the training of officers to coordinate government-funded external works. Middle-level government officials must also be provided with training and orientation to support this work effectively.
5. The role of international agencies and their consultants must change. They must establish processes and procedures so that the community can be partners in development with the government.

Lessons learned

The OPP's integrated area development approach has significantly improved the living conditions of the urban poor in Orangi. Its research and extension approach has led to the development of programmes that are rooted in the local development process and include the local actors.

The focus of the OPP's work was to lower the cost of sanitary latrines and sewerage lines to such an extent that the house owners of Orangi could afford to pay it. Without this drastic reduction in cost it would not have been possible to persuade the low-income families to undertake the responsibility of self-financing, self-managing and self-maintaining the underground sewerage lines. Bringing the cost down through extensive research enabled them to have a successful community participation programme.

Some of the noteworthy features of the sanitation programme that we may be able to transfer and adapt in other settlements are:

- In order to undertake the project effectively and let the lane residents be in charge of the project, no master plan was done and no time targets were fixed. Necessity, ability and strength of social organization dictated the timing.
- Community participation involved only the implementation of the project; the design and research were done by professionals.
- Political involvement was minimal and all residents were treated equally.
- The project itself was simply organized without any fanfare; only when the project became widely accepted did local councillors organize their neighbourhoods to do the work.
- Bureaucracy and red tape were completely eliminated. The official hierarchy was only maintained in documents, otherwise all workers were treated similarly.
- Local technology and materials were used. The suggestion of plastic pipes instead of reinforced concrete was not accepted as plastic pipes are manufactured using imported technology and the local building suppliers would not be able to deal with it.

Now that the OPP has officially been accepted by the mayor as the agency for implementing the principle of 'internal' development by the residents and 'external' development by the Karachi Municipal Corporation, it will be under pressure from the government officials to show results. Therefore it must try and deal with those problems it can control and refrain from moving into the business of lending money.

Its success in adapting simple technology and in drawing on the ingenuity of local institutions and skills available in the community has important lessons to offer to other communities. It has provided us with an opportunity to take a new look at housing and community development. It has shown that housing and its services can be divided into two categories: 'external' and 'internal'. External activities should remain the responsibility of the municipality or other government agency, and 'internal' those the local community should control. Several approaches need to be worked out that can be applied to solving the housing problem in developing countries.

The sanitation programme showed that it is possible to bring the community together in small manageable groups to undertake what is otherwise perceived as a government responsibility. In its housing programme, however, the OPP wisely did not attempt community participation in its traditional sense of forming a community association to address the housing problem. They recognized that housing is an individual activity and instead concentrated on those members of the community who play a direct role in providing housing, that is the thallawala and the mason, and on improving their product and skills. This development of technology and skills will have a lasting effect, even after the OPP has stopped playing an active part, as improved technology and building skills will now be developed and available in the community. This is its success, which can be replicated in other housing projects as well.

The OPP's research and extension approach fundamentally questions conventional service delivery systems, taking a new look at how communities can assume responsibility for services formerly considered the responsibility of government. In none of these four programmes did the OPP see its role as providing a service to the community, a solution which would simply substitute NGO for government services. Instead, it researched existing community potentials in order to develop them by providing appropriate technical assistance. In the end, the community would provide the service for itself. This approach to community development demonstrates the flexibility required for successful NGO intervention in low-income urban settlements. Applying its methodology to a sequence of problems, the OPP developed organizational and technical capacities in a particular problem area before moving on to address another. As a result of this flexibility, the OPP projects stand on their own, but together demonstrate the effective long-term role of an NGO working in a single community on an ongoing basis. The effectiveness of the OPP's flexible research and extension methodology, reapplied to a number of projects in a single community, is its true achievement and the measure of its success.

CHAPTER 4

Multi-Sectoral Partnerships for Environmental Micro-Enterprise Development

Cairo has become one of the largest cities in the world, with an estimated population of fifteen million on an area of 1,000 km^2 and growing at a rate of almost one million every eight months. As a consequence, immense strain has been put on basic services, especially the collection and disposal of solid waste.

Greater Cairo generates around 6,000 tons of solid waste per day.[1] Responsibility for the management of the solid waste system in Cairo is shared between the Cairo Cleaning and Beautification Authority (CCBA) and two traditional groups, the Wahis and the Zabbaleen, who have worked together to collect and remove the city's garbage; the Wahis control the routes and contract with home-owners, while the Zabbaleen collect the waste and transport it to their settlement, where it is sorted and recycled or used for animal fodder.

As the city grew and the amount of daily garbage sky-rocketed, Cairo's garbage collection needs began to overtake the Zabbaleen's capacity to provide services. The Zabbaleen were a marginalized and undervalued community with little or no organization or power. They lived in settlements with few basic services, and suffered from environmental devastation, little economic opportunity, lack of education and a host of other problems endemic to urban slums. Even worse, with the government threatening to look elsewhere to more 'modern and efficient' systems to meet the city's need for trash collection, the Zabbaleen faced the possible loss of their traditional livelihood.

In response to these problems the Zabbaleen Environmental and Development Programme was initiated in 1981. Founded on the premiss that the Zabbaleen already provided a valuable service and filled a necessary niche in the infrastructure of greater Cairo, it sought to improve radically the living conditions and to build the capacities of the Zabbaleen community in the Moqattam area, where over 50 per cent of Cairo's garbage collectors live in deplorable environmental and sanitary conditions. A variety of partnerships involving local organizations, government, technical assistance groups, NGOs and international funding and development organizations has resulted in a number of projects designed to extend services to the Moqattam area, create economic opportunity and generate income through the development of micro-enterprises, consolidate waste management, expand collection services and build human resources. These projects have collectively worked to preserve the Zabbaleen's livelihood, begin the creation of more powerful community organizations and legitimate their role as valuable service providers entitled to basic services.

History of solid waste management in Cairo

Cairo's immense size and explosive growth results in political, economic, social and environmental imbalances that negatively effect the quality of life in the Greater Cairo Urban Region. The demand for services is great, often outpacing the ability of the government to provide them. One area of especially pressing concern is the collection and disposal of solid waste.

Responsibility for the management of the solid waste system in Cairo is shared by the CCBA and the traditional private sector waste collection system that has evolved within the last 50 years and which includes the Wahis and the Zabbaleen. Wahis were the original garbage collectors. They initially came from the Dakhla and Kharga Oases, migrated to Cairo about 100 years ago and entered the trade of garbage collection and disposal. The Wahis took control of the household waste disposal system by subcontracting with the owners of the building, thus gaining proprietary rights.[2] The Wahis dried the waste materials they collected in the open air, selling the end product as fuel. Due to the rapid population growth in Cairo during the 1960s, the Wahis could no longer handle all of the city's solid waste. Moreover, as new sources of fuel supplanted dried organic waste, the Wahis were confronted with new economic pressures.

The Wahis were able to maintain their control of the garbage collection industry with the help of jobless and landless pig breeders from Upper Egypt, who had moved to Cairo in search of work. With very limited skills, these pig breeders fell into the trade of garbage collection by default. An agreement was reached between the two groups; the Wahis kept control of the trade by subcontracting with the owners of buildings and served as administrators of the system, and the migrants took over the role of collection. The Wahis collected the money from the buildings while the migrants (now called Zabbaleen, Arabic for garbage collector) collected the garbage and ensured fodder for their pigs.

This system of waste removal served the old city of Cairo well over the years, providing economical and effective household waste collection services. Nevertheless, the service is now constrained by various factors. The relationship between the Wahis and the Zabbaleen is strained despite having been renegotiated over the years, because the Wahis' position in the hierarchy of the trade is a privileged one; they control the routes and contracts and make the most money. Other constraining factors are the rapid pace of urbanization experienced in Cairo, pushing the traditional trash collection system beyond its limits, the harsh environmental and health conditions found at the Zabbaleen settlements which interferes with their ability to work effectively, the image of the Zabbaleen as an unproductive burden on society and the absence of a shared vision among the Zabbaleen about the future of their community and the potential of their trade.

Currently, the Zabbaleen collect and process approximately 80 per cent of Cairo's trash, while the remaining 20 per cent – which is predominantly street waste – is picked up by the Cairo municipality.

The problem

Perhaps the most severe and immediate problem of the Zabbaleen was the horrible living conditions in their settlements. In 1981, at the time that the Zabbaleen Environmental and Development Programme was initiated, the majority of houses were of brick or stone; however, in the Moqattam Settlement the conditions in the settlement remained poor, as evidenced by this description in a report by Environmental Quality International in 1981:

> Despite the major change in living conditions implied by the construction of permanent homes, the physical environment at The Gabbal (Moqattam) remains appalling. The settlement has no water supply, and very few of the homes are supplied with electricity (main lines have been strung in only a few streets). The sorting of the refuse inside the houses leaves them cluttered and often filthy. This situation is mirrored by the condition of the roads, which are heaped high with waste paper, piles of animal manure mixed with organic residues, tin cans, and often animal carcasses. Millions of flies swarm about, and the air is usually filled with the smoke of fires which have either been set deliberately to dispose of unwanted paper or result from spontaneous combustion of organic residues.
>
> Climatic conditions are also severe at The Gabbal. The site is high and has no protection from the wind. There are few trees. The natural sand and dust blown in from the desert combines with the powdery residues of fires and fine particulate wastes to make visibility nearly zero on windy days. On hot days, the stench of garbage, animal manure and carcasses is overpowering.
>
> There is no government school, no consumers' cooperative, no health clinic or pharmacy. While there is an abundance of grocery shops, greengrocers and butchers, prices are quite high for some essential goods such as meat and sugar, at least partly because of the absence of competition from a cooperative. There is no sewerage system, not a single telephone, and no means of transporting emergency patients to the hospital.[3]

Moqattam also suffered from increased overcrowding, in part because of the new trend of two-storey brick and stone dwellings. Families who used to live in one-storey houses now build two-storey houses on half their land and sell the other half, raising the population of Moqattam and putting an even greater strain on the environment and the almost non-existent services.

In the face of a solid waste crisis, the Zabbaleen system was considered obsolete and the Zabbaleen themselves were perceived to be a primitive community incapable of meeting the requirements of modern-day urban life. Neither the government nor the general public knew very much about the Zabbaleen community or their trade. The value of their services was underestimated and taken for granted. The Zabbaleen themselves lacked the resources, the political organization and the vision to expand their economic opportunities and protect their own interests. Over the years, it became increasingly apparent that the survival of the Zabbaleen as effective service providers required a major intervention on the part of governmental and non-governmental organizations to improve the living conditions in garbage collector settlements and to upgrade waste collection and processing systems for an expanding Cairo.

The solution: the Zabbaleen Environmental and Development Project[4]

Despite the general view of the Zabbaleen as an unproductive, backward community, a small minority of Egyptian and international environmentalists began to take a serious interest in their life and work. They were impressed by the industriousness of the Zabbaleen in providing waste collection and disposal services to a city as large as Cairo, and were particularly intrigued by their ingenuity in creating work from waste for tens of thousands of low-income residents. Environmental Quality International (EQI) received a grant from the Ford Foundation to assist in upgrading the living conditions of the Zabbaleen.

Another major participant in the Zabbaleen Environmental and Development Programme was the Zabbaleen Gameya. The Gameya was first established by the late Bishop Samuel, Bishop of Social and Ecumenical Services of the Coptic Orthodox Church, as an association that represented the interests of the settlement. Members of the Gameya were the heads of the most prominent families in garbage collection and acted as its leaders. The Gameya was concerned with the interests of the garbage collectors, especially the very poor.

However, since many of the garbage collectors lived in one area, namely Moqattam, the association was able to provide the community with services and hence was transformed from an NGO to a CDA, or community development association. EQI was instrumental in helping the Zabbaleen Gameya develop into the current garbage collector's association, with the

The Zabbaleen Environmental and Development Project organizational structure

- *The Zabbaleen Gameya*: Established in in 1970s by the Coptic Orthodox Church, the Gameya, or Association of Garbage Collectors, is the community's governing body. It serves as the primary liaison between the Zabbaleen and other interested constituencies and has been instrumental in channelling the necessary human resources, and organizational and financial support.
- *Environmental Quality International (EQI)*: A profit-making consulting firm serving as the primary organizer and implementor of the project. It has created a common vision among the Zabbaleen and identified the requirements and potential contributions of their services. EQI has been instrumental in encouraging both governmental and non-governmental support for the project.
- *The Association for the Protection of the Environment (APE)*: It was established to manage and operate the compost plant with the aim of increasing profits while at the same time improving the surrounding environment. APE also played a crucial role in establishing the Primary Health Care Programme and the Health Immunization Programme.
- *The Ford Foundation*: Provided both funding and resources for undertaking an investigation of the life and work of the Zabbaleen and also assisted in the design and implementation of several interventions.
- *The International Development Association (IDA)*: The IDA of the World Bank started the Zabbaleen infrastructure and facilitated the programme by funding the first Egypt Urban Development Project.
- *The Egyptian Government*: The Governorate of Cairo obtained financial support from the national government, and then integrated the Zabbaleen into Cairo's waste management system. Finally, the government created the regulatory mechanism for the institutionalization of previously informal waste collection services.

goal of expanding to represent the whole area and ultimately other garbage collector areas in Cairo Governorate.

The programme consisted of a number of projects initiated over a span of five years, and was based on an exploratory, experimental approach whereby project ideas and designs emanated from the learning experience acquired by EQI's team in the field, and from their interaction with the environment and the community. There was no blueprint for the development of the settlement, but the projects evolved out of a flexible process based on experience, local participation and collaboration.

Although the programme has generally been extremely effective in creating positive change in the Moqattam settlement and in the garbage collection industry in Cairo, individual projects have met with varying degrees of success; the programme is an untried, innovative solution to difficult problems. Such an approach is by necessity a learning process prone to unforeseen hurdles and stumbling blocks.

Programme components[5]

Before the introduction of the project the Zabbaleen had little social, political or economic power. As a result, their ability to collect and process garbage was seriously hindered. A combined effort involving a broad cross-section of the urban landscape, private consultants, NGOs, CBOs and governmental actors aimed to broaden the scope of the garbage collection and processing. This involved the following: (1) consolidating waste management potential; (2) expanding basic services to the Moqattam settlement; (3) creating increased economic opportunity through the introduction of micro-enterprises; and (4) enhancing the human resource development capacity of the Zabbaleen. To achieve this over the last ten years the following projects have been introduced.

Area upgrading and infrastructure extension project

The government of Egypt, in cooperation with the International Development Association of the World Bank, financed this project for the construction of basic infrastructure and facilities to upgrade the Moqattam settlement. It provided basic infrastructure services and addressed the settlement's need for educational and health services. Piped water, electricity and sewerage networks were installed. The streets were levelled and paved. A map of the settlement was drawn; names were given to the streets and numbers to the buildings. A primary school and a health centre were established.

This led to a dramatic rise in the value of land, and gave the residents a feeling of security that there would not be any more evictions as there had been in the past. Thus, many of the Zabbaleen sold parts of the land they occupied at prices that were very profitable considering that the land theoretically belonged to the state. The Zabbaleen were able to bypass this point legally, by stating in the contracts that they were finding derelict buildings or dumps on the plot of land being sold. The Governorate of Cairo later evaluated the land at LE 50 (about US$ 15) per metre, and invited informal settlers to buy the land legally and to own it. However, unresolved conflicts remain over prices and other property issues.

In addition to land tenure problems, the infrastructure project had other unforeseen consequences. At the time the study for this project was initiated, the number of buildings in the settlement was estimated to be between 700 and 800. To date, this number has more than doubled. The infrastructure that was appropriate at the beginning of the project is no longer able to withstand the increased demand placed on it, and breakdowns of the system abound. Visitors going to Moqattam for the first time are dismayed by the physical appearance of the settlement. This physical deterioration could have been somewhat reduced if the engineering component of the area upgrading project had been designed with long-term growth in mind, and if provisions for system maintenance had been ensured. Nevertheless, despite the limits of this project the construction boom and increasing demand on utilities point to higher income levels, the result of successful development.

The internal clean-up project

This project received multiple funding from the Ford Foundation, Oxfam and the Soeur Emmanuelle Fund. The aim of the project was to improve the level of cleanliness and sanitation in the settlement. Zabbaleen residents, under the direction of the Gameya, removed tons of accumulated waste and manure from their settlement. This was done on a daily basis until 1987 using four trucks that were acquired through the Gameya.

Recently, however, the project has faltered, and the settlement is once more home to piles of refuse. There are numerous reasons explaining why this project, which was quite successful, has now, for all practical purposes, stopped; however, the main reason is that the project ceased to be economically viable. Once the instalments on the trucks were paid, the owners had no incentive and were no longer as committed to collecting the settlement's household waste.

Had the internal clean-up project allowed for an awareness-related component, or had the programme effectively changed people's attitudes concerning hygiene and sanitation, the issue of economic viability, though crucial, would have mostly affected only the logistical aspects of the project. The project's problems were further compounded when the nearby municipal dump was closed, and the truck drivers were ordered to drive 50 kilometres away to Katameya dispose of the garbage. With the service becoming erratic, people started throwing their waste in the local dumping grounds established higher in the settlement, or anywhere else in the streets.

The Small Industries Micro-Enterprise Development Project

This project, funded by Oxfam, was designed to provide the Zabbaleen with new business opportunities related to their trade. The project concentrated on establishing small community-based recycling industries designed to maximize the resource value of waste. Counting on both a technological and a credit extension component, the Small Industries Project enabled the Zabbaleen families to buy plastic-granulating machines to recycle plastic and rag-pulling machines to recycle rags.

Yacoub Girgis is one of many Zabbaleen that have benefited from the Small Industries Project. An 80 year-old garbage collector, he and his sons have collected garbage for over 20 years and are pig breeders or zarrabas in the settlement. As well as collecting garbage, Yacoub was a scrap dealer. He was one of the first garbage collectors to receive a loan for the Small Industries Project. He bought a rag-pulling machine at the end of 1983 and worked it with rags gleaned from sorting garbage. As the mechanization project came into being, Yacoub Girgis could not afford to buy a truck and so he stopped collecting garbage himself and started to buy garbage from other collectors, continuing his work on the rags. While working on the machine Yacoub modified some of its mechanical aspects to increase its productivity, and, in fact, he was one of the first people to make a maintenance workshop in his recycling area for other rag-pulling machines and plastic machines in the settlement. He even went further, inventing a modified version of a rag-pulling machine. Yacoub Girgis is still a scrap dealer, a pig breeder and still sorts garbage as well as working on the recycling of cohna, or rags, into a secondary material of great value in the recycling industry.[6]

Like Yacoub, many other Zabbaleen of Moqattam provided invaluable inputs to the design of resource recovery and recycling technology in the Small Industries Project. Their participation facilitated operations and ensured that both production and market requirements were met.

The Women-Headed Households Project

This project, funded by the Ford Foundation, was designed to provide income-generating opportunities by extending credit to widows, divorcees and women with unemployed or disabled husbands. These women represent the poorest and most vulnerable group in the settlement.

Loan recipients in the Women-Headed Household Income Generating Project were identified through a self-selection mechanism. Instead of being screened by an outside committee, clients participated in selecting recipients from among their relatives, friends and neighbours. Beneficiaries also decided what type of enterprise they would use their loan for. Loan repayment guarantees and support for female borrowers were obtained through the formation of credit groups, following a tradition that is deeply embedded in the culture of low-income women in Egypt. The idea behind this tradition is the collective saving of money by a group of people who all contribute a fixed sum of money on an agreed-upon date (usually once a month), then take turns to draw the full amount deposited.

The key to the success of the project has been the role played by the extension workers, described as the lifeline of the Women-Headed Household Project. Their respected position within the community and their commitment, encouragement and follow-up have made the project, which is still in operation, one of the most successful components of the Zabbaleen Environmental and Development Programme.

Despite its success in reaching and catering to a targeted and vulnerable group, the project has not yet become self-sustainable, even after six years of operation. The main reason is that the revolving fund does not cover the administrative expenses. There are other problems in the project related to marketing.

The Animal Health and Production Project
(the veterinary centre)

This project, which was initially funded by the Catholic Relief Services, addressed the community's animal husbandry practices and the inherent health hazards to both human beings and animals. A veterinary centre was established in 1986, and was managed in its initial phase by EQI. Since 1989 the centre has been managed by the Gameya. The project was, and still is, extremely successful, though it is now beset by funding and management problems. In 1990, the funding agency discontinued funding the Animal Health Project, and the membership fees for the clinic as well as fees for medical services do not cover the total running costs of the centre. The Gameya is increasingly hard-pressed to make up this deficit. The veterinary centre cannot keep up with the increasing demand for services, and unless its funding problems are resolved, the centre may not survive.

Another aspect to note about the Animal Health and Production Project is that although it addressed the community's need for maintaining the health of the animals, the project design did not involve the Zabbaleen in the decision-making process nor in project implementation. In the initial phase, the project provided charge services, and to date the fees charged are minimal. Thus, in this project, the Zabbaleen were and still are recipients rather than participants.

The route extension project

In response to an increased demand for services, Oxfam funded this project to extend the waste collection routes of the Zabbaleen to low-income areas which had previously been neglected. Initially, the Zabbaleen could not see a business opportunity in marketing their services to other low-income settlements in Cairo because of the low value of the waste from these settlements. Indeed, once initiated, maintenance of this service was hampered by the fact that the garbage collected was of little value to the Zabbaleen. This problem was solved through the Garbage Collectors Association (Gameya), who started collecting fees from the households and paying the garbage collector a fixed sum for his services. Even though collecting fees from households was not an easy task at first, it now presents no problem; low-income communities are quite willing to pay for an appropriately designed and reasonably priced sanitation service. The Zabbaleen, under the supervision of the Gameya, continue to provide a reliable service to previously unserved low-income areas.

The mechanization project

This project was initiated by EQI and the Gameya when the Governorate of Cairo issued a decree in 1987 banning the use of donkey-drawn carts for garbage collection. Consequently, the Zabbaleen had to mechanize or else lose the right to pursue their trade. The project, which was funded by shareholders and supplemented from the Soeur Emmanuelle Fund, was designed to provide the Zabbaleen system with the capacity to respond to government requirements for upgrading waste management and service delivery standards. This process, by necessity, involved the Wahis, who controlled much of the traditional system, and whose interests were sometimes at odds with those of the Zabbaleen. After years of dialogue, the Wahis and the Zabbaleen resolved their conflicts and began harnessing their financial and human resources to respond to the new regulatory framework imposed by the government.

In 1987, the Environmental Protection Company was established by EQI and the Gameya to provide vehicles for the settlement. Soon after, Wahis and Zabbaleen organized themselves into more than 50 small private companies, funded mostly by the wealthier and more powerful Wahis, and operating in the neighbourhoods they had both traditionally serviced. Electing to stay as small independent companies and working closely with their traditional clients enabled the Zabbaleen to introduce reasonable increases in prices that were sufficient to cover their additional costs without losing their client base. This strategy provided the Zabbaleen community with the human and technological resource base to respond effectively to a major portion of Cairo's current and future waste management needs.

The project has had both positive and negative implications. On the positive side, mechanization has enabled the garbage collector to finish his rounds in a shorter time, thus giving him more time for leisure or other productive activities. Mechanization has also reduced the need for child labour and increased children's chances of being sent to school. Moreover, mechanization has definitely improved service delivery standards.

On the negative side, the project has proved costly due to the frequent breakdowns of the trucks and to the lack of experienced drivers and mechanics. Trucks, which are perceived by garbage collectors as their source of livelihood, have become a priority item in their channelling of expenses. Indeed, some claim that the increased income in the settlement is offset by the expenses incurred by the trucks. In response to this, the poorer Zabbaleen prefer to rent rather than to buy trucks.

Taken together with the route extension project, the mechanization project has enjoyed high participation and success. It focused on linking environmental improvements with enterprise promotion, benefiting to the maximum possible extent from an understanding of the social structure and kinship relationships among the Zabbaleen. The programme also capitalized on a thorough analysis of market conditions and opportunities for Zabbaleen services, and the development of a workable strategy for capturing larger segments of the market over time.

The composting plant

This project received multiple funding from the European Community, the Ford Foundation and the Soeur Emmanuelle Fund. The aim of the project was to develop a composting plant based on simple rudimentary technology, with a view to easy operation and maintenance. This plant would provide an outlet for the vast amounts of accumulated organic waste in the settlement by transforming it into fertilizer, and generate income to fund and support other development activities.[7] Responsibility for the management of the compost plant was assumed by the Association for the Protection of Environment (APE), established in 1984 as a registered Private Voluntary Organization. Its role was to manage the compost plant and to provide for other development activities.

Despite the wide variety of programmes the directors of the composting plant have been able to initiate and encourage, the plant itself is plagued by various problems, mostly technical in nature. The composting machines, despite their simple design, suffer from frequent breakdowns and receive low quality input from the *zeribas* (cattle shed owners).

Rug weaving and paper recycling programme

The APE has also helped initiate a school for rug weaving, literacy classes, a paper recycling project and a health awareness programme for pregnant women. At the APE rug-weaving school girls from the community are invited to learn how to make rugs by working school looms. Girls are trained for several months and at the same time receive a monthly salary until they start producing carpets; then they are paid according to the amount and quality of rugs they make. Carpets are made from scrap material donated by textile and garment factories.

The rug-weaving school provides classes in literacy, personal hygiene and health awareness. The underlying objective of the school is to motivate girls to learn to read and write while they are earning money by making rugs. Since its inception, 160 girls have graduated from the APE literacy school, 70 of whom have looms at home to make rugs.

A good example of someone who has benefited from this project is Samia Wadie, a 28-year-old woman from a garbage collector's family in the settlement. She has been working with APE at the rug weaving school for the past 8 years. In the beginning Samia used to make rugs on her loom at home in the spare time she had after she finished helping her family sort garbage. During her training months at the rug weaving school she also attended literacy classes, obtained a certificate equivalent to the primary level education in Egypt, and continued to the next level of education in an ordinary school. About 3 years ago, Samia, because of her strong enthusiasm and motivation, became a trainer at the rug weaving school and is responsible for receiving rugs produced by girls who work on looms at home.[8]

The paper recycling project is another activity connected to the compost plant. After having been nominated to attend a workshop on recycling and to give their personal experience of the Zabbaleen, two APE employees learned the simple process of paper recycling from a participant at the workshop. They returned to their home settlement and initiated a paper recycling programme, producing greetings cards made from waste paper donated by offices and companies.

APE employees are involved in other recycling projects as well. Ezzet Naim Gindy is a 29-year-old man from the Zabbaleen settlement. He is one of the few people in the settlement who has a university degree. Before joining the APE three years ago, Ezzet and his family had a small business recycling plastic with the use of plastic-granulating machines. They were so successful they were able to stop collecting garbage, obtain their supplies of plastic by buying from other dealers in the settlement and hire extra labourers. Ezzet himself has now stopped working in his family recycling enterprise and contributes his management skills to the APE as director of several development activities and assistant manager.

Health care projects

There are a variety of health care projects serving the Zabbaleen in Moqattam and raising awareness of health issues, especially among women.

The APE Maternal Health Care Programme trains girls from the community as health visitors to promote general health awareness for pregnant mothers. At the same time, the midwives project from the Order of St Mary's Dispensary works in coordination with these health visitors. When mothers near their term of pregnancy, the health visitors inform the local midwives who can supervise the deliveries, mitigating possible hazards of a delivery carried out alone.

The health visitors of the Health and Immunization Programme, a project run by the Association for the Care of Garbage Collectors, carry out similar services. Being chosen from the community, the health visitors have easier access into the homes of the community members than complete strangers. They have played an essential role in increasing the number of people vaccinated and educating parents who are often ignorant of the importance of vaccines or fearful of a vaccine's side effects. In turn, infant mortality rates have dropped appreciably during the last ten years.

Changing attitudes about early marriage, frequent pregnancies and other related health issues concerning women are but a few of the main object-ives of the health visitors in the settlement. The health programmes, whether organized by the Association for the Care of Garbage collectors or the APE or the Dispensary of the Order of St Mary, are full of examples of families and individual girls who have greatly benefited. Sawsan William is a 20-year-old rug-maker and health visitor engaged to be married. She is an example of the changing role of women in a community which was once very strict about women leaving the home to work. She works, leaves her home much of the day and at the same time is well aware of the value of health education and promotion. Sawsan is also a representative of a generation of women who are about to marry and become mothers. As a health visitor, Sawsan not only contributes to improving the health of the members of her community, but also acts as a role model for other young Zabbaleen women.

Elements of project success

Gauging the full impact of the Zabbaleen Environmental and Develop-ment Programme is difficult; the overall indirect impact by far exceeds the direct impact of the programme's individual components. The very fact of intervening in the community has activated a process of change that has its own dynamics. For example, a tile factory, several carpentry and blacksmith workshops and the rug-weaving and paper recycling industries have all grown out of the programme. Projects in the Zabbaleen Environ-mental and Development Programme have also worked in coordination with other development activities, such as the services provided by the local Coptic Church, the school established by the Order of the Daughters of St Mary and the polyclinic, literacy classes, sewing classes and nursery provided by the Integrated Care Society. These efforts have helped trans-form the settlement.

Direct results, on the other hand, are easier to account for. These can be summarized as follows.

Environmental benefits

The internal clean-up project led to the upgrading of living conditions in the Zabbaleen settlement. The mechanization and route extension projects led to instituting sustainable low-cost waste management systems in Cairo and the expansion of coverage in high-, middle- and low-income neighbourhoods. The recycling of organic and inorganic waste created employment opportunities, increased Zabbaleen income and significantly reduced the environmental burden that would have resulted from the ultimate disposal of large quantities of municipal solid waste. The compost plant, established in the Zabbaleen settlement, enhanced the natural cycle of conversion of organic matter to a useful compost product that is free of chemicals and harmful contaminants. In all instances, the above-mentioned projects have been designed to be cost recoverable and replicable to ensure sustainability and safeguard environmental gains.

Within the Zabbaleen community itself, environmental improvements are reflected in improved sanitation and hygiene throughout the settlement. The installation of appropriate water connections in the households involved in recycling has been a by-product of recycling practices requiring a dependable water source. A rough comparison of yearly infant and child mortality rates between 1979 and 1981 indicates a dramatic decrease in mortality, from 240 per thousand in 1979 to 117 per thousand in 1991. The infant and child mortality rates projected for the city of Cairo for the period from 1990 to 1995 were 33 per thousand. In 1990, the rate was 45.6 per thousand. Though still considerably higher in the settlement than in Cairo, these rates indicate an average annual rate of improvement within the settlement of 8.3 per cent, significantly higher than Cairo's overall rate of 7.8 per cent.[9]

The move from garbage collection to recycling has relieved many community members from the arduous process of sorting garbage, and therefore from the health hazards associated with working with fermented organic material. In terms of hygiene and sanitation, the health hazards associated with the recycling activities are much less serious than those associated with garbage collection and sorting.

Economic development and benefits

Until the Environmental and Development Programme was launched, the Zabbaleen were a fragmented group living in abject poverty under extremely harsh environmental and health conditions. The importance of their services had not been recognized by the government or the general public. Their future in the trade was threatened by a general trend towards replacing the Zabbaleen with a high-technology waste management system operated by Cairo's municipal sanitation force.

The programme succeeded in reversing the trend. The emphasis placed on institutionalizing their trade has maximized the productivity and revenue-generation potential of community residents. It provides them with the security, dignity and confidence to help themselves and sustain their economic and social gains. The benefits have helped the entire family, increasing household income by approximately a multiple of 20 over the past ten years.

With recycling activities the settlement has transformed from a specialized rural economy to a diversified urban economy where industrial and commercial activities abound. This shift is reflected in both the income levels and the employment profile of the community. The income derived from recycling activities represented an addition to the original income generated from garbage collection. The decrease in the number of pigpens from 500 in 1981 to 450 in 1993, despite the settlement's expansion, confirms that activity has shifted away from garbage collection towards recycling and related occupations.[10]

The Small Industries Project provided a limited number of loans for the acquisition of plastic-crushing machines. However, a large number of machines were bought without the assistance of the project. Of the 30 projects which received loans from 1983 to 1986, 50 per cent were recycling projects, and 50 per cent were service projects; there is an increasingly diversified employment base in the community. This diversification, together with the construction boom, has actually resulted in Cairo residents from outside the settlement moving into it for employment.

The increase in the overall income of the community is invariably reflected in people's life-styles. Both the standards of construction and the materials used are of better quality. The finishing materials used within the houses are also more luxurious. Residents possess such amenities as washing machines, gas stoves, televisions, videos and refrigerators.

Capacity building and human development

The programme has stimulated voluntary action through the Zabbaleen Gameya and has encouraged the participation of community residents in implementation. Gameya staff have been trained in programme management, administration and extension work. From the outset, the Zabbaleen Environmental and Development Programme has relied on innovations in simple technology to enhance productivity and accelerate the development process. The underlying theme guiding all technology development was inspired by the capacity of residents to make effective use of the technology, the availability of raw materials and the Zabbaleen's ability to add value to traditional products and to access new markets. This, in part, explains the rapid transformation of the main Zabbaleen settlement into a mixed-use residential and cottage industry estate, where residents have increased control over their lives and are capable of applying their technology to serve their best interests.

Educational opportunities have improved dramatically for the children of the Zabbaleen settlement. As a result of introducing motorized vehicles to replace donkey-drawn carts, child labour has been reduced, affording children the opportunity to pursue their education. School enrolment is higher for both boys and girls. Presently, 50 per cent of children between the ages of 6 and 14 are enrolled in school, and 73 per cent of those children do not work. The nursery run by the local church started with four children in 1975. In 1993 there were 430 children enrolled. The Catholic primary school started in 1985 with 25 students. In 1993 the school had expanded to include secondary grades, and served a student body of 1,000, of which 62.8 per cent were boys and 37.2 per cent were girls.[11]

Since its inception, the income-generating project for female-headed households has been a source of empowerment for poor women who for various reasons had to support their families. As of October 1993, 506 families participated in this project, which had extended loans to 87 borrowers and has a waiting list of 19 women.

The most visible transformation in the settlement is its physical appearance. In 1981, there were 735 houses in the settlement, all of which were one-storey structures consisting of a large room with an attached courtyard and pigpen. Now, there are 1,394 houses in the settlement, many of which are multi-storey structures. Most of the houses were built using concrete and brick. Tin shacks, which in 1981 made up a fifth of all houses, have totally disappeared from the settlement.[12]

Enhanced public image

Until recently, the Zabbaleen system was considered obsolete and the Zabbaleen themselves were perceived to be a primitive community incapable of meeting the requirements of modern-day urban life.

Today, local administrators and the general public alike have become increasingly aware of the environmental, social and economic merits of the Zabbaleen system. A case in point is when the Cairo Cleaning and Beautification Authority (CCBA) abrogated their agreement with the Zabbaleen and awarded Misr Service, a private company, a contract for the collection of the street waste in Zamalek. This gave rise to a heated controversy, as the Zabbaleen had no other means of supporting themselves. For the first time, the public was sympathetic to the position of the Zabbaleen. The Egyptian national newspapers publicized the Zabbaleen's plight and favourably acknowledged their system, a stance they had never taken before. Because of the public pressure to have the Zabbaleen back, the CCBA recontracted with the Zabbaleen, issuing them official licences to serve households in Zamalek.

Perceived problems

Despite considerable success, the Zabbaleen Environmental and Development Programme is far from perfect and falls short of its goals in several areas. The programme consisted of a number of projects initiated over a span of five years, and was based on an exploratory, experimental approach whereby project ideas and design emanated from the learning experience acquired by EQI's team in the field, and from their interaction with the environment and the community. There was no blueprint for the development of the settlement, which meant that even though the projects that were initiated addressed real needs, the fact that they were not based on a comprehensive integrative framework curtailed the potential of some of them to evolve and accommodate the growing and changing needs of the settlement. Moreover, such potential was also cut short by the inevitable fact that most of these projects had limited objectives. These limitations, which are stated in retrospect, are based on the actual ongoing assessment of the programme. They do not, however, detract from the developmental impact of the programme, nor from the value of the lessons learned.

At the onset, EQI's upgrading programme in the Zabbaleen settlement in Moqattam did not plan for long-term projections of the different programme components. Many of these components were a spontaneous outcome of the presence of a development agency in the community, in the sense that project initiation was a result of the individual efforts of many EQI employees after coming into close contact with the people of the settlement over an extended period of time. Projects were formulated on the spot as they were deemed necessary. It would be difficult to identify what fell short of, or differed from, expectations, as there was no actual blueprint to start with.

Lack of coordination

In retrospect, one of the major problems encountered at the Moqattam settlement is a general lack of coordination between the different organizations in the community. The various bodies working in the community, although well intentioned, do not share a common objective, nor do they necessarily share the same interests. Their policies and management therefore operate individually rather than collectively, and even when there were tentative attempts at cooperation, no policy consensus was reached.

This lack of coordination led to a lack of awareness. Although there are several organizations working for the community, very few are aware of the services and the projects undertaken by other organizations. Consequently, there is a general failure to learn from each other's experience, or to avoid duplicating services and replicating mistakes. Instead of the desire to cooperate, the prevailing sentiment seems to be the urge to compete; and although this can sometimes be to the benefit of the people, it can also have its drawbacks.

Poor management and leadership skills

Even with a development programme as extensive as that conducted through EQI, little provision was made to equip the Zabbaleen to deal with the changes that were about to take place. Not enough efforts were geared into developing human resources, whether by concentrating on creating a cadre of community members trained and skilled to manage and take over the organizations or by preparing them for the changes that would ensue. Although some organizations have taken this component into account and have trained certain members of the community to equip them for leadership roles, management and leadership training is generally lacking. This has become apparent recently on occasions which necessitated a conflict resolution or crisis management and has led to a state of dependency on organizations like EQI.

Dependency and lack of initiative

The influx of donors and funds in the area has created dependency: the Zabbaleen have got into the habit of receiving. They are prone to ask for money to start up a project rather than improvise or be innovative or even productive. For instance, in the absence of a nearby dump site, the Internal Clean-up Project has faltered. Presently, the only organization in the community willing to take action for the cleaning up of the new improvised site is the Association for the Care of Garbage Collectors (ACGC). The ACGC has enlisted the help of the CCBA, which has offered to transport the garbage to another dump. However, the Zabbaleen are unwilling to pay a nominal fee to cover the CCBA's expenses, and the situation remains unresolved.

Uneven level of community participation

In the early years of the programme, representation of community members in committees of the association representing garbage collectors was in the range of 70–80 per cent, with outsiders constituting the remainder. As the years went by, however, representation from outside the settlement became the predominant feature while community representation became restricted to the more powerful families in the settlement. The programme, while taking into account the need for community participation, did not sufficiently ensure that this participation adequately represented the community. Representation relied to a certain extent on the boards of directors, most of whom, being outsiders, did not always reflect the needs of the community as a whole. Moreover, their personal interests and gains some-times took precedence over the needs of the people, thus generating a state of apathy and indifference amongst the masses. Many people in the

Zabbaleen settlement are sceptical about the true intentions of organizations because of the deeply embedded suspicion they have of the nature of representation on the board of director committees.

Uneven distribution of benefit

Access to projects was largely restricted to the more powerful people in the settlement, and this they gained through familial solidarity – a characteristic of the settlement kinship structure of the community, which is Upper Egyptian in origin. In addition, the more powerful families were a step ahead of the less advantaged because they were more willing to adapt and try new ways, a risk the more vulnerable, poorer, families were not willing to take.

As a result, the distribution of benefits, particularly economic gains, has not been equitable. Those in powerful positions benefited to a far greater extent from the development programmes than the poor majority. The gap between rich and poor has grown wider, thereby strengthening existing power positions and exacerbating previous sources of conflict and tension. Such a situation is difficult to avoid altogether, but it could be considerably diminished through more activities targeted at the 'poorest of the poor', and at the most vulnerable groups in the community so as to empower them and help them maximize the benefits derived from the development process.

Sustainability

Despite demonstrated need and high community participation, some projects have yet to become self-sufficient financially or self-sustainable. For instance, the Income-generating Project for Female-headed Households is still funded by a donor agency, despite many years of implementation, while the veterinary centre does not yet cover its running costs.

Despite its shortcomings, the Zabbaleen Environmental and Development Program is a practical example of the importance of investigating the potential of, and building upon, existing natural and human systems before engaging in a search for substitutes. The approach adopted has afforded the programme the strength of synergy among different social, technological and economic elements. It has significantly reduced the need for the importation of high-cost materials and energy-intensive equipment. It has allowed hundreds of thousands of small-scale enterprises to access a cheap and renewable source of raw material from waste, providing essential products in the market-place at affordable prices to low-income buyers. It has protected the environment from the annual accumulation of hundreds of thousands of tons of waste by instituting a low-cost waste management system that is capable of converting waste to useful products. And it has enabled local government to keep a low-income group, which would have otherwise been an economic burden on society, gainfully employed in a productive urban service at no cost to the city.

Potential for transfer and adaptation

Faced with exploding demand for waste collection services, many modern cities have implemented completely new programmes. The resultant systems are often not only technologically complex and financially draining, but they frequently destroy employment opportunities for groups which have traditionally provided services privately or informally.

The Zabbaleen Environmental and Development Programme is an innovative solution to Cairo's solid waste disposal problems and takes advantage of existing traditional and informal systems. This project is an attempt to develop existing human resources and make them adaptable to new and challenging conditions, instead of discarding existing systems and investing in expensive technological solutions.

The Zabbaleen Environmental and Development Programme can serve as a model for other cities to solve problems of solid waste disposal. Through the Urban Management Programme, aspects of the project are being transferred to other cities in the Middle East. Also through the Mega-Cities Project, components of the project are currently being transferred to Bombay and Manila. In both cities the projects are at various stages of implementation. As in these cities, several necessary conditions must be first satisfied, before a transfer of the programme can be attempted. The government must recognize the worth and potential of the traditional garbage-collecting community and be willing to work with a variety of actors, including the community, to achieve project goals. The group that is providing waste disposal services must be willing to participate in the project as well. The support of organizations with experience in solving technical and human resource problems in under-served or unserved communities will be needed.

Community and resource development must also be a large element in the project: access to basic amenities, such as health care, education, suitable infrastructure, water, sewerage and others is essential. Finally all stakeholders in any programme that uses the Zabbaleen Environmental and Development Programme as a model must adopt an open and flexible attitude towards an informal trash collection industry and its potential in serving the needs of large, modern cities.[13]

Lessons learned

It is an indisputable fact that the Zabbaleen Environmental and Development Programme has radically transformed the Moqattam settlement, which houses 50 per cent of Cairo's garbage collectors. As of 1981, the variety of projects implemented in the settlement have had economic, social and environmental benefits.

The major success of the project has been achieved because it has been able to balance its concern over improvements in environmental and living conditions with an equivalent concern for income generation and enterprise development. The core programme design recognizes that there is a cost associated with improvements, which must be met by an increase in revenue-generation capacity. Improvements in the quality of life are matched with enterprise development. The complementarity between environmental upgrading and credit extension programmes has enhanced the potential of the Zabbaleen in expanding their services and institutionalizing their trade.

Finally, the design of this project focused on linking environmental improvements with enterprise promotion. The small and micro-enterprise project administration, after acquainting the Zabbaleen with market conditions and the prices of raw materials and machinery, relied upon the interwoven web of social structure and kinship relationships to do the rest. As expected, the Zabbaleen soon established their own informal information system, whereby names and addresses of scrap dealers and prices of raw materials were circulated through relatives and friends until an impressive network of data came into being, extending beyond the boundaries of the settlement. Moreover, a tacit understanding existed that it would be in their interest to avoid competition and form a solid front; accordingly, prices hardly varied – if at all – from one entrepreneur to another.[14]

The Zabbaleen Environmental and Development Programme also capitalized on a thorough analysis of market conditions and opportunities for Zabbaleen services, and the development of a workable strategy for capturing larger segments of market over time. The strategy included the linking of the evolution of the Zabbaleen system with the growth of the city, and selecting and applying low-cost rudimentary technologies for waste collection and processing activities. Wahia and Zabbaleen were organized into more than 50 small independent companies, operating in the neighbourhoods they have traditionally serviced. Electing to stay as small independent companies and working closely with their traditional clients enabled the Zabbaleen to introduce reasonable increases in prices that were sufficient to cover their additional costs, without losing their client base. This strategy provided the Zabbaleen community with the human and technological resources base to respond effectively to a major portion of Cairo's current and future waste management needs.

The continued reliance in the near and medium term on launching Zabbaleen companies from their traditional service areas should provide an excellent opportunity for expanding coverage in Cairo and for replicating this model in other urban centres in Egypt and cities around the world. The careful selection of appropriate technology, and the emphasis placed on enhancing improvements in living conditions and recycling operations, are essential ingredients for sustaining and replicating this project. The benefits gained from linking improvements in environmental and living conditions with enterprise promotion are central to the successful implementation and sustainability of community development programmes world-wide. Community action is best achieved when needs and priorities as perceived by the community are incorporated into the development programme and when opportunities for enterprise and revenue generation are also explicitly incorporated.

The project has demonstrated the following lessons:

- The programme must provide the informal sector with increased economic opportunities and services, utilizing appropriate technology that is inexpensive, easy to use and maintain and takes advantage of available resources.
- The programme must respond to the needs of the community. However, although need can be capitalized upon to enhance community interest and participation, need alone does not necessarily determine the success or sustainability of a project.
- Sustained public participation is a necessary ingredient in development programmes. This depends on effective human resource development and education so that participants are increasingly productive, empowered and aware of the importance of their work.
- Coordinated and cooperative partnerships between funding, development, government and community agencies are necessary in order to achieve complementarity rather than duplication, and in order to optimize resource allocation to areas of need.
- A problem encountered in the Zabbaleen experiment, and indeed in many development programmes, is that of human resources. It is vital that more emphasis be placed on project and crisis management training programmes. Such programmes would pave the way for the eventual exit of external funding or development agencies, and would enable the project to survive, expand, or even to shift its orientation once its initial objectives were fulfilled.

CHAPTER 5

Local Government and Private Sector Partnerships for Land-Sharing and Incremental Development

Squatting on private or public land has been a common, and at times the only, option the urban poor have to find a piece of land in the majority of the cities in developing countries, but that situation has changed, as empty urban land developed for non-profit purposes is disappearing in many countries.[1] Squatting on vacant land was the way people occupied land in the city, creating squatter settlements or 'unauthorized colonies', as they are called in the subcontinent. But the practice was in fact the brain-child of middlemen (colonizers/developers) who marketed peripheral land to cash in on the gap between the demand for land and shelter and the formal sector supply. In spite of all its efforts, the public sector's land and shelter programmes have been limited and the prices in the legally operating private market are too high for a majority of families. Developers of illegally occupied land, on the other hand, are able to bring land into the market cheaply and quickly by eliminating the provision and therefore the cost of infrastructure – water, electricity, sewerage and drainage, roads, parks and schools. Official sanctions are not obtained, and no time is spent getting them. Entry cost into these settlements is kept low, and slowly over a number of years services are brought into the settlement as it becomes regularized. Colonizers as well as landowners manage to make huge profits, even though rates are kept as low as Rs 2–3 (7–10 cents) per square yard.[2] Today, given the shortage of housing, the large number of property dealers operating in unauthorized colonies are progressively moving towards serving the middle and upper-income class who want to build their houses or start small industrial or commercial enterprises. It is not uncommon for plots to change hands three to four times. Paradoxically, government intervention, either in the form of regularization and provision of services, or in improving links to the city centre, hastens the rise in property values, and prices have in some places soared to 50 to 100 times the original cost. In Orangi, for example, plots which originally cost Rs 120 ($4.8) now cost from Rs 60,000 to Rs 70,000 ($2,400–2,800).

Since illegal developers are aggressively seeking more middle- and upper-middle-income clientele, for the poor, entry into unauthorized colonies is becoming increasingly difficult, unless they are willing to settle for plots as small as 20–25 square yards. Poor households are bought out or squeezed into older settlements. Thus the picture of low-income households buying land illegally at low prices and building incrementally to improve housing conditions, with the government stepping in as the facilitator, does not completely fall into place.[3]

Given this development of the land market, it is difficult for the informal process to supply land for housing the poor. Governments can no longer rely on the informal processes to provide for the growing numbers of poor. It is estimated that by the year 2010, 70 per cent of the urban population in developing countries could be living in impoverished and environmentally hazardous conditions.

The need for governments to become involved in the supply of land, participate in the land market and facilitate NGO initiatives is increasing. There are many theories which favour governmental intervention in land markets, but only a few methods appear to work, and then only in special circumstances. One of those methods is land-sharing, where land which does not belong to the squatter is negotiated by the owner and the occupant to formalize the rights of the latter. Another method adopted by some agencies is incremental development, where unserviced land is given to the very poor at very low cost. In both, the roles of private developer and of community involvement are important. Two case-studies, Citra Niaga in Samarinda, Indonesia, and Kuda-ki-basti in Hyderabad, Pakistan, point to the advantages and risks in undertaking such developments and also highlight the importance of well-conceived, well-planned, and well-thought-out design in both processes.

Land-sharing

Land-sharing is a simple proposition involving the division of squatter land between the original owner and its occupants, with recognition of the legal rights to the land of settlers who have illegally occupied it for an extended period of time. This partition of land for use by the landlord and by the occupants of the site is seen as a pragmatic and constructive resolution of conflicting claims. It is also a realistic compromise between landlords and slum dwellers that has the potential of creating new and better living conditions for the occupants.[4]

One crucial factor that is absolutely necessary before any land-sharing process can be initiated is the threat of eviction. Once the threat is imminent, the process can be initiated either by the residents themselves, or by the owner, or by the government, or by a non-profit organization. If there were no threat of eviction then most involved parties would not be interested in upsetting the status quo to seek a solution. Therefore, for land-sharing to be considered an attractive proposition, there must be serious development pressure on the land that threatens imminent eviction.

Land-sharing works in societies that have a history of negotiation and compromise. In societies where there is a total mistrust of government policies or private investment intervention, attempts at land-sharing may lead to protracted negotiation and eventual collapse of the process. However, under circumstances where land-sharing may be possible, questions arise about how planners could develop policies regarding its use.

An important aspect of any land-sharing project is the negotiation between the owners of the land, the occupants and their representatives. This involves the actual division of the property and the negotiation of land price, a process that often requires tact and patience on the part of both parties. This negotiation is important as it eventually determines the overall composition of the community, i.e., the number of people who are to benefit from the scheme, the actual land that is being made available, and at what price. This has a direct influence on the eventual quality of the environment, as it is through these negotiations that the overall density, the road widths and road lengths, and the size of the open spaces of the project are decided.

Forming a community organization is necessary as it is this organization that will eventually be responsible for negotiating an agreement and then carrying out the various tasks that are involved, such as selection of the households and individuals eligible to participate in the scheme, plot sizes, subdivisions and financing of both the land purchase and rebuilding the houses. Before any agreement can be worked out, an analysis of the number of households and people living there has to be made. Also, the length of stay of these households and individuals has to be determined in order to arrive at a selection criterion. This is often a difficult issue as some households or individuals are bound to be left out of the process and be asked to leave, which could lead to dissension among the residents and stop the process. Therefore it has to be handled through a criterion agreed upon by the participating groups.

Criteria need to be established for the location and sizes of the plots. Who should be given priority and the reasons for this have to be clearly worked out. The criteria may be based on the length of stay, or the size of households, or the size of plot presently occupied. Whatever the criteria they need to be discussed and worked out, as the actual available plot size is going to be less than what residents have at present. Division of the site will involve rehousing the existing community on a smaller site, which will increase the density of the site. If the original density in the settlement was already high, the new density will be even higher, unless some of the residents are excluded by the new scheme.

The increase in residential density and the need to clear parts of the site will necessitate the reconstruction of houses unless original densities were low enough to permit infilling. Rebuilding may also require new forms of construction, using more permanent or more solid materials than that which may have been used in the original structure. Recycling of building materials may be impossible, and this would mean an increase in cost.

Financing the purchase of land and the rebuilding of houses is an important issue which has to be worked out in detail. The actual cost to each member and the payment pattern needs to be established early on. Schemes that are flexible in nature have to be created so that they can assist the very poor; each household should be allowed to pay on a daily, weekly or monthly basis. The cooperative also needs to work out a payment plan for the purchase of the land and other infrastructure construction costs. Cross-subsidy by the owner or other outside agencies may have to be negotiated by the cooperative.

The above points highlight the principle of land-sharing, explain the process involved and briefly discuss some of the problems associated with it. As stated, land-sharing is a complicated and lengthy process and its success depends on the strength of the cooperative and the willingness of all parties involved to ensure a smooth process. Some of the actors that are involved in this process include:

1. The residents on the piece of land and its community organization.
2. The owner of the land: either the government or a private individual/s. The approach in each case will be different. The landowner may be able to provide some financial assistance or provide cross-subsidies during the development of the project.
3. NGOs or a state agency that negotiates on behalf of the community and helps form the community organization.
4. The lending and financial institution that lends the money to the cooperative to buy the piece of land and moneys for the actual construction of the infrastructure and the houses.
5. In large projects international agencies may also get involved to provide financial or other assistance.

Land-sharing has been used in a few countries with success. In the Lines Area project in Karachi, Pakistan, the land was owned and re-developed by the government. It incorporated 72,000 of the original occupants in the scheme, with cross-subsidies made available through the auction of commercial plots to finance infrastructure development on the entire land.[5] In Bangkok, six communities (Klong Toey, Rama IV, Wat Ladbuakaw, Sam Yod, Manangkasila and Soi Sengki) have managed to initiate land-sharing agreements, often after long mediation by the National Housing Authority. Klong Toey is the most successful of the six land-sharing projects. Approximately 6,000 households have settled on 65 hectares of land belonging to the Port Authority of Thailand. After a 30-

year struggle for permanent housing, an agreement was reached in 1983 in the form of a land-sharing agreement with the port authority granting the dwellers a 20-year, legal lease.[6] In Citra Niaga, Samarinda, Indonesia, the land was government-owned, but was redeveloped by a private developer and the occupants either incorporated within the scheme or relocated. In all three countries the experiment has produced different results as the schemes were motivated by, and initiated to achieve, different ends and were therefore handled differently. The rate of success of land-sharing projects is low, partly because there are so many steps and the complexity of the negotiation process invariably leads to delays. Yet the process holds great promise if the government and owner/developer are willing to come up with projects with clear objectives and strategies.

Citra Niaga Urban Development Project

The Citra Niaga project is one project where government and developer cooperation led to successful land-sharing and urban renewal. The project redeveloped a slum in the city centre and next to the port into a commercial complex with kiosks and stalls for the pavement traders who were living in the slum, new shop-houses, and a shopping complex. The owners of the shop-houses (who had legal rights) and the pavement traders (who did not) were both accommodated in this project. The project has become the focal point of the city, where people gather in the evenings for shopping and entertainment. The project also provides a mix of commercial activity in keeping with traditional Asian markets.

Citra Niaga Urban Development Project was an innovative approach to land-sharing addressing the issue of slum consolidation and urban renewal of central city land. It was developed by the local authorities as a strategy to tackle the problem of street hawkers who were choking the city's roads. It was one of the first land-sharing projects to focus on commercial, non-housing rehabilitation for the poor.[7]

This particular programme of rehabilitation and land-sharing was developed by a local developer and a group of architects as an alternative to the proposal made by the local authority. The local development agency had first proposed a typical shopping complex as part of a slum clearance strategy. The typical supermarket solution was not accepted by the mayor and the governor, as it did not address the informal sector nor did it solve the squatter problem. The mayor and the governor were alarmed at the rising squatter population and were concerned that if something was not done to improve the city of Samarinda, it would soon become a vast slum. Their aim was to allow the city, in addition to functioning as a centre for the local state government, to express the spirit of modernization without discriminating against any of the economic sectors. The principle of development was based on the belief that spatial improvement of the city's facilities should include the participation of the people and should not only express the 'image' and the spirit of development in the Samarinda municipality but should also increase the economic development at all levels of the society.

Samarinda is the provincial capital of East Kalimantan (Borneo). The population of some 360,000 persons in 1987 has shown a steep rise recently due to emigration from the hinterland because of extensive deforestation. There is also substantial emigration from other parts of the country because of the economic opportunities available in the region due to logging, oil exploration and mineral exploration, and these industries are mostly in the hands of the Japanese, South Korean or Taiwanese companies.

Samarinda, located on the banks of the Mahakam River, acts as the trade depot for the region, and the port accounts for half the total timber exported out of Indonesia. Even though the town attracted migrants, a large number were unable to find jobs in the formal sector and therefore sought employment in the informal sector, opening some retail facility as hawkers or pavement traders. The *kaki lima*, or pavement traders, increased dramatically from 1,000 in 1983 to 5,000 in 1985. These are official figures which only reflect a trend; the probable figure was closer to 6,000. A large number were located within the town centre because of its proximity to the port and other commercial interests. The slum population increased substantially, creating not only a housing problem but also a social problem, as the crime rate rapidly increased in most of these settlements.

The project site is located in the centre of town, in close proximity to the port and a block away from the warehouses. The slum on this site developed on what was an existing piece of open recreational land. In 1982, a devastating fire destroyed the shop-houses around the park. The shops were quickly rebuilt but the park was taken over by squatters and became a slum.

Legal shop-houses fronted the main street with the slum behind them. In the middle of the site was a swamp which became used for noxious small-scale illegal industries and presented a serious health hazard. About 100 families occupied the site, a majority of whom were pavement traders; the others worked in workshops or light industry.

On the site were also a large number of prostitutes and criminals: the area was notorious as a red-light district. The bad name that the area was giving to the city prompted the city fathers to do something about it. Then a large fire in Balipapan, another large town in the region, in the fishermen's section of town, cost a large a number of lives. The bad name and the fire gave the authorities the impetus to redevelop this area.

The initial proposal of the city planning board was to develop a supermarket-type project, but it was found to be unsuitable and was also seen as unable to address the complex issues of the site, which was on a prime location in the centre of the town and close to the harbour. The supermarket proposal also did not address the problem of the street hawkers who were choking the city's roads, and who needed to be accommodated in or near the site. Indonesia is unique in the attitude of its government agencies, which try and accommodate the needs of slum dwellers. The Kampung Improvement Programmes established by the government have been in existence since 1975, and have made people aware of the plight of the urban poor. The ex-governor of the state of East Kalimantan was particular distressed by the slums in the city centre and was impressed by some of the urban renewal programmes in the United States, which he had visited. It was his enthusiasm that led to the support for an urban renewal project to be undertaken at the site which would revitalize the city centre. His son Didik, a local developer, was invited to redevelop the town centre. Didik, along with his friend Antonio Ismael, an architect working in a community-based project in Mexico, got in touch with Adi Sasono from the Institute for Development Studies, an NGO that was already working in Samarinda, and Michael Sumarijanto of PT Grivantara Architects, to help launch the project.

The project

The project as visualized by this group involved not only the owners of the shop-houses, who had legal right to their property, but also included the pavement traders who were part of the slum. The scheme proposed by this group was a commercial complex which included rebuilding of the shop-houses that had been destroyed, a shopping complex, an area with kiosks and stalls where the *kaki lima* could sell their goods, and an open plaza which would become the focus of the project and serve as an open space where various activities could be held. This idea was accepted in principle by the authorities and a detailed programme worked out. The government decree promulgated on 27 August 1985 stipulated that 30 per cent of the shopping centre at Citra Niaga would go to the *kaki lima* and 70 per cent to other trades. The project was to be developed on two levels simultaneously. The buildings were designed in the regional style and at the same time organizational aspects were being tackled.

Before the project was actually started, a complete inventory of the settlement was undertaken. An attempt was made to keep the intention of the survey a secret so as not to alarm the dwellers or give out word that redevelopment of the area was being proposed. This would stop the people from taking undue advantage of the situation. If redevelopment plans were made public too soon, people would show up with false claims to property in the area and create unnecessary problems. It was also feared that if the nature of the scheme was disclosed early on, before the community that would eventually occupy the shops and houses was

brought in on the project, a number of people would speculate on ownership rights and push prices up.

From its inception the scheme was seen as a commercial development;
the shop-houses would be the only residential part of the scheme. Displacement was therefore a crucial issue which had to be addressed very
cautiously. Through a preliminary survey, it was determined that a place
to live was not of primary concern to the occupants. They wanted to be
allowed to continue plying their trade there. The survey and inventory
undertaken thus helped to determine which activities would support the
overall success of the development. It also became the basis for selecting
who could participate in the scheme. About 60 per cent of the occupants
could be accommodated on the site, but the other 40 per cent had to be
displaced.[8] Activities such as workshops and light industry were relocated
elsewhere by the *muspidah* (local authority), and in some cases the resettling
costs were paid by the developer. People involved in prostitution or crime
were evicted. This eviction involved a protracted dispute between the
residents and the gangsters for about six months, but after the formation
of a community cooperative they were eventually able to withstand the
pressures from the gangsters. The developer also bought off a number of
adversaries who were blocking the project.

The formation of a cooperative and their participation in all aspects
of the scheme was important in its success. The innovative aspect of this
scheme was twofold: the involvement of the local government, the central
government and the private sector; and the process undertaken to ensure
the participation of families who occupied the area and had been selected
to be part of the new scheme. The NGO worked closely with the
community in identifying what their needs were, explaining the scheme to
them and showing them how they would improve their economic conditions at a cost no greater than that which they had been paying to the
local slum landlords for water and other services. The scheme was designed
not just as a self-cost recovery and self-sustaining project, but as a profit-
making venture.

The programme

The programme brief and the functional requirements of the project
emerged through a series of discussions that went on for three years
between the government and the users. The principles that governed the
brief were as follows.

All classes of users should have the same rights, treatment and facilities
because all of them would contribute to the prosperity of the area; land
use must be mixed; the design must be traditional in character and be
physically attractive; the layout should permit integration of users easily;
and rigidity in design should be avoided. The users were to be shop-house

owners of high and middle income; kiosk/corner shop owners of low income; and pavement traders from the lowest economic class.

The ratio of land use between the informal sector and others was specified by the government. The developer therefore had to work out his project finances very carefully because 30 per cent of the built space in phases I and II would go to users who were receiving free facilities and 70 per cent to users who had to purchase the property to generate profit and cross subsidize the scheme. The terms under which the projects were sanctioned were that the developer would receive government land at no cost, but the local government would not finance any part of the development. The management of the shopping centre would be appointed at the discretion of the local government and would include the local shop-keepers. In phases I and II 60 per cent of the shops were designated for the informal sector and 40 per cent for other tradesmen.

The programme was conceived in three phases, with the first phase concentrating on a totally commercial development to finance the second phase, which related to the informal sector. The first stage was designated area A and B, where 58 shop-houses would be built. This area was vacant; it too had been destroyed by fire and was included as part of the scheme to allow for capital generation.

Area C was the second phase of the project and included 25 kiosks and shops, facilities for 224 pavement traders and 27 shop-houses. The informal sector was developed in one go so as to minimize displacement time; this also ensured that the bulk of the scheme and the development of the plaza were built simultaneously. The development of the informal sector in the second phase also gave the developers and the NGO time to form the pavement traders' cooperative and to agree terms with all the occupants. It also allowed time for sorting out the relocation issue. During construction a temporary settlement was supplied by the local government nearby, but only for trade; housing had to be found elsewhere. The NGO helped the pavement traders form a cooperative, which then purchased a 10-hectare piece of land on the outskirts of the city. This was made possible through a bank loan given to the cooperative, with the members' kiosks and stalls used as collateral.

Area D was the third phase of the scheme and included 56 shop-houses and 54 kiosks aimed at the higher income group. This phase gave the developer his highest returns and subsidized area C. In addition to the retail outlets, the other facilities provided include a tower to serve as a symbol and focus of the scheme, an open space which forms the centre of the scheme, a performance space that is covered, public toilets, parking spaces and a new traffic road between phases II and III.

The developer limited the kind of activity that was given to retail outlets. For instance, six major types of retail activity were permitted in the informal sector; garments and sewing occupied 40.6 per cent of the total shops; general merchandise, 9 per cent; coffee and drinks shops, 17.4 per cent; food, 17 per cent; shoes, leather, 6 per cent; medicine, 3 per cent; and others, 7 per cent.

The site area is 2.7 hectares; the total built-up area for all three phases was set at 1.83 hectares plus 1,800 sq. m. 9,500, sq. m. of open space and walkways and 1,200 sq. m. of roads. In all there is 16,870 sq. m. of built-up space for the shop-houses, 1,443 sq. m. for kiosks and 1,800 sq. m. for the *kaki lima*. A total of 1,800 sq. m. of free area was given to the members of the informal sector cooperative for retail outlets. The stalls are only lent; they are owned collectively by the cooperative. The shop-houses, on the other hand, were sold outright to individual owners.

Maintenance

The complex is maintained by a board comprised of representatives from all users. Service charges, parking and toilet fees generate an annual income of Rp 124.5 million (US $70,140) and the maintenance comes to Rp 114.5 million (US $64,507).[9] The service charge to each *kaki lima* in the informal sector is Rp 1,500 per day (US 85 cents); this Rp 1,500 is allocated as follows: Rp 200 to the government, Rp 72 for rent, Rp 200 for electricity, Rp 200 for water and Rp 828 for the Management Board. For the *kaki lima* these are very favourable terms. Before the project was built they were paying Rp 2,000 per day (US $1.14) in extortion and another Rp 1,000 (US 56 cents) for water. The money is now paid to the cooperative on a daily, weekly or monthly basis.

The total cost of the project was Rp 3.9 billion (US $2.2 million), of which Rp 1.1 billion was for phase I, Rp 1.3 billion for phase II and Rp 1.5 billion for phase III. Resettling costs for those who did not participate in the project was Rp 0.4 billion. The developer, after the gross subsidies of Rp 700 million (US $394,366) got a rate of return of 27 per cent before taxes, which is high. Four years ago the shop-houses in area D cost Rp 75 million (US $42,254) and they are appreciating rapidly. The shop-houses in area C are selling for Rp 35 million (US $19,718) and those with road frontage for Rp 60 million (US $33,803). The gross daily sales at the kiosks selling food are in the vicinity of Rp 75,000 (US $42.25).[10]

Lessons from Citra Niaga

The Citra Niaga project represents a breakthrough in commercial projects for Asian and developing country cities. It has been functioning for five years and has had a tremendous impact on the city. With this innovative experiment the city was able to reclaim its prime land for public use, provide an urban centre, and re-establish the link between the city and the harbour.

The success of the project has many ramifications: it was developed successfully by a private developer in partnership with the government and the community for the benefit of the larger community. It was a profitable business venture and yet included the usually ignored social and ecological aspects. It not only managed to upgrade a squatter settlement (although at a cost of resettling a large number of people), but it also developed a public plaza in the heart of the city and re-established the link between the harbour and the city. The scheme developed a successful shopping centre and created an urban environment out of a slum which ordinary people shunned. It was financially viable. This suggests that even in small towns profits can be made if projects are well thought-out and if innovative complex financing schemes, through a mixture of cross-subsidy and self-finance, are used.

The success of this project has given the government confidence in its ability to solve at least some aspects of its squatter problem. It has also shown that a positive and profitable government/developer joint enterprise is possible. Other such projects are now under way in the area and the government is developing the adjacent sites in a similar manner. The attractive architectural features are being copied by various projects, and the whole area around the port is being revitalized and is teeming with life.

The community has been galvanized into achieving success in running and maintaining the project. With the help of the NGO, which was involved in the project from its inception, the community had a voice in the planning and design of those aspects of the project that affected them directly. Because in this particular case location for economic opportunity was more important than housing, the formation of the community organization helped to finance housing which was then built elsewhere.

The architectural achievement was that it provided a central focus of urban space and character to the town.[11] This not only created a popular public space, which can be compared to Boston's Fanneiul Hall Market-place and other similar developments, but has understood the characteristics of the Asian commercial environment. In Citra Niaga there is a great variety of merchandise being sold to all income levels. This is the contribution of its design and planning. The typical shopping centre provides a wide range of goods but primarily caters to the middle class or the upper middle class. Citra Niaga's achievement lies in its mix of retail outlets in both variety and price range. This gives the project an enormous dynamism and makes it pleasant to visit. The large choice offered is representative of retail outlets all over town in a small area.

This combination of creative land-sharing and urban renewal has produced a scheme which is not only financially successful, but has also provided that mix of commercial activity which is in keeping with the traditional Asian commercial fabric. Citra Niaga has therefore achieved a truly Asian urban development, and its relevance to other developing countries in terms of creating a shopping complex, a city centre, squatter upgrading and an appropriate environment cannot be underestimated. It is a crowded, active part of town: on Saturday nights it teems with people. In the covered stage in the plaza are performances for both children and adults. The plaza is filled with street entertainers – fortune tellers, magicians and so forth. Ninety per cent of the promenaders are teenagers looking for entertainment. The project has provided a choice for young people who otherwise hung around streets corners and got into trouble. Now they have a place to go that provides fun for the whole family.

Five institutions have been linked together by this project. They are the developer; the non-governmental organization and its consultants; the banks; the cooperative that was formed as a result of the project; and the state and national government.

Land-sharing, in general, has not yet had widespread appeal and success, because of the complexity of the operation and the necessary cooperation of the participating groups. Problems generally arise as a result of the inability of the occupants of the land to form cohesive units. Long periods of negotiation often cause problems in completing the project. Yet, when successful, as in the case of Citra Niaga, the results are spectacularly successful and this has resulted in spatial patterns that respond well to rapid urban growth.

Potential for transfer and adaptation

The success of the Citra Niaga project has been documented and the information disseminated to many cities within Indonesia and in Asia. Although land-sharing schemes have traditionally required extensive time, energy and effort, the Citra Niaga model is transferable, keeping in mind a number of issues and preconditions.

A strong partnership of appropriate individuals to organize and facilitate the project is needed which should include government officials, private developers, architects, NGOs and community groups. All eventual beneficiaries of the project should be involved from the onset in order to promote the maximum sense of ownership, and to address any issues threatening the project's success. Flexibility must be maintained in facing the numerous obstacles and issues that may arise, as was obvious from the issue of displacement. Finally, flexible financing schemes must be allowed and promoted, to ensure that the project is not only self-financing but profitable.

The Citra Niaga approach has now been adopted in Jombang in East Java. The project was developed by the same team of developers and architects. However, in order to comply with the local conditions in Jombang, the original developers entered into a partnership with a local developer and formed a new company, PT. AFDOL, to carry out the work. This project has also achieved the success that Citra Niaga achieved, proving that its approach can be transferred to other cities in the region.

Incremental development

The idea that the poor can build their houses more economically than can the authorities is based on the assumption not that labour costs are saved, but that the houses can be built at a pace affordable to each family. A family purchases the land it can afford and builds pieces of its dwelling as its resources permit, a flexibility not found in the formal housing sector. The family also acts as its own contractor, controlling the purchase of materials and overseeing construction.

The incremental development approach to housing evolved out of the site-and-services approach. It formalizes the methods found in informal settlements, where squatters provide shelter for themselves at prices and at a standard that they can afford. In incremental development schemes, infrastructure and urban services are also provided incrementally, that is, just as the house grows over time, reflecting the resources of the occupant, so, too, the services grow as they become affordable by the group of people living in a particular cluster or block. This reduces the initial cost to beneficiaries and allows more of the poor to participate.

Fundamental to the success of incremental development is that the scheme be affordable to the very poor from the start. A very low down-payment is therefore required, and the initial services are limited to the basics: for example, a public water supply and public transportation to the city. But over a long period, house-to-house water connections, sewerage, electricity and road paving can be installed, when and how much depending on the ability of those living there to pay for it.

From its inception a community organization has to be developed that will collect instalments. The instalment schedule has to be flexible so that dues can be paid on a monthly, weekly, or daily basis, depending on the earning patterns of the individuals. An NGO would assist in forming the cooperative but would also make clear that neither it nor the development agency was responsible for providing the services themselves and that each block or neighbourhood unit would have to pay for its own.

Standards for projects of this sort have to be flexible. Creative site planning is needed to allow community participation at the block or neighbourhood level, independent of the rest of the project. The layout of the scheme should be fixed, but no standards pertaining to the quality or plan of the houses can be imposed. Professional guidance, however, should be provided to avoid unsafe installation.

To reach the target group, residency in the scheme must be mandatory for receiving a plot. Plot titles can be held in the name of the cooperative

to reduce speculation. The time-lag between plot development and allocation also has to be kept to a minimum if the project is to be a success.

Khuda-ki-basti Incremental Development Scheme

The Hyderabad Development Authority (HDA) has sponsored one of the
first incremental development schemes in Khuda-ki-basti. The results have
been far from spectacular. It has run into problems, but it can also teach
some lessons about how government agencies can plan and design for the
provision of cheap land for a large number of poor families.

Hyderabad is situated about 10 kilometres from the River Indus. The
small towns of Kotri and Guddu lie at its outskirts. The Sind Industrial
and Trading Estate (SITE) is located near Kotri and is a job source for
those living nearby. City growth is mainly to the south, along the Karachi–
Hyderabad superhighway. South of the superhighway lies Gulshan-e-
Shahbaz, a mixed-income site-and-services project, which had remained
underdeveloped. In 1986 the HDA planned an incremental scheme that
integrated features of an illegal land subdivision into a government-
sponsored scheme in order to provide affordable housing for the poor.
For this they chose sector 6 of Gulshan-e-Shahbaz, because it bordered
on the illegal subdivision of Ismailabad and the squatter settlement of
Sikanderabad. The settlement that developed there was eventually called
Khuda-ki-basti (Settlement of God) by the people who live in it.

The HDA wanted to simplify the allocation process and reduce the
initial costs to make it easier for the people to receive a plot and to keep
the cost low by providing virtually unserviced land and by not establishing
standards for house construction. They also wanted to allot plots immediately and encourage the development of infrastructure and services
incrementally, based on the residents' requirements and ability to pay.[12]
Households for allotments were identified by the HDA with the help of
local councillors in Kotri and Hyderabad. The HDA granted 32 households
possession of 80-square-yard plots for an initial deposit of Rs 460 (US
$18.4).[13] The only condition imposed was that they had to put up a
structure within one year and leave a three-foot setback in the rear for
ventilation.

On monitoring the project during the first few months HDA found
that only 2 of the 32 allottees had complied by starting construction. The
rest lacked resources to build, or simply did not want to because there
was no guarantee of tenure. To overcome this problem the HDA started
afresh in sector E4 of Gulshan-e-Shahbaz. This time possession of plots
was granted, but the titledeed was withheld until the household had
constructed a house and moved in. The period of construction was
reduced to three months. Even this did not improve the situation.

The HDA then decided to cancel the previous allotments and to re-allot the plots to applicants on the waiting list. Their conditions were that they had to start construction immediately and move in within a month. The plots were made non-transferable except by inheritance. The allottee forfeited the deposits if the allotment was cancelled. After an initial period of activity, development slowed down again. This time it turned out that on the recommendations of local councillors, the allotments had been given to a lower-middle-income group whose housing situation was already adequate. They even enjoyed amenities in their present dwellings that they would not have had in Khuda-ki-basti. There was no incentive to move.

At this stage the HDA decided to enter into partnership with the local *dallals* (professional land speculators and land-grabbers) and let them find households in the *katchi abadis* (illegal settlements) of Hyderabad who would want to resettle in the Khuda-ki-basti. The HDA issued cards which had a schedule of payments printed on them instead of a title-deed. The initial down-payment was still Rs 460 (US $18.4) with a subsequent monthly development charge of Rs 60 (US $2.4). On completion of the full payment of Rs 9,600 (US $384) the allottee would be given the deed. But the *dallals* had their own vested interests; they very diligently settled households and made money through speculating on the plots.

The concept of the reception area

By this time the HDA had come to recognize that the allotment procedure was crucial to ensuring the success of any scheme.[14] When a family on the waiting list and in dire need of shelter turned up at the site with all its possessions and simply occupied a plot, HDA officials began to realize that, if a family was really serious about moving in, it would bring all its belongings to the site.[15] This realization became the basis for the idea of a 'reception area' as an effective mechanism to find the right people and filter out all those having aims other than living in the project.[16]

A reception area, in the form of an open plot, was provided where families could temporarily live in makeshift dwellings while they waited for a plot. From there the HDA could observe the household and decide whether or not its intentions and its need were real. To overcome the reluctance of families to pass through the reception area the HDA built a few semi-permanent houses and rented them to those who could afford it. This scheme worked; 16 days after its initiation on 2 November 1986, 350 families had moved through the reception area onto a plot. The HDA made the reception area a permanent feature of its allocation process.

Today to receive a plot an applicant submits a photocopy of a national identity card along with an application to the HDA. After the stay in the reception area and the screening process, the beneficiary is allotted a plot and makes a down-payment of Rs 1,000 (US $40). If the allottee does not stay on the plot the allotment is cancelled and the plot is reallocated.

The monthly instalments of the development charges are deposited into a separate account for each block of the scheme. Block residents decide in community meetings which services they want. When sufficient money is collected in a block account, the residents meet with the HDA to decide by popular vote what it should be spent on. Once the decision is taken the HDA hands over the supervision of construction to the block leaders. Since the community does the supervision and the community contractor works for a marginal profit, no kickbacks are involved and the development cost is reduced by about 25 per cent. The block organization is also responsible for maintaining services and action against defaulters and absentee owners. It disburses small loans for house improvements and income generation.

Evolution of the settlement

In most new developments, the moment a scheme is announced, a number of local leaders, self-proclaimed social workers and other middlemen try to take advantage of it. The middlemen capture as many plots as they can, by encroaching or by using fake applicants or through contacts inside the implementing agency. Anticipating an increase in land value in the area adjoining the scheme, they also establish illegal land subdivisions there. This happened in Khuda-ki-basti, and may be one of the reasons there were so few settlers in the beginning.

When the scheme was still vacant a *dalal* encroached on the land and began to build houses overnight. Noticing that development was about to start, customers for adjacent plots showed up. The *dalal* then sold plots on the condition that they start construction immediately with himself supplying the building material. When the *dalals* were given the responsibility for identifying prospective households by the HDA, the cards that HDA used in place of the title-deed became an important source of income and influence. *Dalals* charged exorbitant amounts for prime plots in the scheme, and made fake cards to populate the scheme as quickly as possible to inspire confidence. When the 'reception area' was established they also took advantage of this by taking bribes to settle people directly, a practice the HDA failed to stop. Obviously there are dangers in involving *dalals*. They operate by making their customers obligated to them, but they also have the advantage that they can attract people to build in the area and resist outsiders with claims.[17] In the case of Khuda-ki-basti, however, they misused their position so frequently that ultimately the HDA had to end its cooperation with them.

In the land registration process the lowest in the hierarchy of public servants is the *patwari* or *tapedar* (clerk), who keeps records of the land titles in the area. Although of humble rank, the *patwari* controls records and can easily tamper with them. In a society where bribery is common the poorly paid *patwari*'s position invites corruption. Through their connivance civil servants, members of the bureaucracy and the police now claim land in and around Khuda-ki-basti.[18]

The *waderas* are a powerful group of feudal landlords who often sell their land to subdividers and also have subdividers appropriating land on their behalf, enabling them to obtain facilities in their areas quickly.[19] Some of these subdividers and aids live in Khuda-ki-basti itself and serve as local leaders in political parties or voluntary organizations. They continually try to occupy more land than they are entitled to in order to speculate.

The local leaders are brokers in a patronage network. By monopolizing access to public means the broker privatizes them. Brokers never attempt to solve problems because, by doing so, they undermine their own usefulness to others. They would rather maintain and even generate tensions to provide the situation in which they thrive. In Khuda-ki-basti some of them are now trying to get more plots and trying to abolish the instalment plan.

The HDA attempted to generate community participation through social workers, but this failed as well. A 'working committee' instituted to keep out non-residents was dissolved because it so often quarrelled. Since then, the community has elected leaders at the block level (a block consists of 250–300 plots). The block organizing committees administer the bank account in which the residents' instalments are deposited and out of which the development of the block is financed. These committees distribute and control loans provided by the HDA on behalf of House Building Finance Corporation (HBFC) for building and businesses. They also manage transfer fees.

Quarrelling in these committees led to the formation of an executive committee with a monthly rotating membership of block representatives and one representative from the HDA. This committee has the power to suspend members if charges of corruption are levelled against them. In spite of this, the community does not have a high opinion of the block leaders because, when the 11 blocks were organized in August 1988, elections were held by show of hands, and most of those elected were middlemen, land speculators and small-time entrepreneurs and their musclemen. Opposition to them from the losing candidates has consequently been strong. The block organizations have also turned into lobbying groups, pressuring the HDA for additional services.[20] The HDA has stopped depending on them for support, and has at the same time surrendered too much control to them. Of late the HDA has decided to stop trying to organize people, and instead attempts to work with a level of organization that is created by the residents. The block committees' accounts are kept in a bank branch in Khuda-ki-basti. Balance sheets are published every month. Transfer fees have to be deposited to this account.

Khuda-ki-basti is too new a settlement to control and effectively make use of such a representative organization. The block organization is also too large – each one represents an average of 200 to 250 families, making it difficult to form a cohesive group. The poor design of the blocks has also been a contributing factor.

Some problems are beyond the control of the HDA. One of them is ethnic sensitivity. After the ethnic riots in 1988 many Mohajirs felt that they could no longer be safe in Khuda-ki-basti; though they would have been in a majority, they would also have been surrounded by Sindhis. This prompted them to stay on in Hyderabad city, where they had moved to during the riots, leaving vacant plots in Khuda-ki-basti.

Poor transport between the settlement and the city remains a problem. The Sind Regional Transport Corporation runs public transport 25 times a day between the settlement and Hyderabad, but the service is unreliable, time-consuming, and expensive – the Rs 5 (US 20 cents) per trip it costs accounts for about 19 per cent of the average household income.[21] A private transport service using small vans is also available between the settlement and the city and to nearby workplaces. This transport is more convenient for the people and is used by them regularly, but also costs about Rs 10 per round trip to the city.

Another problem is that, though in principle no octroi tax[22] was to be levied for building materials bought in Hyderabad by Khuda-ki-basti residents, the three octroi posts between Hyderabad and Khuda-ki-basti invariably levy a tax. The police, leaders and the court have been of no help. Finally, the public agencies that connect services and infrastructure are very corrupt, adding to the hardships of the community.

Conditions in Khuda-ki-basti

Surveys have shown that the average household size in Khuda-ki-basti was seven persons.[23] More than 50 per cent of the households were employed in the informal sector, 17 per cent in the manufacturing sector, 16 per cent in the service sector, 9 per cent were government employees and 6 per cent did not have a job. A comparison with the adjacent illegal subdivision shows that both settlements house nearly the same income groups. About 78 per cent of the residents are Urdu-speaking Mohajirs and Biharis, 16 per cent are Sindhis, and 4 per cent are Punjabi. About 40 per cent were squatters before they moved to Khuda-ki-basti; one-third rented their previous house, and about 20 per cent came from villages. Previously 66 per cent of the residents lived in Hyderabad, 17 per cent came from Sind, 14 per cent lived in Kotri and 4 per cent came from outside Sind.

Physical conditions

The HDA did not give adequate thought to the design of the scheme, a standard sites-and-services layout. The plan was based on potential uses that were unrealistic. The streets are too wide and designed for cars. The main roads between sectors are even wider, but they are used for public transport. Open spaces are vast and their location is not based on any functions. The plan is a grid with no hierarchy of spaces between public and semi-private. Community facilities are distributed randomly within the site.

The project would have been better planned in clusters with community spaces protected from vehicular traffic; this would have kept land from being used for the wrong purpose and would have guaranteed safety from traffic. The number of units per acre could easily have been increased from 26 to about 40 and would have conserved land. Back lanes should have been eliminated, and the HDA has also failed to enforce its condition that three feet be left open at the rear of the plot to guarantee light and ventilation. A clear segregation between external and internal infrastructure should have been part of the physical plan, and to allow for effective block organization one block should not have consisted of more than 100 houses.[24]

The lack of physical planning has resulted in monotonous unattractive spaces as one walks through the settlement. In this hot and dusty climate, the lack of shaded and protected spaces makes it difficult for children to play outside and the parks are unused and poorly maintained.

Housing conditions

Of the houses, 16 per cent are *pucca* (built with permanent materials), 45 per cent are semi-*pucca* (semi-permanent) and 39 per cent are *kutcha* (built from temporary materials), though there are differences within these categories. The average investment in a house was about Rs 19,000 (US $76). The major source of financing was through loans from relatives and employers; a minor one was the House Building Finance Corporation, which charged 15 per cent interest for its loans. The average household income was Rs 1,500 (US $60) per month; if a household can afford to spend about 20 per cent of its income on housing (Rs 300) after paying Rs 110 for the development charge, it has Rs 190 left for house construction. With this amount, a household can repay a loan of Rs 11,500 (US $460) from the HBFC in ten years. Rs 11,500 (US $460) is sufficient to build a semi-*pucca* house.[25]

The quality and design of housing in the settlement were poor by the standards of informal Karachi settlements but average by Hyderabad standards. The HDA gave no help in design and construction and made no attempt to develop ways of improving them. Minimum guidelines could have been provided in terms of effective layout, ventilation and how to construct foundations and keep damp out. But apparently the HDA had no personnel for this purpose.[26] They had not learned from the Orangi Pilot Project, although similar services could have been provided.

Infrastructure

The allottee in Khuda-ki-basti at first used bucket latrines for disposal of human waste, and the public health hazards from this practice were serious. When the HDA became aware of this problem it tried to increase the down payment from Rs 1,000 to Rs 1,700 (US $40–68) so that it could supply the plots with ventilated soakpits with concrete toilet squatting tops, but the residents objected to the cost increase. The HDA is only now providing concrete toilet tops with the plot, as most residents have by now built a soakpit. However, the soakpits themselves are quickly filling up because of the rocky soil conditions.[27]

The HDA has adopted the Orangi Pilot Project approach for the delivery of services. Once sufficient funds from development charges have accumulated in a block account, the community then decides what kind and level of infrastructure is needed. There is a direct relationship between the level of community organization and the availability of infrastructure. By the middle of 1988, 72 per cent of the residents had piped water in their lanes and 24 per cent had sewerage lines, although there are problems with their functioning since they were put in by the community. While lane lines have been laid and are utilized, the secondary lines have not been laid. At some places sewage is seeping out of the ground and collecting in puddles, posing a potential health risk.

Delays in the delivery of services after payment has been made is another problem, because the community refuses to bribe the officials of the Water and Power Development Agency that is responsible for providing water and electricity so there are delays. Residents have had to wait anywhere from two and half months to nine months before these services are provided.

Unlike the Orangi Project, where a non-governmental organization was involved in motivating the people and providing the technical expertise, in Khuda-ki-basti the HDA is trying to play the role of an NGO, but is having limited success. Residents still feel that the HDA is responsible for providing the services. Since the block organizations are politicized, they also put pressure on the HDA that does not necessarily reflect what the people may really want. Given these conditions, the community does not have a clear agenda and therefore participation is very difficult to get and sustain. For that reason it has not had the level of success achieved at Orangi.

Community services

There is no hospital and no ambulance in the area, though doctors serve the community on a part-time basis. There are five private schools, and six clinics including one women's centre. A home-school project initiated by the HDA encouraged educated women to open basic schools in their homes, but, like most of the NGO programmes, which were to have been appropriated by the local social welfare or block organizations and were not, it has ceased to function. The majority of the residents feel that they did not benefit from the NGO programme. The NGO programmes did not work because they were not related to the local organizations, nor was there an official HDA connection. Civic strife also did not help.[28]

Cost recovery

The scheme achieves full cost recovery as the price of the unserviced land is collected from the allottee in the down-payment. The only direct government subsidy admitted by the HDA are the administrative costs. The cost of infrastructure is bound to rise with inflation so full cost recovery may not continue; it depends on the ability and willingness of the population to continue paying for it. The cost of the developed plot is borne by the beneficiaries in instalments spread over eight years.

However, the reason services can be provided so cheaply is that the HDA had subsidized the major services in the Gulshan-e-Shahbaz development. Although the rest of the development is still vacant, Khuda-ki-basti has been able to connect up with its infrastructure. To expect that housing can be provided to the poor without subsidies by the government is unrealistic. The question here is not whether the government should subsidize housing developments for the poor or not, but how governments can supply housing for the poor at a cost affordable to both occupant and government, where tenure is secure, and where there is an equitable and sustainable environment.

Potential for transfer and adaptation

The basic premiss of incremental development schemes is that it can benefit the poor households. However, the down payment of Rs 1,000 (US $40) is still high, especially for a place that lacks job opportunities. For a poor family to pay Rs 110 (US $4.4) per month for infrastructure and still have money left over for house construction and other daily needs is difficult. In addition, a sizeable number of respondents reported a drop in income as a result of moving to the scheme. To be successful there should be more income-generating activities in and around the site, and the number and quality of social services in the scheme must be increased.

The mechanism of the 'reception area' does seem to help check infiltration by middle-income groups, but as facilities are added to the scheme, over time land value is bound to rise and with it the possibility that its poorest residents will be priced out of the project by the upper-income groups.

The success of the scheme depends on the allottee occupying the plot and staying there. As the scheme grows, it is becoming more and more difficult to police the settlement and ensure that this is happening. After the ethnic riots of 1988, many people moved back into the city and have not returned.

The scheme is managed by three or four officials. The pressure to accept bribes, particularly by those who have built there but for some reason do not want to stay, is very high. To evict an allottee once the house has been built, even as a temporary structure, is difficult. The problems with the block organizations have exacerbated the situation, as most middlemen and land-grabbers are quick to claim vacated plots and houses.

For incremental development projects to be successful, two issues have to be resolved. The participation of middlemen or *dalals* in the scheme has to be controlled. In Khuda-ki-basti the role of the middlemen grew as the scheme developed. The idea behind involving middlemen was that they had financial ability to promote development. They were supposed to check illegal subdividers. Jan Van der Linden, in his evaluation of the project, said that it was 'probably the right thing to do since it is sometimes impossible to work through proper channels'.[29] However, in practice this has caused the failure of the scheme, because depending on middlemen to control speculation has given them power over the HDA, and eventually the leadership role of the community. They act as patrons and they tend to divide rather than unify the people living there. Without an NGO or other organization that could focus the community organization on solving its own problems, middlemen favour one group to the disadvantage of the other and the project fails.

This project shows that incremental development schemes do not provide land as cheaply as illegal subdivisions, but they do offer tenure and provide cheaper infrastructure faster. They also reach their target population more effectively than conventional site-and-services projects and at least initially prevent infiltration by higher income groups into the scheme. The HDA's approach has challenged conventional wisdom, and offered an alternative to the World Bank approach of site-and-services, which even the Bank itself has come to question.

Future directions for incremental development schemes

In incremental development, the role of the private developer has to be regulated. The advantage of private developers is not their ability to provide cheap services, but their ability to be opportunistic. Profit is their incentive; they develop settlements illegally because they can make a profit doing so. They are able to provide land at low cost to the poor because they do not provide services. However, there is a cost incurred in paying off government officials, the police and the landowner, if it is private land, and the cost of undertaking the subdivision. This cost is charged to people at a rate that ranges from Rs 700 to 1,000 (US $28–40). Plots are also given free to widows and disabled people to settle the people as quickly as possible. Most developers move on once the subdivision is filled, but the more streetwise among them keep choice plots for themselves until the settlement is consolidated and services are brought in, and the price of the plots rises rapidly. The developer then sells these plots to the highest bidder and makes large sums of money in the process.

In Khuda-ki-basti, the middlemen are trying to buy up plots allocated to the poor through their intermediaries so that they can then sell them once the settlement is fully developed. The HDA was unaware of this, but once it became aware it tried to cut them out of the process, leading to a power struggle. In incremental development schemes the role of the private developer should be limited to developing the settlement and giving them a certain number of plots as payment. The issue of community organization, beneficiary selection, settlement design, densities and level of services to be provided should be handled by the development agency and the NGO.

To improve the level of community participation and to ensure its success it is necessary to redefine the role of the implementing agency. The charter of the HDA requires only that it develop urban land; it does not have to administer the settlement once it exists. One possibility is to have staff carry out community development activities; another is to use the services of an NGO to implement the project. The HDA would demarcate the land and the NGO would be responsible for settling households on it using the reception-area approach. The NGO would be responsible for collecting down payments from the residents and transferring them to the HDA. Once the households have settled the NGO could upgrade and provide services as they did in the Orangi Pilot Project. The NGO would also be in a position to pressure the authorities not to delay in putting in infrastructure, just as the *dalals* did. This approach showed in Orangi that the community can improve its living conditions with help from the NGO.

Suitable urban design and settlement layout is lacking. The HDA gave no thought to subdividing the site to create spaces the community could use. It is a typical site-and-services layout, whose prime objective was to install infrastructure cheaply and to follow the World Bank land-use criteria for percentage of built-up space, open space and circulation space.

In incremental development schemes as in site-and-services projects the quality of the environment is important. Arif Hasan, Jan J. Van der Linden, Brian Brace Taylor and others who have evaluated the project have commented on how Khuda-ki-basti reflects people's ingenuity and hope. However, designers and government officials have a duty to assist in ensuring a qualitative development of the settlement. If it takes ten years to provide a decent habitat, it is ten years too late for all the children who have grown up in it and ten years lost for their parents.

Who is responsible for external and who for internal development has to be clearly defined and agreed upon. The development agency should be responsible for the first, the community for the second. But if this is not made clear, conflict over rights and responsibilities will arise. It is also important to ensure that even though the community will be responsible for internal development the government should bear responsibility of providing assistance through NGOs. Communities should not be expected to come together on their own to undertake such large-scale efforts and sustain them over time. Standards and quality need to be maintained and the government should ensure them.

Given all these shortcomings, Khuda-ki-basti has still shown that without government resources, without loans, without any experts from the World Bank or the Asian Development Bank, the people, with modest help from an urban development policy instituted by the HDA, can develop new communities through government and private partnership.

Lessons from Citra Niaga and Khuda-ki-basti

More projects like Citra Niaga and Khuda-ki-basti are needed where government, private investment and the community together participate in providing housing for the poor. The partnership, however, does have its problems, as evidenced in Khuda-ki-basti. The government tries to provide housing for as many people as possible at as low a cost as possible. Private developers want to derive the maximum profits from their investment, and the community wants the best environment at a minimal cost.

If the role of the private developer is clearly identified, as it was in Citra Niaga, the process has a chance to succeed. Designers, NGOs and development agency officials all worked together in Citra Niaga to arrive at a plan that would best satisfy all demands. Can the efforts undertaken in Citra Niaga be replicated in housing schemes? In Citra Niaga the development was commercial in nature so that the developer could make a profit. The prime location in the city centre also played a large role in its success.

In most housing projects, however, available land is at the city's fringes and opportunities for quick returns are limited. Yet a cursory analysis of city growth in developing countries shows that land that was once at the fringe ten years ago is now well located and in demand. New housing projects using private developer money and ingenuity can be developed if the development authority would provide the land and also the external services, such as main roads and electricity, at nominal or no cost. The developer would then be responsible for the internal development of the scheme and provide the internal infrastructure. Restrictions on what the developer could charge and the precise percentage of the plots for sale on the open market could be established, as was done in Citra Niaga. Certain plots could be given to the developer for commercial or other facilities. An increased floor space index could also be allowed at certain locations in the development so that an effective cross-subsidy could be worked out. Housing allocation and residential development would be controlled by the development authority, the community organization and the NGO.

Land-sharing is also now being tried in Bombay. The Bombay municipal corporation has invited private developers or owners of the land in 15 selected slums to redevelop them. Slum dwellers are to be given 180-square-foot houses costing Rs 65,000 (US $2,160) each at a subsidized cost of Rs 25,000 (US $833). The landowner or developer is expected to recover the subsidy and make his profit from the free market sale of other houses on the site. The density on the site has been increased to 2.5 FSI (floor space index) to allow additional houses. Seventy-five per cent of the slum's residents would have to agree to this redevelopment. Those who do not want to participate would be given land to build houses elsewhere.[30] The proposal has only been recently introduced, so we do not yet know if such an approach can be successful. However, what is important is that governments are realizing that to solve the urban problem the active participation of private developers and the community is needed.

CHAPTER 6

Local Government and Private Sector Partnerships for Low-Cost Housing Design

The city of Indore is the commercial centre of the state of Madhya Pradesh in Central India with a population of over 1.5 million. Aranya township is a large-scale housing and mixed-use project in Indore designed to provide low-cost dwellings for the poor. Designed by B. V. Doshi, director of the Vastu Shilpa Foundation for Environmental Design and Research (VSF), this project redefines the conventional site-and-services approach to include an innovative cluster and underground infrastructure system, models for future dwellers, house types, suggested materials and steps for implementation, while at the same time remaining flexible. It has about 6,500 housing units in various income categories – but predominantly for the poorest people categorized by the government as the economical weaker section (EWS) – facilities for social welfare and infrastructure. All told, the project amounts to setting up a new town for 40,000 people, looking for a middle ground between the site-and-services at one extreme and fully serviced housing on the other.

Project history

In 1982, an estimated 60,000 households in Indore lived in informal settlements with no adequate facilities: 41.4 per cent of the households lived in one room in a tenement, and 74.12 per cent households lived in rented quarters.[1] Housing in Indore is the responsibility of two government agencies – the Indore Development Authority (IDA) and the Madhya Pradesh Housing Board (MPHB). To deal with the shortage, various schemes were undertaken by the Indore Development Authority (IDA) as part of its development plan along the Bombay–Delhi National Highway.

In 1981–82 the IDA embarked on what became known as the Aranya township. The programme required evolving a master plan for a community of 6,500 families with individual plot sizes ranging from 35 m² for the EWS to 500 m² for the middle and higher income groups. The project was tendered, and construction work commenced in 1984–85; it was completed in 1989, largely as it was conceived and designed. The site measures 220 acres and has been designed to provide 3,985 EWS plots of the 6,500 total. The EWS scheme was designed as a site-and-services project; the rest of the site as serviced plots. Of the 3,985 EWS plots only 171 had been occupied as of the end of July 1991, but more houses are under construction. The total of 220 houses represents only a 4.29 per cent occupancy rate for the entire project and a population of over 1,000. These figures are small for a number of reasons, of which allocation and unavailability of services are only two of the most important.

The money for this and other urban development projects came directly from the government of India and indirectly from the World Bank, and from the Housing and Urban Development Corporation (HUDCO). This is common in such schemes, for which the money comes from an international financing agency to the government of India as part of a larger development package. The central government then approaches a state authority, and between them an allocation agreement is reached. The state authority in turn asks local development authorities to prepare the project.

The first plan was developed in 1981 by the IDA for the Aranya township. It was a typical plotted development, with areas allocated for roads and other services. Fifty-five per cent of the land-use was utilized by the IDA in this plan.[2] The project was then sent to the technical committee at the state level, where representatives of the World Bank and HUDCO reviewed it. The technical committee, including its World Bank members, thought the design inappropriate and unaffordable and suggested that the project be revised. The plans were twice revised before it was decided to bring in a consultant to prepare the plan and do the design work. Mr Doshi and Vastu Shilpa were invited to Indore along with other architects, and Vastu Shilpa was eventually awarded the project.[3]

The World Bank suggested that Doshi do only the overall plan, but he insisted on doing the total project, including the services, and an agreement was entered into with the IDA and HUDCO to that effect.

Project financing

The project had been budgeted at Rs 97.5 million, of which 70 million was spent on construction and civil works, 15 million on electricity and power, 3.7 million on land acquisition and 1.8 million on consultants; the balance was on other development and overhead costs.[4]

A surplus of Rs 11.7 million has been generated against the investment of Rs 97.5 million based on 1982 prices. This has been achieved by judiciously locating the upper-income plots and the commercial facilities in the areas which would fetch the maximum prices. The surplus generated has provided seed capital for further EWS schemes.

The sale price to the poorest people is also subsidized to the tune of about 35 per cent on average, again from the sale of upper-income plots.

The revenue in terms of the investment is, therefore, quite substantial. This was the first scheme in India where the World Bank has financed a mixed-income housing project.

The World Bank and HUDCO were joint financiers of the project, each with a 50 per cent commitment. World Bank charged 12 per cent interest on its loans but gave generous subsidies to the government in terms of its repayment plan which is extended over 20 years. HUDCO funded the project with a variable interest rate ranging from 4 per cent for the EWS plots, 6 per cent for low-income plots, 8 per cent for middle-income plots and 12 per cent for the higher-income plots.

Site context

The site, 6 km north of the city centre, on the Delhi–Bombay highway is well linked to the city, and is near employment: both existing and proposed industrial areas are within a radius of 2 km. Suburban growth has almost reached the southern boundary, but toward the east and north the site is surrounded by agricultural land earmarked for future growth.[5]

Of the net area of the site (88.6 ha), 1.85 ha has been set aside for light industries on the highway along the eastern boundary. The square site measures about 1 km by 1 km. A commercial-cum-industrial complex for the eastern boundary will be for large-scale commerce and warehousing (*mandis*). Another major commercial, educational and administrative centre is proposed about 1 km south of the site towards the city. A 30-metre-wide city road flanks the northern, southern and western boundaries. The site is flat, with no notable features; a natural rainwater channel runs diagonally across from the east to north-west.[6]

Planning and design

The Vastu Shilpa Foundation (VSF), through research work already undertaken in other areas, had found that low-cost urban housing schemes often generated unpleasant and unbalanced environments resulting from disregard for the traditional life-styles of the people, uncomfortable and ill-thought-out use of spaces, uneconomical and disorganized use of land, costly or inadequate infrastructure, poorly designed housing and lack of community, recreational and commercial support. There was seldom any provision for flexibility and elasticity of spaces, particularly in the poorest pockets, where dwelling densities were highest.

Linear cluster

The studies that the VSF had already undertaken found that contiguous linear open spaces work much more efficiently when big areas of open space are also included.[7] This led to their decision to use a 'linear cluster' instead of a regular cluster model. Other studies on squatter settlements in India were also undertaken to study how poor people use and live in these spaces.

Doshi's own experience over the last 20 years, in both the housing projects that he had designed and the studies undertaken at the School of Architecture and Planning and at the VSF, was fundamental in developing the design.

The guiding force in the design of the township and one of the important innovations was the development of the 'linear cluster', which represented a change in the development of the cluster. The 'linear cluster', as the name suggests, is long and narrow in plan, much like a dead-end street. In most culs-de-sac, the houses are set back from the street. However, here the houses edge the road, which is narrower. It is unlike a cluster model, which is a closed system, where according to Doshi 'services terminate, traffic terminates and maybe even life terminates, the spaces become very individual and personal'.[8] The 'linear cluster', being more like a street, brings low-cost infrastructure to the house as efficiently as possible. It also borrows heavily from the traditional Indian street in providing an outdoor living room for the community. Unlike a usual cluster model, where the outdoor living room is in the shape of a courtyard, the 'linear cluster' space is like a street without a central focus.

In contrast to the models proposed by Horacio Caminos, where the street is a service channel, the street here is treated with beauty and character, and open spaces are not large squares but are in the form of linear areas.[9]

To help families re-establish social contacts, the dwellings are arranged around short streets. The courtyards form clusters of manageable size to foster group activities. Good use has been made of public squares, landmarks and variations in widths of streets and in house elevations. The front porches (*ottas*) help the inhabitants to set up income-generating activities to supplement incomes. All the essential utilities – water supply, sewerage, surfaced roads, storm-water drainage, electricity lines and street lighting – are provided. Every dwelling has direct access by a surfaced road. Though initially the construction will be limited to the service cores, a demonstration cluster to influence future development has been built.

Infrastructure design

As water supply and sanitation constitute the major cost components of any site-and-services scheme, the design of the service core and the supporting infrastructure become the critical elements of the design. Individual toilets and wash facilities were provided for each dwelling, and placed at the rear of the dwelling unit to isolate them from other household activities. Pit and borehole latrines were avoided because of soil conditions. Service lines from the core to the service plots were short; manholes and main supply lines were reduced to one per nine or ten dwellings, and the main service lines were halved to one every other street. These numbers are much lower than usual and resulted in cost reduction. For maximizing common walls and minimizing foundations, the service cores were generally grouped into fours over suspended platforms. Simple, repetitive, pre-cast components were used to encourage the 'self-build' spirit. When assembled, this system also overcomes many of the problems of excessive ground shrinkage caused by the local soil conditions.

The linear cluster model allowed 18 houses to be connected to a single manhole. Service pipes from nine houses on either side of the street are brought into a service plot which has been left open and provides another entry into the houses. The service plots can also function as open spaces for children to play in and for other outdoor activities.

Economically weaker section dwelling

The planned dwellings have traditional features such as front porches (*ottas*), verandas, courtyards and roof terraces. Variations of these elements combined with various plot size make each house different. Entrances and balconies are staggered to avoid views into opposite houses across streets. Every unit has adequate light and ventilation. The basic core can be easily absorbed into any future ground-floor extension. Maisonette-type row houses optimize built-up areas in relation to plot areas and plinth perimeters. The common party walls and their shared foundations are also maximized. Deep plots (12' × 30') reduce service lengths. The internal subdivision of each dwelling is simplified to give maximum efficiency for the net usable area with minimum circulation space.

Three type of core plots are available for the EWS: type E1 has a water closet only and plinth for bath; type E2 has a WC and bath and plinth for one room; and type E3 has a WC, bath and one room, and complete plinth.

Planning at the sector level

The town as a whole has been planned so that the sectors function as intertwined villages, a characteristic of traditional Indian settlements. In each sector a relationship is established between the dwellings, clusters and streets to maintain contact with the land at all levels. To avoid segregation caused by income differences, while at the same time maintaining the value and marketability of the upper-income plots that help subsidize the economically weaker sector (EWS) housing, plots are laid out in concentric rings. The outer rings have the largest and most expensive plots and the best vehicular access. Behind them are the lowest-income core units, which can be built over time. These inner lower-income plots cluster around open spaces with the emphasis on pedestrian and slow-moving vehicular traffic. No direct vehicular road links all the different income levels areas; however, links between the various income areas are reinforced with pedestrian linkages.

The project has been divided into six sectors, called 'slices' by the IDA in order not to confuse them with the sectors at the city level. Each slice is designed and developed as a self-sufficient community. Lower-income and EWS plots are distributed among all but one of them; slice 6 is reserved exclusively for the highest income. All the other five slices have a mix of income groups in established proportions. The highest proportion is for the EWS.

To avoid friction income groups were not mixed. That meant that the allocation of plots had to be done with care and subtlety. As one goes towards the interior the plots grow smaller, but so gradually that one does not perceive the change as one moves from one group to the other. From the highest-income plots located closest to the highway, one moves to the middle-income plots in slices 5 and 3, and then to the lower-income. The lower-income plots are in front of each main cluster fronting the wider roads, and, finally, the EWS plots are located behind the low-income plots and in the interior. Most of the type E3 plots are located at the edges of the cluster adjacent to the lower-income plots and the E2 and E1 plots are in the interior of the cluster.

Schools, dispensaries and open markets combine or overlap with gardens, play areas and other recreational facilities. By planning the green areas as usable and not merely ornamental spaces, as well as by assigning large spaces to social activities, the open spaces have better chances of being maintained and remaining free of encroachments.

Complementing the formal vehicular network is the pedestrian network, which links all the service buildings and the central commercial zone. Small shops are located within clusters based on the number of families located around them, so that they do not have to go to the central market for all purchases. A five-minute walk from any dwelling to a community facility has been set as the design target. This has been done by allowing the pedestrian tracks to short circuit formal road patterns.

Planning at the township level

Though Aranya had to fit into the urban fabric of Indore, it was designed so that it would acquire its own identity as a township in which social and economic activities could flourish. The multi-storey commercial, residential and community complex rises above the low-rise housing to accentuate the physical as well as the functional centre of the town. The main sports field is integrated with the centre to emphasize its importance to the whole community.

The vehicular and pedestrian networks converge in the town centre, binding the different sectors. The central facilities such as the cinema hall, community hall, restaurants, etc., are surrounded on three sides by EWS housing and are directly connected to the highest-income housing by a spine road, allowing easy access to the low-income communities and securing the patronage of the upper-income families who will provide the essential income for the survival of the city centre. For safety, the major traffic intersections are Y- and T-junctions and the sector roads are staggered to control vehicular speeds.

A hierarchy of roads were designed ranging from 60 m and 30 m-wide highways on the periphery, to 4.5 m-wide internal roads, largely for pedestrians and bicycles, but they are wide enough for emergency vehicles. There are also 3.56 m-wide (average) pedestrian links that have no carriageway.

Open spaces

The underlying principle in the design of the town's open spaces was to provide for the various activities that take place in any Indian community. The first task was to distinguish between activities for earning money in the organized or formal sector and in the informal sector, which is also in its way organized, but whose owners are not formally registered and therefore are not paying taxes. The designers determined the kinds of spaces required by each sector and designed them to accommodate both formal and informal activities. For example, in the informal sector hawkers, tailors, laundrymen (*dhobi*), cobblers, etc., usually work outside, so the VSF provided areas for these kinds of work, including the space required to keep, store and maintain the tools.

Service lots where manholes are located were also designed to accommodate informal sector activities. In some of these, trees were planted, and in others a concrete platform was built where small-scale economic activities could take place. In addition to the service lots within each cluster, there is an open area at the crossroads of the street clusters where small shops are located. These spaces could house a tobacco shop (*panwalla*), a newspaper stall, a barber shop, milk booth, or even small building material storage areas. It was expected that building material areas would also provide employment and training to local people for house construction. In addition to these small squares is the main large area of open land connecting with the town. Planned for this space are small dairy cooperatives, primary, middle and secondary schools (with the school children utilizing the open space as a play area), an orchard, vegetable gardens, and a playing field and football ground.

The town centre and commercial facilities for the city at large were planned to act as a magnet to the commercial zone. The town centre is meant to serve a much larger population than just the township itself and people from surrounding communities are also meant to use it. This will provide a viable economic base and avoid the area's being stigmatized as belonging to 'poor people'.

The primary road into the centre will link up to a city-level main road so that buses and other transportation will be able to come to the centre to help provide a lively and cohesive environment for the residents.

The problem in designing these large open spaces was how to control activities like grazing and other forms of encroachment. The designers believed that control would be exercised by the community once a use for these public spaces was established. In a community of 40,000 people these spaces will be used, and community maintenance of open spaces is well documented. A recent example in India which inspired the designers was the work done by P. S. Athavlay, a contemporary reformer, who inspired the planting of thousands of trees in villages by explaining to the people that planting trees was their offering to their God.[10] The approach was very successful, and the people who planted the trees are now maintaining them.

The issue of social organization and community development is very important in the design of a number of public spaces. Unfortunately neither social organization nor community development happens overnight. To initiate community development and to bring unknown people together for a common cause is a difficult process, and to sustain it over a period of time is even more difficult. Professional assistance to organize and to act as a catalyst is important. Designers most often use successful examples of social organization and community development as a means of justifying the design of their projects and showing how these spaces can be effectively used. However, the most important aspect of forming community organizations is neglected. Both designing and implementing agencies are unsure of whose responsibility it is, and the majority are unaware of how to bring about community organization. Lack of a community organization plan has also been a problem with this project.

Commercial and economic activities

According to studies undertaken by the VSF, there is a shortage of commercial facilities in India. Planning norms call for about 2 per cent of the land to be reserved for commercial activities. However, surveys of existing towns show commercial activities take up around 4–5 per cent of land. In Aranya 3.5 per cent of the land has been allocated to commercial activities, spread over the whole area, from the individual cluster level to the main commercial centre.[11]

A wide variety of uses has been planned for the commercial centre but the VSF was not involved in designing the buildings for it. It was only responsible for assigning spaces and allocating uses. It felt that if this were left to the market forces, non-profitable uses such as libraries and community centres would be left out.

In the central commercial area, land for both the formal and informal sector has been allocated. Spaces have been provided for businesses ranging all the way from up-market boutiques to street vendors and repair shops. In the commercial sector, hotels, apartments and office buildings will be developed. Institutional buildings such as schools, health centres, police stations, and post offices have been provided. Exclusive shops will be located in five-storey buildings, together with car showrooms. Nearby will be semi-permanent buildings for weekly markets, and next to those sheds and finally platforms.

Population density and land-use

The gross township area is about 100 ha, including open spaces and peripheral roads. It is designed for an initial population of about 40,000, which is anticipated to eventually rise to 65,000. The gross density is, therefore, 400 persons per ha, rising with time to 650 persons per ha. This compares favourably with densities in the inner cities of India of over 1,000 persons per ha. Studies have shown that housing and infrastructure costs are optimal at densities of between 300 and 600 persons per ha.[12] Of this area, 21 per cent will be used for roads; pedestrian walkways and squares will take another 1.5 per cent of the net planning area. About 8 per cent of the planning area will be left open, which falls within the planning norms in India of between 8 per cent and 10 per cent.

Cross-subsidy and affordability

Cross-subsidy was successfully achieved in this project. By cross-subsidizing the services with the upper-income housing, standards for the economically weaker sector were not cut: on the contrary, they have been made cheap enough to be affordable. Cross-subsidy is also expected to raise revenue through commercial development, which is expected be sold at a profit, and developing residential areas for upper and middle incomes. It is expected that these people will eventually pay for much of the development. Without cross-subsidy, most of the standards would have been compromised, as the lower-income groups would have had to pay for the services by themselves, and this would have made them prohibitive.

The costs of the EWS plots have been worked out to achieve monthly repayments of Rs 45 for the families in type E1 up to Rs 125 per month for families living in type E3. VSF studies suggest that the monthly incomes of the EWS groups are underestimated in the national statistics, as they do not take into account income generated from the informal sector.[13] The practice of subletting parts of dwellings to augment income is one such unreported income source. All these factors can speed the growth of the dwellings from the basic core to the final built form.

The EWS demonstration project

The goal of the township at Aranya is to provide decent housing, infrastructure and work opportunities to the economically weaker sector. Although the site-and services approach ensures that a large number of people with very limited resources can be reached, it has the drawback that the built form that eventually defines the character of the development cannot be controlled. As a result, many site-and-services schemes in the past have turned into slums because there was not enough emphasis on built form and the way people live.[14] It was to avoid this that demonstration clusters of EWS houses were proposed. The idea was discussed with World Bank representatives in June 1983. It was agreed that the construction of demonstration houses was imperative if the success of the township was to be ensured.

The objectives of the demonstration house were to show the different stages of growth from basic sanitary cores to final two-storey houses; to show the variation of form attainable within simple, repetitive house layouts; to provide control of quality and workmanship for other construction to follow; and to set a planning control model for the growth of other EWS houses in the future. Written regulations are much less likely to work than the built examples that people can emulate. They would also demonstrate pre-casting and other technologies to encourage the use of self-build elements; set a pattern for landscaping and street furniture in the EWS streets; examine the possibilities of setting up material banks and other services to channel the available resources more effectively; provide an opportunity to architectural and engineering students to study such developments through participation; and provide a nucleus of a well-established community around which the immigrant population can settle.

Analyses of the demonstration project

Two hundred demonstration houses were to be built with an average built-up area of 30 m² per dwelling. Some units would be completely built, and others only partially built to show various stages of growth. Altogether they were expected to cost the IDA Rs 20 million, which would be recovered from the sale of these houses.

The houses, according to Doshi, all followed a single design. He expects that not everyone will use the same colours or style, that the staircases will be changed and the roofs will vary. The aim is that each house be built for under ʳs100 a square foot. He wanted to demonstrate that low-cost housing can be built through a private agency or a contractor and sold to people at a price otherwise not possible in the market. In this the demonstration project was successful.

Most of the demonstration houses were designed by the VSF; however, the Center for Minimum Cost Housing from McGill University designed some of the other demonstration houses.[15] The McGill group's design kept the same plot area, but increased the frontage of each plot. From their studies of Indore slums, they felt that low-income people needed more frontage because of their use of the street. Orienting more of the house to the street also makes it appear much larger. The house itself was otherwise essentially the same as Doshi's, but the cost may be higher because the common wall between the houses is shorter; also the cost of installing the services increased as more manholes had to be introduced. The same efficiency as in Doshi's layout could not be replicated.

The McGill group did not really experiment. They fell back on typical site-and-services projects with a small variation from the standard 6 m² plot size, to get their longer frontage. Because the room is not deep, more of the house has natural light and ventilation.

This part of the demonstration has not been completed, and the McGill group has not returned to follow up on the project. Only the plinth has been laid out. It will be interesting to compare the two solutions, once the McGill part has been developed, to determine which layout is more functional.

A number of the ideas used in the demonstration houses have not worked, but in any case the beneficiaries now building in Aranya have used only a few of them. No attempt has been made to assist people to draw lessons or ideas from the demonstration project. For the IDA it is primarily a source of revenue, though the houses have not yet been allocated, probably because the authority is under pressure from various vested organizations to have the houses allocated to it. During the survey, the demonstration project was visited on a number of occasions by politicians, senior police officers and so forth, who expressed interest in them. The IDA's asking price is quite high; it ranges from Rs 160 to 220 per square foot.

The planning and design process

When the VSF started work on the project it had no clear picture of the complexities of site-and-services projects and the process of development involved. It undertook the design in order to learn as it went along. It was very fortunate that the development authority permitted it to do this and gave it time to study the situation and survey the site. It was also able to make spot surveys of land prices, the social and economic composition of the families that were going to inhabit the township, the income mixing that was proposed by the IDA and the various alternatives and options available. The VSF was not familiar with the territory. It had never worked in Indore before, so it chose to concentrate on its strengths and learn what the problems were through the process of designing and implementation.

The VSF held certain ideas right from the beginning. It discussed hierarchies and understood the complexities of the design and the various scales involved. It also knew the budget would be tight. Given these limitations it concentrated on its strengths in architectural design and built form. Urban form was crucial; the premise was that there has to be some kind of built form which could dictate the overall physical shape of the community.

It was unfamiliar with the group it was designing for, nor did it know what their space requirements really were or how fast the town was going to grow. As far as the site-and-services idea was concerned, it was given no choice; that path had already been agreed on when VSF was hired.

To overcome some of these drawbacks, the VSF studied a number of slums – their built form, street sizes and use and the spaces within the community. According to Himanshu Parikh:

[W]e in our design were imitating the existing urban patterns from slums and traditional urban areas. We started to superimpose our idea of scale and hierarchy on these physical patterns. Sense of scale and time was not appreciated at the beginning. Allocation process was totally fictitious when we started. When the work had progressed sufficiently and we had some idea of the overall structure of the project, then the idea of phasing was introduced. Even then phasing was introduced for the agency's convenience not in terms of people taking time to move in over a period of time.

Implementation

The scheme was divided into six 'slices', not so much to phase the work as to divide it into manageable areas so that if for some reason there was a problem with a single contractor, the entire project would not be held up. Each of these six 'slices' of the site were tendered to a different construction agency. Each contractor was to provide complete services for site work, road work, underground sewerage connections and electricity connections.

The designers expected that work would not be done simultaneously, but phased, so that problems that arose during construction could be rectified. The IDA, however, insisted that the work on all sectors proceed simultaneously, so that services could be connected without problems. A small water drain and storm-water drain ran through the site as well. According to Mr M. L. Bhatt, chief engineer and head of planning at the IDA, 'because of the site complexities it was very difficult to do one slice at a time. If the site had been a more normal piece of land it may have been possible.'[16] But the designers attribute the lack of phasing to pressure from the financing agencies and the state government, who wanted the project completed as soon as possible. Correspondence from the IDA to the VSF argued that the project should be further split into even smaller pieces to facilitate work on the scheme and to reduce the cost of each slice so that it did not exceed Rs 4 million. The IDA was reluctant to spend any more time on the project than was necessary.

On the face of it, the proposal to split the project up into further slices made sense, since it meant having more contractors working on it and finishing sooner. The VSF, however, refused to split the project into more slices than the six already planned for, arguing that further division of the project would render coordination impossible and would increase costs. They urged the IDA to retain the six slices and, if necessary, place house construction, the public buildings, landscaping and construction of the water reservoir and oxidation pond out to separate tenders to reduce the cost of the individual slices.

THe VSF's approach reflects the reality of construction work being done in India. To achieve what the IDA was suggesting, a group of contractors who would work well together would have to be found and their work would have to be coordinated and somehow phased. Generally most public projects lack management and planning; in many cases it is almost non-existent. For a public agency to have 10 to 12 contractors working on a project simultaneously would have involved making sure that all aspects of the scheme dovetailed into each other.

Lack of this kind of expertise in managing projects led the VSF to insist that the project be handled in larger chunks, where at least there is some integrity of the whole and there is some scope for compartmentalization. In the six-slice arrangement it is possible for a single contractor to work on one slice at a time, the civil and other works in the entire slice could be integrated and the contractor could complete almost the entire package. The degree of overlap with the next slice in terms of connections was limited and could be controlled between the six different contractors without great difficulty.

It would also have been possible to divide the project in a number of the different ways. It could have been divided either in terms of different work allocated to different agencies, where one agency does the water supply, the other does the sewerage, and another does roads, etc., but that approach works well only if a project is well coordinated. Disputes between agencies because one has to wait for the other to finish its work are common. To undertake a project of this scale when using this approach, the IDA would have had to bring in a professional project management team. A project of such scale and complexity requires professionals to control, oversee coordination and organize all the activities that are required over a period of time.

Given all its shortcomings, the IDA on the whole managed the project quite efficiently and completed the scheme within its budget and within the specified time. To this extent the project has been a success. The Public Works Department people are often said to be corrupt, but, although the VSF had no control over which construction agencies were chosen and the same government people and the same government agencies executed and supervised the project, it was still finished within budget and within the specified time.

Although generally in EWS schemes the standards and the level of services that are provided are minimal, the VSF designed underground systems for both services and electrical wiring. They argued that because of high population density, above-ground connections would be a potential hazard. In addition to safety, aesthetics, shortage of land, flexibility for further expansion of dwelling, narrow streets and high dwelling densities argued for the decision. These design decisions caused friction with the implementing agency; they highlight the complexities of such a project, and point to the problems projects continue to face even after they are completed and occupied.

Wet services were finally taken below ground when the VSF's cost analysis showed that it would not be expensive; cost cutting was achieved by eliminating extra manholes through an innovation in design.

Running electricity cables below ground posed problems: the electric system, the power system and the street lighting system were designed by the VSF and their placement was planned in the normal way and was to be executed in each slice by the contractor doing the job. However, the Madhya Pradesh Electricity Board (MPEB), which provides the electricity, was adamant that wiring be done by themselves.

The second problem arose after the MPEB took over electrification; it was not used to installing electrification underground and insisted on open wires and overhead cables. The VSF compromised with a mixed system. At the periphery where the density is low and houses are high-income, overhead wiring was used; in the EWS areas and in areas where the densities were high and maintenance seen as a problem, it was placed underground, which proved much more economical. With the underground system more connections were possible, eliminating expensive overhead junction boxes.

Allocation process

The allocation process in any housing scheme is important, but in low-income schemes it takes on additional importance and complexity. The IDA first issued a call for applications in 1989, after the project had been completed to the point at which it stands today. Applications were invited through advertising in local papers. Various categories of applicants were based on income group. Three levels of EWS plots were available, ranging from Rs 200 per month to Rs 400 per month (the type E3 was eventually raised to Rs 750 per month). To be eligible, applicants could not own other property. After the announcement, 40,000 applications were received, of which 20,000 were found eligible. Of the 20,000 eligible, income was verified for each through the local administration. After eligibility was verified, the final selection was done through a computer.

Once the beneficiaries were selected, a list of houses according to slices was then prepared. According to beneficiary eligibility in terms of house type (E1, 2 or 3), names were matched to plot. No other criterion was established for plot allocation, nor was any choice of location given to the beneficiary beyond a choice of slice. The process was random. The winners were named and another 10 per cent put on a waiting list. No complaints were made about the lottery, and the allocations have been registered with the IDA, but the IDA faced many problems. It was not geared to deal with so many applications and there were computer problems along the way. There were also problems in the lottery and final handing over of possession. People have been given possession only in the last six to nine months.

The lottery for low-income plots has also been held. The middle-income and high-income plots were to be sold at market rate but the high-income sale has not yet started. Over a hundred middle-income plots have been sold. In this project 22 per cent of the plots were reserved for various groups: politicians – 2 per cent, IDA staff – 2 per cent, 'backward classes'[17] – 15 per cent, IDA corporation members – 2 per cent, and the chairman of IDA quota system – 2 per cent.

The demonstration project will be allocated separately. Any individual can apply. People put in a bid and the highest bidder is given the house. Various categories of the house have been sold at prices ranging from Rs 160 to 200 per square foot.

The allocation process was not well thought out. The lottery system is fair, but when it comes to forming communities it does not work well. People were given no choice of location or preference of neighbours. In India there are a fairly large number of socio-religious groups, and people prefer to live with the group they belong to. Today's changing values and family life-styles mean that there are different needs that have to be provided for. A straight lottery does not provide these choices.

Some way of forming a community has to be established and the allocation made more refined than the one adopted by IDA in Aranya, so that a sense of community will be fostered. According to Himanshu Parikh:

> As the work started progressing it became clear to us that since we were developing a community we should therefore try to bring in communities as groups if possible rather than select randomly. This was one area where the implementing agency was not flexible, knowingly inflexible, because they felt that if they let the door open for any kind of negotiation, there would be other political forces and special interest groups asking for special consideration and the process would become unmanageable.

Land speculation

To keep speculation out of the scheme also proved very difficult. Keeping out speculators is virtually impossible in any housing scheme, as the demand for housing is so great that speculators eventually will come up with a method of getting around the rules set by any development agency. However, the IDA's attempts to control speculation have had some amount of success. When a beneficiary took possession it was verified that it was the same individual or family who had applied and been given the allocation. Each applicant had to submit a photograph, which was checked before the plot was handed over. These checks may ensure that the plot is given to the rightful beneficiary. However, it does not stop the beneficiary from selling the property shortly afterwards.[18]

Once the beneficiary had been selected and verified, the plot was handed over and restrictions on selling and transferring property were imposed. Nobody is allowed to sell the plot; it has to be returned to IDA. However, when the house has been built there are no restrictions on selling the plot and house; only the sale of empty plots is illegal. In the survey one of the type E3 plots has since been sold for Rs 14,500, a profit of Rs 2,000. In this case it was legal because type E3 plots already have a built room. Mr Bhatt said that legislation avoiding this would never be passed. He also felt that if a beneficiary had built a house he had the right to sell it. Sales involve the IDA and include certain transfer fees. The new owner can be anyone from any income group. It would in any case be difficult to ensure and verify income at this stage, nor could a poor family afford to buy a completed house.

The IDA did not look into other patterns of ownership such as collective or community ownership, whereby people buy into a cluster and have a right to live there, sometimes for 40 years, sometimes for ever. Change or transfer of property is otherwise handled by the cluster community. Projects using community or collective ownership schemes have managed to reduce speculation, but they are no panacea and they work better in some places than in others. In Thailand, for instance, the Thais prefer mediation to confrontation; in such situations this approach has worked. In India, too, there are community and cooperative housing programmes, but they were formed to finance and develop housing, not to restrict ownership transfer.[19]

Even though it is a good idea to control land speculation, and for this reason community ownership should be encouraged wherever possible, in cities like Bombay and Delhi where pressure on land is extremely high and prices on serviced land increase immediately, the poor have more incentive to dispose of land for a good profit than they do to keep it. In these situations ownership patterns, such as cooperatives, cannot solve the problem. Fundamental changes in property ownership must occur. All other approaches are only stopgap measures, which eventually will be overcome by the pressure of development.

In Aranya not much 'filtering' is taking place. All but five of the houses surveyed were occupied by beneficiaries. However, controls are minimal, so the chances of beneficiaries selling out to speculators once the property value increases significantly and once all the services are in place is high, especially since the title is in the name of the beneficiary and not in the name of a cooperative or other institution.[20]

Only 171 families are living in the project a year after the beneficiaries were able to move in. There are a number of reasons for this. Three of them are the perceived shortage of housing in Indore, which was mis-calculated; not all services are yet available at the site; and the beneficiaries have been given two years to move in. According to the law, the IDA cannot revoke the allocation or take any action, unless after the two years beneficiaries still have not moved in. Then they will have to pay penalties, but their claim over the plot cannot be revoked. This law could only be changed in the legislative assembly, which would be very difficult to do, but M. L. Bhatt would like to see the time reduced to one year. To construct a house is an expensive undertaking, however, and even though the plot is cheap and subsidized, the cost of constructing the house must be collected.[21]

Plot cost and payment process

The cost of each type of EWS plot and the instalment payment is as follows:

Type E1	4,595 Rs	45 Rs/month instalment
Type E2	5,670 Rs	56 Rs/month instalment
Type E3	12,565 Rs	125 Rs/month instalment

Loans for the serviced plots are paid in monthly instalments. According to the IDA, beneficiaries are paying regularly and are not defaulting on the loan. Building loans of up to Rs 10,000, are also available from the

IDA towards home construction, but the World Bank requires the beneficiary to construct part of the house, the wall up to a certain height, or the flooring, with their own funds before the IDA loan can be released. This stipulation has not worked. The IDA has been unable to give out many loans and utilize the fund properly, so the World Bank agreed last April to allow IDA to process loans without the stipulation.

Project analyses

A survey of 27 EWS houses, several from each slice, was undertaken to evaluate the project. Two houses under construction in the middle-income area and two schools, one secondary and the other middle level, were also visited. The survey evaluated change taking place within the township, the profile of the people living there, how they build, how they raise money, the facilities available for them in the township and their opinion of the township as a place to live.

Of the 27 houses studied, 9 were type E1, 6 E2 and 12 were E3. Twenty-two houses are still occupied by the original allottee and 5 have changed ownership. Fifteen houses are built to the level expected according to type. Eight are partially constructed and four are minimal or of temporary construction. Of those surveyed 16 families have an income level above the Rs 750 per month threshold and 11 have incomes at or below the threshold.

Of the slices that were occupied, slice 4 and 2 had the most people living in them; slice 1 and 3 had the fewest. In slice 5, part of the demonstration project has been built, but only two of the houses were occupied, both by people working for the IDA. One of them was the security guard for the site.

Family size, composition and social groupings

The average size of the family in the houses surveyed was five to six people, usually a couple and their two to three children, but sometimes one or both parents of the couple. In one house a sister of the wife was living with the family. Most of the families had young children either going to a kindergarten or who were in school outside the township. Only one elderly couple was living there.

Since the allocation had taken place only a year earlier the residents have been living there for less than a year: From the total of 171, 15 families had moved there in the beginning from Arjun Singh Nagar, a slum in the city, and all were from the same neighbourhood (*mohalla*). They had been allocated plots under a special category because their houses had been condemned by slum improvement projects and were in low-lying areas prone to flooding.

Among these 15 families a certain social bonding and sense of community was evident that was absent in the other clusters. A large number of the houses were built as temporary structures, even though the families have lived there for a year. They are wooden frames packed with earth and tin roofs. Some have internal partitions; some do not. Some are being converted into more permanent structures using brick walls and internal partitions. The five families interviewed were all earning Rs 700 a month. Four of them worked as tailors in garment factories. Some inhabitants worked as labourers outside. They had to walk to Vijay Nagar, about 15 to 20-minutes' walk, to take a *tempo* (a three-wheeler van) ride into the city. Most of the wives did not work at all or did only occasional work.

In this cluster, one unoccupied type E3 plot which had a built room was being used by some of these families to store their belongings: they were making the best use of the available resources. In other clusters people were more likely to live within the boundaries of their own plot; spaces outside were very rarely used, aside from open spaces for playing and sitting. Not knowing one's neighbours within the cluster and, in most cases, not having a neighbour living next door led to a lack of community cohesion.

Income and occupation

Most people living in the township are regularly employed in some factory, shop or mill. Of those who are employed, income varies from under Rs 600 per month to over Rs 2,000 per month. In most cases wives do not work, or are involved in some cottage industry like making incense sticks or stitching clothes. But because the township is away from the city centre and there is as yet no market for these goods in the community, most women are idle. In two of the houses surveyed, shops selling groceries and other small items had been opened on the front veranda. One is run by a 12-year-old boy and another by an elderly couple. The couple only earn about 100–150 rupees a month; the boy earns between Rs 5–10 a day. A shop selling building material has opened in slice 2.

The shops built as part of the design at cluster corners for small household goods have not yet been sold. The IDA is still holding on to all commercial properties.

Social and community facilities

To date four kindergartens are operating from houses; all are privately run. They charge about Rs 25 per child. All four kindergartens are run by individuals who do not live in Aranya. One kindergarten in slice 2 is run by a lady teacher who lives outside the township and bought the house from the preacher who lived in it first.

There are at present three schools in Aranya: a secondary school, a middle school and a private school in slice 5. However, most children in Aranya go to school outside the township, because the schools do not give preference to children living in Aranya and admission is based on merit. If a child fails, then he or she must continue with the same school and cannot transfer to a school in Aranya.

Often this means a long commute. But principals of the Aranya schools are keen to maintain standards in their schools and do not want children who have failed. There is a shortage of schools in this area, which guarantees enough children from the surrounding community. No children from Aranya attend the private school; the fees are far too expensive.

No other services are available: there are no doctors yet, and the health clinic has been built, but not opened, because of a shortage of government nurses. No postal service has come to Aranya, so people receive no mail.

Construction quality and financing

In the houses that have been finished, most of the work is quite well done. Floors are made either of terrazzo tiles or of cement. The walls are brick, and the roof is flat and made of stone tiles. Houses have doors and glazed windows. Most houses are also whitewashed inside, and some are painted outside.

Permanent construction in Aranya is done mainly by masons. However, in most houses the family does provide some labour. The survey showed that in 90 per cent of the houses, the occupants had played some role in the construction of the house, ranging from unskilled labour to doing part of the work on their own, such as finishes and flooring. In most cases the owner also acts as the contractor and supervises the masons and the work done.

From the houses surveyed one can make the following generalizations: a completed house costs Rs 40,000, and includes a front room, covered veranda, a kitchen, toilet and bath, and a courtyard. The cost of constructing a staircase is additional. In two of the houses, the staircase and the house were built for under Rs 40–45,000. However, neither house has any interior or exterior wall finishes, or any tiles in the kitchen. In both cases part of the work on the house was done by the owners.

A partial house costs on average Rs 18,000; the house has only one room, kitchen, and toilet and bath. The house has minimal external and internal finishes and it did not have a staircase or courtyard walls. Some storage space was built in.

A minimal house costs about Rs 3,000. It has mud-brick walls and a semi-permanent roof. The interior of one of the houses was neatly finished, using mud as a finishing material.

The most expensive was a one-storey house costing Rs 85,000 on a type E3 plot. It has a covered veranda, a front room, a kitchen area, a bath and toilet, an enclosed courtyard, a staircase and a finished terrace upstairs. A similar two-storey house would cost at least Rs 30,000 more. At the low end, houses made out of temporary materials cost about Rs 2,000.

Houses are constructed by borrowing money from outside sources: place of employment, relatives and money-lenders. Some families also sold their jewellery to raise some of the funds. In two cases the family received gifts either from relatives or from elsewhere. One was a gift from the occupant's father upon his marriage. The other was built by the church for its occupants, who are Catholics. About eight such houses were built by the church at a cost about Rs 40,000 each.

A small number of people actually took out IDA loans, but only received Rs 3,000. People are more comfortable taking loans from their employers or through their pension funds. Only those with no other resources have taken out IDA loans. Loans are also available from the National Housing Bank (NHB), but no occupant had one.

Another form of assistance or loan for constructing the house is through material on loan either from relatives who may be in the construction industry or from building material shops. In Aranya there is only one building materials shop, however, and most people do not use it, in contrast to the Orangi Pilot Project. In Aranya there is no consolidated building industry in the township, and the IDA has not encouraged local building material suppliers to set up their outlets there.[22]

The houses discussed above were entirely built by masons and the owners moved in after the house was completely finished. Of the other 40 houses that are under construction, most are being built by masons and supervised by contractors. In these cases the occupants will move in only after the house is complete.

Water and electricity connections

Of the houses surveyed, the majority did not have legal electricity connections. Wires were run from street light posts or through junction boxes. The families have resorted to these illegal methods because the electricity board has not given them a legal connection. Electricity and a meter do cost money, however, so it may be that the people are unwilling to pay the fee if they can get it free.

Most people do have water connections, but almost everyone complained of low water pressure. A few had no water at all, even though they had been living there for six months. Most people have to go to the main overhead water tank located in each slice to supplement their water supply.

Water is supplied during certain times of day. The water comes through a looped system and, because the number of people living in the township is so small, to preserve water pressure certain areas are not given water at all. The IDA claims that if it releases water in pipes where there are few houses the pipes may spring leaks. But the water supply is also not adequate in the township. When the main Narmada River canal is completed, the water supply should improve. For now water is being drawn through tube wells and then pumped into overhead storage tanks.[23]

Transformations

Observation of the people living in Aranya can provide clues to the quality of the environment. The design and implementation supplied amenities such as the underground sewerage system, water connections and underground electricity to each and every house. The service-lot concept has led to a reduction in the cost of the services and also provided breathing spaces within the cluster. The location and provision of various commercial activities and large and generous open spaces distributed evenly over the site are things one rarely sees in low-cost housing and site-and-services schemes. The linear cluster is a design decision that will ensure a good environment.

Given all the important features developed in this project, the important question then is, how do people respond to this environment and how do they use the spaces? Shanker Rao, a resident of slice 1, summarizes the occupants' evaluation of the project best.

> In this project all facilities have been planned for. There are schools, electricity, water, underground sewerage, community hall, parks, nursery. However we are seeing that those that are responsible for its maintenance are not involved in its maintenance and upkeep. We feel that IDA is not paying any attention to this project. Holes that are dug in the roads for any purpose are never filled up, even if a person or child might fall into it at night. Even if there is an accident or there is a complaint, there is no one to complain to. The street lights do not work, water is not enough. Like this are many other problems and inconveniences here. When all of these problems are addressed and solved, then I think that this will be a good colony for low income people to live in.

Shanker Rao's complaints are frequently heard in the township. There is a tremendous gap between what was proposed and what has been built. By no stretch of imagination is this environment worse than a slum or squatter settlement, but the full potential that the design had to offer has not been realized. The chasm between project implementation and project occupancy management is very wide.

Linear clusters and open spaces

The linear clusters were designed to have attractive spaces, but even Doshi admits that he does not expect the clusters, once occupied, to look as he envisioned. The open spaces designed for common use, particularly the service lots, are not regarded by residents as common spaces to be used by all cluster residents. The 15 families who moved from one settlement and located in slice 4 do not understand the idea of common space. They believe that it should be used by the residents of those houses that are adjacent to it, that living adjacent to the open spaces gives them user rights. Residents have in fact already started to appropriate these spaces for their own use. In slice 2, one of the residents has erected a small wire fence around part of the open space directly adjacent to her rear courtyard, which she uses as a kitchen garden.

The designers expected that groups, once they formed a sense of community, would control their open spaces. However, this same group is unclear about the use of common areas and, even though the people came from slums where it is generally thought sharing of spaces is common, this is simply not the case; in slums there is actually a much higher notion of territoriality and this emphasis on individual spaces is reflected in Aranya.[24]

The space provided is certainly useful; all communities need 'breathing space'. However, the issue here is whether the space will be used by the community or misused by a few. To stop the misuse or ensure communal use, an organization that sets forth the uses of these spaces and enforces those rules has to be formed.

Among the EWS there are great disparities of income as more prosperous families move in. Without control, these newcomers will be even more likely to appropriate open spaces whose use is not entirely clear. The concrete platforms in the clusters were designed by the consultants to be used as work platforms and as places where small shops or hawkers could set up their stalls for selling goods, but it is unlikely that they will ever be used for this purpose. There is no shade over them for people to sit under, and most residents in a cluster who want to sell anything will either do it from their house or go to the commercial centre where the most customers are. These platforms might be used by hawkers for selling fruits and vegetables. However, they too could just as easily wait in front of a house to attract the same group of people. Most likely they will be used by children to play on.

The point here is that such spaces might be both attractive and useful, but unless some collective understanding of their use is established, the residents cannot reach that conclusion on their own. Models that are successful because of an already established social order will not be successful without that order, and order does not miraculously appear; the link between social issues and those of design is not always apparent. Manuel Castells said it best: 'although spatial forms may accentuate or deflect certain systems of behavior, through the interaction of the social elements that constitute them, they have no independent effect, and consequently, there is no systematic link between different urban contexts and ways of life. Whenever a link of this order is observed, it is the starting point for research rather than explanatory argument.'[25] Under the present conditions, it is difficult for any individual living in Aranya to figure out for themselves what the overall structure and use of open spaces were meant to be. At present they are not maintained and are fenced off. Snakes and scorpions breed in the vast open fields.

Commercial spaces

No commercial spaces have yet been allocated. The design envisaged a central commercial area as the spine to the city, but it ignores a major site condition, namely, that the site is adjacent to a national highway which is a prime location for commercial and other development. In the new master plan, a new ring road will be built, and the national highway will move further out, but will still remain a main spine. Because Doshi and the VSF wanted a commercial centre in the township, they deprived the township of a commercial location adjacent to the highway that would have served the community much better.

Office buildings, large shopping areas and small-scale industries could have been located on the highway without compromising the integrity of the scheme. Small and medium-size commercial facilities could still have been located inside the scheme, along with institutional buildings such as schools, health centres, a library, a police station and a post office. The town centre could have been split into two areas, one connected to the city and the other serving the immediate population. It was not necessary to locate all of these facilities in the town centre.

The house

The EWS house plan allows very few ways to build. Basically it is a series of rooms, one behind the other, with an inside or outside staircase. Most houses have been constructed in this way. Variety is achieved through the incremental nature of the building and the stages each house has reached: whether it has an upper storey or not, how the façade and parapet has been treated and where the staircase has been located. The staircase is either open-to-sky or covered, either in the front of the house or in the rear courtyard. If it is in the front it is either outside the front room where a veranda would be or inside the house as part of a covered veranda.

Most residents are not aware of the importance of locating elements of a house. Building a staircase in the rear courtyard makes it difficult for the owner to rent the upstairs space, unless the house has access to the service court and a separate rear entry. A staircase located in the front and outside the veranda allows use without entry into the lower floor. If the staircase is in the front but within the covered veranda space it can also be used separately without entering the main living space, but it shares the veranda with those living upstairs. This arrangement may be attractive when the house grows to accommodate a family.

Inside the house, the courtyard offers some possibilities for variation. In one of the houses surveyed, the courtyard had been covered and converted into a kitchen and the kitchen partition wall had been moved to form two equal rooms. The drawback was that covering the back courtyard blocked ventilation into the back rooms. Since the house adjoins the service plot, it had been possible to make a window in the side wall to bring light into the small connecting space.

People should be advised to leave the courtyard open. They may not understand the advantages of the courtyard and, for short-term gain, may lose out on future expansion possibilities or create an internal environment that lacks both light and ventilation.

Potential for transfer and adaptation

Planners and designers all over the world are re-evaluating the role of site-and-services projects and developing new models for giving these settlements a better environment and quality of life. The design of the Aranya project provides an innovative approach to site-and-services projects and how one can achieve social, physical and aesthetic goals within the severe financial constraints of low-cost housing. The Aranya project has developed new norms and methods for settlement planning and design relevant to and in tune with the needs of the urban poor. Cultural, social and economic needs were taken into account in the design process to realize these objectives.

This project makes it clear that, in a site-and-services project, land and infrastructure become the critical cost components, making efficient site planning essential. A fresh approach to infrastructure design was evolved to enhance the economic viability and performance by using new materials, design methods and computer-aided models. This, and the concept of the linear cluster, are elements that can be transferred and adapted in other site-and-services projects all over the world.

This scheme has both a fully designed dwelling component and also one that can grow incrementally over time, and the settlement design attempts to bring together a community. As the settlement grows incrementally, new networks are bound to develop, which will help build the settlement. As of now, the one demonstration cluster of housing has been built to give an idea of what the urban fabric will look like. The stress that has been laid on flexibility and elasticity at all levels of planning should ensure that it can respond dynamically to any feedback received during construction and even after occupation. The settlement design methods that have been developed here can be used and improved upon to help resolve the problems of housing the poor.

Lessons learned

Aranya, in both its success and its failure, presents lessons fundamental to the development of any low-cost housing scheme, whether or not one chooses to use the models or housing-delivery systems.

First, it has shown that to create a quality environment the role of the designer is fundamental, as is a comprehensive site plan that learns from existing housing and understands the modern urban township. The development of a mixed-use pattern, the careful planning of open spaces, the linear cluster and finally the provision of urban services are all important developments that will be used as models for future housing developments.

Second, a careful design should be complemented by a careful technical and financial analysis. Both large- and small-scale projects operate under tight fiscal control, but even in low-cost housing, through judicious design and fiscal control, a quality environment can be made to serve the low-income population.

Third, and tied to the first two, Aranya has shown that through both judicious design and fiscal control, improved standards can be provided, and that standards, though dependent on the design and finance, need not be sacrificed to them.

Fourth, the evaluation of product, process and values in Aranya township has thrown light on the various intricate connections that exist between the financing, implementing and designing agency. A clear and positive manipulation of these linkages goes a long way toward guaranteeing an effective project.

Aranya has also provided us with important lessons in its shortcomings. First, the city centre and commercial design of the project were seen to be equally important by the designers; however, the idea of creating a township centre and hoping to bring the city to it was flawed at best. This does not mean that large townships need not have their own commercial and institutional centres. It means that one should consider how the township centre will meet the city and explore all possible linkages.

Second, the commercial potential of the township was not explored to the maximum. The Indore Development Authority held on to the commercial properties in the hope that selling them after the site developed would bring top prices. It is only now beginning to dispose of the commercial properties and the price of the land has in fact gone up some two to two and a half times. However, it has been at the expense of township development. In retrospect, having identified the commercial areas, it may have been much more opportune to sell them quickly. It would have accelerated the settlement development and lessened the demand for resources. A large loan from HUDCO, of which land acquisition is only a tiny proportion, would not have been necessary. If the IDA had sold the commercial land in 1982, the project would have cost half as much. It would have carried a smaller loan and saved on interest.

However, the reasons for selling the commercial land are not just financial. By selling it off earlier the IDA would have gained a five-year head start on the entire development process. A trade-off between prices and starting activities would have been to sell at least half of it earlier.

The IDA's holding on to the commercial property waiting for the prices to rise also defeated the VSF's plan to provide spaces of various kinds that would be affordable by various groups. The commercial spaces to support small traders or hawkers are today too expensive. People are instead opening shops and other services in their own houses.

Third, the effectiveness of the demonstration project was diluted by not providing an adequate system for showing it to the people. It was a source of satisfaction only for the designers, the implementing agency and the politicians. The lessons that ought to have been learned were completely lost on the occupants. The project shows that even in an obviously well-thought-out project, people can be least important.

Fourth, the people were left out of the system. From the allocation process to actual occupancy of the project, both the designers and the implementing agency were out of touch with the occupants. The designers were as keen as the IDA to hand over the project. They are now doing a post-occupancy evaluation with a grant from HUDCO, but evaluating occupancy has not occurred to anyone.

The IDA claims to have started community development with its new slum upgrading project, but it has not yet developed a comprehensive occupancy plan for the township and is not even sure how to go about doing it.

The allocation process must be changed to a system designed to allow beneficiaries a choice of location so that groups can move into projects together and be located in one cluster. Slum dwellers being relocated for various development and upgrading projects should be relocated in the same way to provide some level of cohesion.[26]

The advantages of phasing the project and developing one sector at a time should be looked into for future projects. In Aranya people are living scattered all over the site, away from anybody else. Each slice or each area should be planned so that it can be filled as soon as possible.

People are not moving into the project for an array of reasons, but mainly because of a lack of confidence in the new environment. Whatever the demand, unless people have no other alternative, they will hesitate to move. Therefore trade-offs have to be effectively worked out. The role of the community and community-based organization is critical in such schemes in assessing community strengths and weakness and providing the underlying confidence that is needed.

CHAPTER 7

A New Agenda for Urban Equity and Sustainability

The problems generated by poverty, including declining health and disintegrating social and environmental conditions, are leading to increased political unrest in countries both rich and poor. Riots in Los Angeles, looting in Rio de Janeiro, racial and religious tensions in Bombay and Karachi are all symptoms of a deep and growing resentment among the poor. The notion that the poor will be able to pull themselves out of their misery without any external assistance has simply to be abandoned. They are caught in an unfortunate vicious circle of enduring poverty, and government programmes aimed at alleviating their misery by providing shelter and urban services have so far had minimal impact.

Clearly, the difficulties that are already apparent will worsen as time goes on as a result of the pace of urbanization and the absolute number of new urban dwellers. By 2020, a staggering 52 cities around the world will have populations of more than 4 million.[1] While cities have a positive role to play in any national economy as generators of wealth, centres of employment and agents of social change, few governments have in place the policies and programmes needed to cope with current rates of urbanization, let alone those of the future. Any government initiative will have to deal with a range of problems facing cities, from environmental pollution to land-use allocation.

Rapid urbanization cannot be written off as an unavoidable crisis or tragedy. Since there is no way to halt it, therefore, it must be tackled as a challenge. Managing and directing rapid urbanization and reaping its benefits are not easy and will require fundamental changes in approach by those involved in urban development. National governments will have to become more proactive in developing policies that promote the required changes and in supporting local initiatives.

The preparatory committee of the United Nations Conference on Environment and Development (UNCED) described its human settlement objective in Chapter 7 of its Agenda 21, entitled 'Promoting Sustainable Human Settlement Development', as improving the social, economic and environmental quality of human settlements, and the living and working environments of all people, in particular the urban and rural poor. For this purpose, it goes on, countries will need to set priorities according to their national plans and objectives, taking into account their social and cultural capabilities. If the objective of development is to broaden people's choices, it must do so not only for the current generation but also for future generations. In other words development must be sustainable. This implies a new concept of economic growth – one that provides fairness and opportunity for all of the world's people, not just the privileged few, without further destroying the world's finite natural resources. Any new model for sustainable development must be based on the five guiding principles identified by Pronk and Haq.[2]

They are, first, to protect human life and human options – the most endangered species in many places are the people; second, to use environmentally sound technologies; third, to place a real value on natural resources in all decision-making (the only effective way to emphasize that environment is not a free resource is to put a price on it); fourth, to make all development participatory and community-based; and finally to ensure that development is fair to all people and the use of resources is balanced.

Reducing inequity

Approaches promoted by UNCED and other organizations stress sustainability and equity in contrast to many other development strategies which remain as pilot projects and are unreplicable. It is a truism that greater equity in the distribution of income and wealth requires wider participation of the people in the economic, social and political processes through which wealth is generated and distributed.[3] If developing sustainable and equitable urban environments is the goal, then national planning has to change and an administrative structure devised that will permit managed decentralization and local autonomy in planning, designing and implementing development programmes. Such a change requires, in particular, a shift in power from groups who dominate the centre to those who have local control. Local empowerment is not a solution in itself but it is critical for achieving economically sustainable and equitable development.

Reducing inequities between people and increasing their ability to participate and make decisions for themselves are the new challenges. As I discussed in Chapter 2, inequities exist at two levels – interpersonal and interregional. Reducing inequity, however, is often thought to be in conflict with economic growth and development; for example, urban planning policies often operate at cross-purposes with markets and with the government's own market-oriented economic development strategies. Urban planners have often sought to steer growth in remote regions in the name of equity or sought to create a new layer of secondary cities in the name of planning principles.[4]

The goal of this book is to develop new paradigms for equity and sustainability. I have argued that inequity needs to be reduced in the manner in which these programmes are planned and developed. An approach to inequity reduction that has been proposed in this study is to increase the choices that the community is given, and to create conditions that promote community decision-making. A second is to optimize the role played by government agencies, private sector organizations, community groups and NGOs, and to assist other subgroups that may have a potential role to play.

Principles for equitable and sustainable developments

Inequity can be reduced in a number of ways, however; if programme sustainability is to be achieved, then planners and policy-makers must understand what makes housing and urban-service programmes equitable. In this chapter, I argue that housing and urban-service programmes have a better chance of becoming equitable and sustainable if they are developed through consensus rather than confrontation; if the role of NGOs and intermediaries, as facilitators, enablers and managers, is acknowledged; and if they encourage and promote private sector involvement under conditions that are clearly understood and instituted. Community accountability and decision-making must also be increased, local management promoted and programme components in which the community has a larger implementing role introduced. The role of local entrepreneurs and developers must be enhanced; and the needs of the broadened client groups understood and reflected in planning and design. Finally, site designs for urban developments have to be integrated to reflect the needs of the immediate and surrounding community. Evidence from the five case-studies – the Orangi Pilot Project in Karachi, the Zabbaleen Environmental and Development Project in Cairo, the Citra Niaga Project in Samarinda, Indonesia, the Khuda-ki-basti Incremental Development Scheme in Hyderabad, Pakistan, and Aranya township, Indore, India – demonstrate that undertaking urban development, housing and shelter programmes is a complex process and that no one approach can be used in all cases and be expected to work.

Urban development through consensus

In the 1960s and 1970s, in most developing countries, the urban poor, both old residents and recent migrants, who were unable to find shelter resorted to illegal means to obtain it, mainly by land-grabbing and squatting. Over the years, squatting became institutionalized, as developers began to use squatters to grab land they could not otherwise obtain. Government-built housing was another avenue for some of the poor to gain access to shelter. The result was that two mutually exclusive systems of housing and urban services for the poor were operating – one dominated by the government and the other dominated by illegal land-developers. Neither of these systems were able to provide safe and clean housing. The living conditions in both squatter settlements and formal housing were very poor. Indeed the poor who moved to squatter settlements in search of cheap shelter moved from one set of economic pressures to another, pressures that were generated by land-developers and slum landlords.

Over the last decade low-income developments have been built mainly with support from government agencies, private developers, community groups and NGOs. In the most successful of them the distinction between government-dictated and community-initiated projects became increasingly blurred. Orangi, Zabbaleen, Khuda-ki-basti and Citra Niaga all show that cooperation between the government, private investment, community groups and their representatives are proving to be an effective approach in procuring land for the poor, having housing built, securing urban services and creating economic opportunities.

Building trust

Cooperation between government agencies, community groups and their support organizations differs from project to project. Partnerships between these groups can be formally instituted or informally achieved, or both. The case-studies show that a new intermediate system, whereby both the government approach and the self-help approach can function, seems to be forming. It is successful when all the parties involved trust the others that they will be able to deliver what they promised, based on their record and the commitment shown.

In Orangi, for example, the Orangi Pilot Project (OPP) did not enter into partnership with the Karachi Development Authority (KDA); in fact, the project was undertaken because the KDA was not providing the services the community needed. The KDA did not try to stop or restrict the project, a lack of interference that was surprising, since in the past government agencies have discouraged such large-scale community-based endeavours, because they were afraid that it would lead to other demands.[5] In this case the government did not interfere because the OPP took great care not to politicize the effort and kept communications with the government open through intermediaries at the local councillor level. One other factor is also important: two of its chief supporters were well-connected and powerful people. Akhter Hammed Khan, the director of the OPP, is a respected social worker and scholar with long-standing links with the government, and Aga Hasan Abidi, the founder of BCCI, which provided the grants from the BCCI Foundation for the project, was even more connected to the government at all levels.

The OPP cultivated community leaders by showing them the proposed infrastructure system first and convincing them of its viability. They then persuaded the rest of the community to participate – in this the women were particularly active because they clearly saw the benefits of the system. Women became very active in local groups; many were elected group leaders and it was often women who found the funds to pay for the sewers out of household budgets. Great care was taken to keep the politicians out of the picture until they could play a useful role, which was to maintain contact with the development agency.

In the Zabbaleen project, the community itself was more central to creating the partnership than were the city agencies. The project got powerful support from international donor agencies and their support for the community organization prompted a metropolitan response.

The Zabbaleen project placed the community at the centre of a variety of programmes that were funded and developed by international donor agencies and administered by local NGOs and community representatives. The important turning-point was the agreement reached with the Cairo Municipality, which agreed to provide services to the community in return for the Zabbaleen extending its garbage collection services to the poorer communities. The Zabbaleen partnership resulted in more dramatic re-structuring of political and economic structures than in the OPP, Citra Niaga and Khuda-ki-basti projects, because it overcame the exploited position occupied by the community in relation to the metropolitan environment.

Citra Niaga used an approach that was the reverse of the Orangi Pilot Project. Here, the Samarinda Development Authority was a partner in a project developed by a private developer, the son of an ex-governor, who had first introduced the idea of redeveloping that particular part of the city. The project got off the ground only after the developer was able to put together a team that included an architect and an NGO. They were then able to convince the development authority that the project was both feasible and important. In this case, too, trust and confidence were established at two levels – with the development authority and with the community. The NGO had already built successful community develop-ment projects in Indonesia and had an established reputation; the community therefore trusted them. The development authority also had a good reputation.

Khuda-ki-basti presents yet another situation. In this case, the Hyder-abad Development Authority sought help from land-dealers in settling and screening the beneficiaries, but the strategy failed because the role of the developers had not been specified. The development authority regarded the *dalals* as representing the agency, whereas the *dalals* saw an opportunity to turn a profit. This led to conflict and mistrust. The HDA did not establish its own connection with the community; the developers did. As a result, those aspects of the project that involved partnership were a failure.

All four cases show that trust and confidence in the organization undertaking the project is necessary for a successful partnership. They also show that a government agency need not be actively involved as long as mutual trust and confidence are established. In all four cases the private developer, the NGO and the city agency had separate agendas, but in three of the cases they were able to work together because they established clear rules of partnership. Each party was willing to let the other achieve its own ends; it was only a matter of working out boundaries and responsibilities and sticking to them. In Khuda-ki-basti no such rules were established. The development agency wanted to use the local developers, but not to allow them to share in some of the success; the local developers wanted to make money and were able to manipulate the situation to their benefit.

The Khuda-ki-basti experience shows that not all market-based and government agencies are able to participate successfully in urban projects. The level of partnership achieved will also depend on the kind of projects that are to be undertaken. Some roles may be mutually conflicting and preclude successful partnership.

What is important, though, is that a clear distinction between government-led and community-based approaches need not exist: there is an intermediary layer, where the top-down approach and self-help activities come together. Successful programmes have managed to find this intermediary level of connection. Those projects that make the connection between those in power and the community have the greatest probability of achieving equitable and economically sustainable development.

Finally, experience suggests that genuine partnerships include the principles of equity, transparency of operations and mutual benefit:

- Equity – partnerships are based on the principle of justice and fairness between sectors that are traditionally opposed. Partners must break down the perception of donor/receiver relationship and identity, and build on the mutual input and the particular strengths of each sector.
- Transparency of operations – the partners have declared their interests (financial and otherwise) and are truly committed to working openly.
- Mutual benefit – all partners gain something valuable and distinct from the relationship and are motivated by long-term rather than short-term goals.

Conditions for private sector involvement

Private investment in public projects is no longer considered by many politicians and development theorists as necessarily negative. Most projects use some private sector investment, and the case-studies here show that it can play a still larger role. With proper controls and mechanisms the private developer can successfully undertake public housing, urban services and mixed-use developments.

In Citra Niaga the project was developed based on an understanding of the requirements of the residents, of the development agency and of the developer. Very early on the Samarinda Development Authority established a clear set of controls and guidelines for the developer to follow. The controls set were reasonable, and in some cases favourable to the developer, encouraging him to participate. The goals set were limited; they did not try to achieve everything in one project. That the developer would need to profit was never questioned. The project was planned to allow it, but at the same time to achieve clear social and communal goals.

In addition, the project was to provide an urban space for city use in order to revitalize the urban core. To achieve this, the actual area to be developed, the kinds of commercial activity to be established, the open-to-built-space ratio, the total amount of profit and the proportion of public to private space were all decided after extensive discussions between the developer, the development agency and the community representatives.

This case shows that by setting clear and achievable goals and by undertaking responsible communication with all parties concerned, a well-programmed, carefully implemented and successfully managed project can be achieved.

Promoting local entrepreneurs and small-scale developers

In most urban development projects the concern for income generation and enterprise development is very limited unless the project is focused on income-generation activities. Also urban development projects rarely use small-scale contractors, because it is time-consuming and because it requires more coordination and more sustained management than using a single large firm.

The case-studies show, however, that the successful projects have managed to balance the concern for improvements in environmental and living conditions by an equivalent concern for income generation and enterprise development. The Zabbaleen project, Orangi and Citra Niaga all generated income for different segments of the community through different kinds of enterprise development activities.

In the Zabbaleen project, environmental improvement was achieved by reversing the move to a high-technology waste management system to improve the productivity and revenue-generating capacity of community residents. The evidence from Cairo shows that not only is the informal sector productive, but it can also be innovative and competitive in providing services at a much lower cost than the formal sector.

Depending on the kind of project, it may be possible to involve small-scale private developers and, when it is, there are certain advantages in doing so. In Orangi, the project was planned so that the community worked in small groups. The sewerage system was lane-based and the technology used was simple and did not require sophisticated equipment. This meant that it was possible for small-scale developers to assist in its implementation. Since the project was divided into small independent segments that were being implemented concurrently, several small contractors could work at the same time. This also meant that work between various contractors did not have to be coordinated, thereby limiting the time lost due to lack of coordination and poor management.

The advantages achieved in Orangi from this small-scale contractor participation has implications for settlement upgrading and new development programmes. One was that, though the major funding for research and technical assistance was provided by national and international donor agencies, the money for the actual construction was raised by the community; a part of it from local private contractors in the form of material loans to the community. Another is that the developers supported the project because they saw in it financial benefit for themselves, and their support helped get the project moving. Private small-scale developers usually live in the community where they operate. They are often respected community members and wield influence. In Orangi, over time, most of the community had received favours from the local contractors, in the form of either building materials or construction loans, so they were indebted to them. The OPP used them to help get the project off the ground. Small-scale contractors usually employ local people and thereby provide jobs for the community. In Orangi, there are approximately 250 of them and each employed about 3–4 local labourers.[6] Any disadvantage arising from increased management responsibilities or construction time was far outweighed in the long run by the advantages provided by their involvement.

Enhancing the role of small-scale building contractors

Low-cost building technology becomes most efficient when it is able to adapt to already existing technologies. If technology is improved on the site and small manufacturers are involved, improvement has an immediate impact. In Orangi, the improvement to local houses were made by improving the technology used by the local thallawalas. This approach was three-pronged: the OPP first refined the manufacturing technology in use by the contractors, for example, by increasing the strength of sun-dried bricks rather than replacing them with kiln-fired bricks; it then introduced a wider range of building components to enhance existing product lines, making the local thallas in the long run more competitive and providing a wider range of choices to the community. The OPP did not compete with thallas in marketing these new building materials; it only provided research and technical assistance to local contractors. Technology was improved not to achieve cost reduction in construction, but to improve the overall quality of the technology used in the community so that the overall quality of housing construction would go up. Even though the unit cost of the new materials was higher, in the long run savings will be achieved through infrequent repair costs and the strength and permanency of the new materials.

The use of the newly improved technologies was not limited to a few building contractors. The housing programme was seen as an opportunity to introduce improved technologies on a much wider scale. At first, however, a few test thallas were selected to work out the problems and other thallas were encouraged to try it. As the thallas became interested, other outside building suppliers also started introducing their version of the improved technology, thereby increasing the competition. The net result was that the community has more choice and a wider range of products to select from.

Improving local technologies is, however, only one part of the equation. To ensure that improved technologies will lead to improved construction, a training programme for masons was also developed. In addition, the OPP offered planning, design and construction management services to the community at no cost, so that quality control was maintained and confidence in the community developed. This strategy is the contribution that the OPP housing programme has made to future urban development programmes

Once the thallas were convinced about improving existing technologies, the OPP introduced new and refined products in the form of batten-and-tile roofing systems and prefabricated staircases. These new products were developed to be applied on a small scale by the local building contractors. The market for the new products was not guaranteed, but grants and loans were made available to purchase the equipment needed to produce the new components.

The OPP then set about forming a thalla cooperative so that the thallas could function more effectively in purchasing raw material and marketing their goods, but this failed. That failure turned out to be a blessing in disguise. Without the cooperative the thallawallas are left to function as individuals; they now have a choice of augmenting their products and technology from sources other than the OPP, and as a result competition has increased and new products are coming into the market more quickly. If the cooperative had been a success it would probably have taken more than the four years it has taken to introduce the technology on this scale. It is also possible that the cooperative might have been perceived as an extension of the OPP, or that those who did not join would feel left out and continue to market the old inferior products. Success would then not have been so dramatic.

All this shows that product improvement can be achieved by improving existing technologies and manufacturing standards. Older products need not be replaced by newer products. Construction standards will improve if manufacturing quality is controlled and maintained. New technologies can be introduced as a means of increasing product range. For example, some of the building contractors supplied roofing materials but did not manufacture it. The OPP developed simple prefabrication technology and gave assistance to building contractors to manufacture it. Retaining the individuality and competitiveness of building contractors is important in expanding the use of the new technologies and products. Grant recovery can be achieved if the technologies introduced prove successful and when building contractors begin to make enough money to pay back their loans.

Risks in lack of control and clear aims when involving private developers

The risk of involving private-sector organizations, whether large or small, is that their need to make money can conflict with the project's goals. Such a conflict was clear in the Khuda-ki-basti project, when *dalals* were used to solve problems of beneficiary identification. When the government could not convince any of the poor to move into the project, local private developers were asked to assist. Since neither their role nor their gains were settled in advance, the *dalals* felt that the development agency was indebted to them, and this gave them the opportunity to gain other favours from the government. They quickly developed a mechanism to profit from their involvement by manipulating the system, assisting some of their own people to get plots from the HDA and also getting them elected on to the community boards, thereby gaining control of the community organization. The HDA lost sight of the role they could best play, and instead involved them in roles that allowed them to gain control of the community and thereby the project.

New partnerships between the government, private investment and the community are being continually forged. If the role of each group is not clearly projected and worked out, the partnership will end up favouring one group over the other. Both the development agency and the private sector organization have to be explicit about what they want the partnership to achieve and then work out a mutually satisfactory agreement that is fair to all parties. Developers should not be viewed as social or charitable organizations; they work for profit, and therefore clear rules for partnership are necessary. The task of the development agencies is to establish these guidelines and controls, so that the private developers can provide the finance and management. Once these conditions are met, the community can be given the responsibility for managing and developing the project. If they are not met the partnership will remain on a tenuous footing, and eventually the project will fail.

Private sector involvement in any programme or project is like building a set of relationships and is a complex long-term operation that has to be actively sustained. For this relationship to be most productive there has to be trust between business and other sectors and include the principles of accountability, transparency and shared purpose:

- Accountability – here involvement is based on a sense of responsibility that is both financial and ethical.
- Transparency – where the business community has declared its financial interest and the community is in agreement with that interest.
- Shared purpose – where both the business and community gain something and the involvement is motivated by long-term rather than short-term gain.

The role of intermediaries

Society and social relationships have been transformed in the city to the extent that we need to be sceptical of an *a priori* assumption that, given the opportunity to do so, community organizations will spontaneously arise and undertake collective action to reverse the environmental deterioration common in most low-income neighbourhoods.[7] Translating the reality of urban life for the poor into active communities faces many obstacles. Local NGOs and other intermediaries – skilled and well-placed community leaders; government officers/agencies (from local or central government); professional consultants; bilateral aid agencies and international NGOs with experience and expertise in partnership-building; and specially formed cross-sector groups or associations – can help crystallize communal concerns and sharpen community awareness.

The role of the local NGO, however, is particularly important and the case-studies have shown that:

1. local NGOs have facilitated the successful implementation of community-based/partnership efforts;
2. they have developed an empowering strategy that has improved the communities' access to important environmental resources, particularly land, and infrastructure, services necessary for environmental management, and economic empowerment; and
3. they have managed and facilitated the implementation of a complex project over a long period of time.

In Orangi, the Orangi Pilot Project, the local NGO, has played and continues to play an instrumental role in developing a participatory development process, creating an empowering environment, forming partnerships with traditionally uncooperative groups and changing the patterns of thinking in the community. From day one, the OPP sought out a cross-section of the Orangi community and convinced them that they themselves were capable of improving their living conditions. Working with a range of people, including local leaders, respected service providers, local businessmen and the women, it developed a supportive network which allowed the community successfully to implement several interlinked programmes on a large scale.

In the Zabbaleen project, multiple organizations played the role of intermediary and became the catalyst for the project. There were three principal intermediaries. The Zabbaleen Gameya or Association of Garbage Collectors, serving as the primary liaison between the Zabbaleen and other interested constituencies, was instrumental in channelling the necessary human resources, and the organizational and financial support. Environmental Quality International (EQI) created the common vision among the Zabbaleen and identified the requirements and potential contributions of their services. The Association for the Protection of the Environment (APE) managed and operated the compost plant with the aim of increasing profits while at the same time improving the surrounding environment, and established the Primary Health Care Programme and the Health Immunization Programme.

In Citra Niaga, the Institute for Development Studies (IDS), a local NGO that was already working in Samarinda, was instrumental in working with the community to identify their needs, explaining to them the proposed project and showing them how they would improve their economic conditions at a cost no greater than what they had been paying to the local slum landlords. The IDS was also instrumental in conducting a community survey to select the families that would be included in the scheme and helped them to form a community cooperative so that they would be able to access loans from banks to build their houses.

In Khuda-ki-basti and Aranya there was no intermediary organization to represent the local communities' interests and assist them in the formation of partnerships with the other sectors. In both programmes, therefore, community organization and formation of community-based programmes were unsuccessful. In Khuda-ki-basti, without any intermediary to protect their interests and help the community mobilize itself, the people were at the mercy of the *dalals* and their proxies in any communal decision that had to be taken for the introduction of infrastructure and other services.

In Aranya there was a similar experience. In the cluster where one particular community that had lived together in a slum was relocated, they were unable to undertake some of the basic community functions. They did not have the capacity to form themselves into an organization that would be responsible for the implementation and maintenance of the cluster spaces as had been intended by the designers and the Indore Development Authority. After two years of project implementation the Indore Development Authority finally opened a community division. But such a move does not help. What is required is a neutral intermediary that can inspire the community interest and work with the other sectors.

Product champion

In all of the case-studies evaluated, the product champion has played an important role in the project's inception and implementation. This individual or groups provoke, stimulate and create the possibility of the programme unfolding over a period of time and bringing together the various sectors. In almost all of the cases the personal integrity, credibility and capacity of this person/s was key to the successful inception and implementation of the programme.

In Orangi, it was Dr Akhter Hameed Khan who had the vision and belief that the community is capable of providing its own services. He made it possible to bring the local community leaders and residents together to solve the problem of sanitation and introduced other programmes in Orangi. His personal links continued to bring other parties into collaboration, including the national government in recent years.

In Zabbaleen, the late Bishop Samuel, who established the Gameya, Dr Mounir Neamatalla of EQI and Dr Leila Kamel of the APE have played the instrumental roles in the inception and development of the project, and organized the Zabbaleen Community into a community. The late Bishop Samuel started an association that represented the interests of the Zabbaleen. Dr Neamatalla, who understood the importance of the work that this marginalized community was providing to the city of Cairo, developed a comprehensive technical assistance programme. In contrast, Dr Kamel developed a comprehensive programme aimed at educating and providing skills to the children so that they can augment the family income.

In Citra Niaga, Didik, the ex-Governor's son, and Antonio Ismael, the architect, were convinced that they could develop a truly Asian shopping centre that would also provide the pavement traders with an opportunity to sell their goods.

In Khuda-ki-basti, Tasneem Siddiqui, the then head of the Hyderabad Development Authority, pioneered the concept of incremental development and was the prime mover behind the project. He spent every night at the project to stop illegal encroachment and made sure that the families that had been given a plot were actually staying there. Unfortunately, once he was transferred the project lost its champion and other members of the HDA were not as committed to the success of the project as he had been.

In Aranya, B. V. Doshi had the vision to develop the linear cluster concept and worked hard to convince the World Bank that this approach was cost effective under the parameters set down by the Bank.

For successful implementation of programmes there has to be an effective intermediary and catalyst. For an intermediary to play an effective role, there are certain qualities and qualifications that need to be fulfilled. These include:

- Transparency of interests (including financial).
- Perceived neutrality.
- Trusted and valued relationship or the clear potential for creating one.
- Appropriate technical knowledge and skills for the specific situation.
- Understanding of the socio-economic and political context.
- Political acceptability to all partners.
- Management capacity (working to a time-scale and managing expectations of all parties).
- Commitment to the development and maintenance of non-dependent relationships between the intermediary and all partners.

Increasing community accountability and decision-making responsibilities

In most urban development projects no group is accountable to the community. Under the present system, when projects are financed by either local or international financing agencies, the development agency is held accountable for the cost of the project. The planners and designers are accountable to the development agency and the development agency is accountable to the politicians. Evidence from the case-studies shows that, when accountability to the community by those involved in the design and development process is increased, the chances of the development being able to meet the needs of the community and becoming economically sustainable in the long run improves dramatically. In Orangi and Citra Niaga, those involved in both the design and development work were made accountable to the community and their representatives. In Khuda-ki-basti, the planners intended to promote community involvement, but that aspect of the project was undermined by the developers, who seized control of the development process. By increasing accountability, a series of checks and balances are established and community involvement in various aspects of the project increases. When accountability is increased, the community can make decisions involving programme planning, project design and the implementation and development agency officials and project planners can become aware of community needs.

Developing accountability in programme planning

When the community is made accountable and is given a fair opportunity to debate decisions, then even those decisions that may otherwise seem unpopular or impossible to achieve can be made.

In Citra Niaga, the community group was given the opportunity to discuss the proposed development and it made the decision to support only the commercial aspects of the project. Given the choice, the community found it most important to have a place where they could sell their goods and earn their livelihood. The NGO group working with the community was also able to convince them that if a small shop or kiosk was first secured from the developers and if they were organized, they would then stand a good chance of obtaining loans for housing as well.

In Orangi, the OPP was able to assist in developing the urban services only because the community was involved in decisions and knew the people in charge to be responsible. The system of lane managers allowed the community to undertake responsibility for management and construction. The OPP was responsible only for providing technical assistance.

Opportunities for increasing community decision-making have to be carefully orchestrated, as it can easily get out of hand. In Khuda-ki-basti, for example, the Hyderabad Development Authority tried to get the community to form block organizations that would be responsible for deciding the kind and level of services, where they would be developed and by whom. However, this did not work because the responsibility that was supposed to have been vested in the community was usurped by the local developers, who managed to gain control of the community groups by getting themselves or their representatives elected to the block committee. This usurping of power by the local developers split the community. Eventually they were unable to decide on what was important and how to obtain it. The community fought over who would be responsible for services. Even bringing in an NGO to act as a mediator did not work because the community looked upon the NGO as an extension of the HDA. The lack of clear responsibility and infighting among community members have slowed the pace of work considerably.

Increasing community accountability in design decisions

Cluster planning is the system most frequently used for housing projects, because it is thought to permit a greater number of dwellings on a site, to allow for natural drainage systems, provide access to sunlight and give community space which is better distributed.[8] Over the last decade a number of projects have been planned in this mode, including Aranya.

One of the problems this system overlooks, however, is that it is overly dependent on physical order. Clustering, or any other formal model, is developed for one set of circumstances and no longer works when the social and cultural conditions that first led to its development change. There is a danger in assuming that recreating a pattern of residential living used in the past, as clustering is, will lead to a better environment.

In Aranya, the architects developed cluster plans based on a traditional layout that include a series of open-to-sky spaces going from the semi-private to public, with the aim of providing the community an opportunity to use these spaces in a variety of ways. The cluster spaces in both these projects were well thought out in terms of scale, ambience and use of materials, but most were never used by the community in the ways envisaged by the designers. Most of the open spaces have been privatized, for example, and only nominal spaces for access and egress have been maintained.

Aranya does not yet have a large enough residential core to allow a comprehensive evaluation of the use of its cluster spaces. Of the people who are living there already, however, most do not appear to know what the designer's intentions for the use of open spaces were. Those who move into the cluster first set the norms for communal space use for those who follow. Without adequate information on their intended use people make up their own. The bolder of them have put barbed wire around the cluster spaces adjacent to their houses and have planted flowers and vegetables in them.

To avoid such problems, it is necessary to increase the community's involvement in deciding what kind of open-to-sky spaces are designed, what they will be used for and how they will be used. In Aranya, the community is not involved in any design decisions, and therefore it has no opportunity to voice its opinion or hold any group accountable for what is being planned and designed. The process of getting the community involved in decision-making may lie in increasing its opportunities to choose and by promoting community management.

Promoting community management

Community management in low-cost housing has several advantages: it improves maintenance and controls cost and, less obviously, it helps create conditions for equitable developments by providing a social structure for new communities, especially where the opportunity for developing social networks and structures would otherwise be time-consuming and limited.

In projects where self-management was undertaken – Orangi and Citra Niaga – reduction in the cost of construction was achieved by eliminating expensive contractors. It was also found that the community had more control over what was being built and that they assumed greater responsibility for the project after it was completed. In each of these projects the open spaces were looked after and maintained. The organization that was formed to manage the development of the project was eventually turned into a management group that oversaw the maintenance and repair of the development and undertook to collect and settle disputes that arose. When local management is installed the environment is well maintained, public spaces last much longer with less wear and tear, and private encroachment on communal spaces is limited, because the community has direct control over the spaces it uses and does not have to depend on a public agency to maintain them. Even carefully designed and planned housing environments will not be sustained unless the occupants can establish control over them so that open spaces can be maintained and used.

Jamel Akbar has shown, in his study of traditionally built environments in North Africa and the Middle East, the importance of the interrelationship between ownership, control and use.[9] He identifies five basic forms of property ownership – unified, dispersed, permissive, possessive and trusteeship – and argues that in each of the five, changes in relationship between the owner, controller and user affect the maintenance and use of the property. From Akbar's study we can postulate that space which is owned, used and managed by the same individual will be the best maintained, and that those areas in which the owners differ from users, and both differ from the managers, will be least well maintained and used. Cluster communal spaces fall into the last category. They are owned by the development authority, used by a few people, and managed or maintained by the municipal corporation. Unless these relationships are changed, these spaces will be misused and neglected, as the case-studies show.

Introducing external and internal components to urban development programmes

In most urban development projects the government is responsible for providing the major trunk services. These include major roads, the trunk infrastructure systems and electricity. In contrast, in low-income projects the development agency is responsible for these. In site-and-services schemes, where all services are provided, it has been found that dividing urban development programmes into external and internal components increases community control over those parts of the development process that affect their day-to-day life most. It also increases the choices that the community has in terms of what is developed and by whom, promotes self-management, reduces development costs and gives small-scale contractors the opportunity to participate.

Dividing low-income development projects into external and internal components means that the government is responsible for site preparation, major roadworks, the main commercial sector, trunk infrastructure systems and electricity. All of this work is supervised by the development agency and undertaken by large contractors. The internal component includes lane and cluster sewerage lines, paving of internal roads, local wiring and building the service core. All of these are managed by the community and built by local contractors. This approach has the advantage of providing employment for a number of small contractors, keeping the jobs in the community and raising incomes. Orangi and Khuda-ki-basti have used this approach. Their experience highlights both its viability and the problems encountered.

In Orangi, the external component was left for the development authority to provide. The internal component was a progressive infrastructure system that worked without a trunk system. Because flexibility of choice can be achieved when the internal component is controlled by the community, in Orangi, each lane was able to choose whether it wanted to participate, and if so when, to raise the funds needed, and to undertake the work at its own pace. This was achieved by treating each lane separately. Not all the residents were convinced of the viability of the system and some lanes were not able to organize themselves sufficiently to undertake the work. Using the lane system prevented those that could not, or did not want to, participate from jeopardizing the whole project. Control of each lane was in the hands of a manager who was a lane resident selected by other lane residents.

When the community installs the internal component, it also assumes responsibility for taking decisions. By undertaking construction management and, in the case of Orangi, implementation, the middlemen were cut out, resulting in a substantial cost reduction – a fifth of what it would have been if the government had provided the services. Material was procured cheaply by the community using many sources.

Dividing the project into its external and internal components is not without disadvantages, however. Resistance from the development agency and financing agencies, lack of adequate planning and design to allow for optimization of the internal process (as evidenced in Khuda-ki-basti) and increased time of construction are some of them. It has taken ten years to install services in Orangi and over three years in Khuda-ki-basti even to start installation.

Implementing external and internal division of projects

Flexibility in programming on the part of both the development agency and the local groups involved in the development process is essential if a project is to be divided into separate external and internal parts. How site planning and the infrastructure are developed and what systems are introduced determine its success.

New technologies that are both innovative and cheap are being introduced all over the world. In Orangi, technological innovation was achieved with the introduction of one-chamber soakpits until secondary and primary sewerage systems could be laid. In north-east Brazil a 'condominial' system treats the block like a horizontal apartment building. The result is a layout radically different from the conventional system, with a shorter grid of smaller and shallower 'feeder' sewers running through backyards and with the effects of shallower connections to mains rippling through the system. These innovations cut construction costs to between 20 and 30 per cent of a conventional system. Since the 'feeder' sewers run through backyards, community consensus and participation are essential to its success.[10]

For such innovations to work they have to become an integral part of the planning and development process. Whether in new housing, old neighbourhoods, or squatter settlements, the system by which solid and wet waste is collected and disposed of may have to be redesigned, and the way project planners envisage such projects might need to change. In addition to adding flexibility in programming, the development and financing agency officials have to change the standards used and their expectations of project quality.

For the community to be successfully involved in developing the internal component, it must be further divided into small manageable groups and the work into comparable segments. The success of the Orangi Pilot Project lay in breaking its infrastructure project up into small pieces that could work independently of each other for a number of years until secondary connections were in place. The project was very large, but the planning and implementation module was only the size of a lane. When bigger block sizes are used, as they were in Khuda-ki-basti, the increased number of people in each block means that the chances that problems might arise increases exponentially, as does the complexity of the work. In Khuda-ki-basti a much larger block size – 300 families for its internal development programme – was used, and it failed. Getting that many people to agree on any aspect of the work to be done was too difficult. Also, because of the large block size, the amount of work to be done in each block was too great and the cost high, and these became both practical and psychological barriers. The lane size was longer than in Orangi; therefore the total length of pipes to be laid was greater. Even though there were more people in each block to do the work, the distance was perceived as a problem. Limiting block sizes and developing clusters that house about 100 families seems to encourage community participation, though the optimal number may differ from project to project.[11] What is important is to design the physical plan so that the project can be divided into small independent pieces involving small groups of people. The design must be such that these independent projects, as they are added on, become part of a larger whole.

Time is an important factor. Most housing developers are under pressure from both politicians and financing agencies to finish construction and have the project occupied as quickly as possible in order to limit cost overruns. When projects are divided into their external and internal components, the internal components usually take much longer to complete, particularly if the community is doing the work. Even though the savings achieved by using this approach in Orangi were significant, the infrastructure has been under construction for over ten years and it is still not finished.

Optimizing the range of choice available to the community

For a development programme to be equitable and sustainable, it is essential that choices on a wide range of decisions be made available to the community. Only through choices can the people make knowledgeable decisions about their living environment and participate in those aspects of the project that may be most beneficial to them. In order to provide a wide range of choices, a number of conditions first have to be developed. Those who are initiating, planning, designing and managing the development process need to understand the client group better. The client group that is served has to be broadened and the specific requirements of women, children, the elderly and the handicapped have to be taken into consideration. Planning and design decisions based on the male-headed family are no longer necessarily appropriate. Family life-styles have changed and so have their requirements and preferences.

Who is to live in a house and whether there will be rental tenants are important factors in its design. In a typical housing project one plot is provided per family whether the family is extended or nuclear. The extended or multi-family organization is a good economic survival strategy, and it should be reckoned with in planning new housing projects.[12]

The requirements of a single-family plot can also differ. A nuclear family can organize its house plan into the kind of narrow-frontage plot developed in Aranya, but a wider frontage or bigger plot that can be subdivided for rental or commercial use might be required by others. Even a plot with more than one side exposed to give separate access to different sub-units of the family may be necessary.[13]

It is not only families that need shelter; there are also single mothers, widows, the elderly and the young unmarried, both male and female. At the present time these are, in general, not considered to have any particular space needs. The elderly are expected to be cared for by their family; others are expected to be taken care of by society without any special effort on the part of planners or designers. Only single blue-collar workers have been catered for by the market in single-room tenements or in rental accommodation in squatter settlements, but today even single white-collar workers are searching for accommodation in squatter settlements, as the cost of apartments rises far beyond their reach.

The plight of the elderly was recently highlighted in a leading Indian magazine: 'A silent revolution, a coup of sorts, is taking place. The patriarch, the matriarch, the eldest son, the aging boss, the village elder are being elbowed aside. The youth are moving in.'[14] The elderly are being forced out by their children; they have no place to go; their earning capacities are minimal. Because of improved heath conditions, they are living longer, but they are spending a considerable amount of that extra time looking for a decent place to live or, having no choice, living on the streets.

Plots sizes in new housing projects should reflect these kinds of changes in society. Creating homes for the elderly may give them a separate place, as has been done in the United States, but it isolates them from the rest of the community. Even in the United States this has been recognized as a problem, and over the last decade a number of new housing projects have incorporated special needs and elderly housing into general developments.[15]

The elderly do not require large houses, but they may require spaces to earn additional income. Many may be able to work in the home, selling groceries or sewing clothes, for instance. One elderly couple started a shop in their house in Aranya. Locating elderly housing along a major roadway with access from the street would encourage others to do the same. The elderly may also be given management and other roles in new developments. They could be responsible for the regular maintenance of the cluster. As elders they are respected in many societies, and may be in a position to act as mediators in community disputes. They may also act as watchdogs since they are on the premises most of the time.

Locating families with small children in upper-level apartments should be avoided for lack of ground access. Families with children also dislike using stairs. Children are outside more if they live in dwellings with ground-floor access, and supervising their play is easier for their parents. In Aranya, the clusters were used by children to play in. These are safe places to play, particularly for small children. In Orangi and Khuda-ki-basti, where there are no clusters, small children have to use the streets, and the streets are already being used by older children who could deal with the occasional traffic that ventured into them.

For single parents, cheap childcare facilities in close proximity to the home are important. In Aranya, schools for children are privately run and cost over Rs 25 a month per child. Some single women could be encouraged to start day-care or crèche services in their homes to gain income and provide a service which otherwise would have to be provided by an outside agency. Houses designed for single-parent households should also be located near open and safe play areas. Most design and planning decisions leave such issues to the market when they should be anticipated and planned for.

The youth and children can also participate in the design of play areas, look after the playgrounds and assist in the maintenance of the projects. When a project is designed, play areas and community open spaces could be conveniently located within each neighbourhood and clearly identified and designated. In Aranya, the playgrounds were placed next to schools and other communal facilities to ensure their use and maintenance by those institutions.

Some of these things might happen in communities in any case – but only intermittently, over time and at their own pace. If both old and young people are to be involved when the community is being formed, it should be when the physical and social environments are at their most changeable and their usefulness can be harnessed more effectively.

Even if design becomes responsive to the needs of these special groups, unless a community development programme is in place in each housing development, the target groups in the community may be unable to benefit from it.

An equitable allocation system

The second issue that needs attention is how and when the potential beneficiaries are selected. The number of potential beneficiaries eligible for plots in a public project is always much larger than the number of plots available. The most common way of solving the problem is to draw lots, a system that provides the plot but does not allow beneficiaries to select the location of their plots or to choose their neighbours. For a housing project to be successful, it is imperative to develop an allocation system that is much more responsive and sensitive to issues of community formation, especially choice of location. In the projects surveyed, it was found that people had in most cases no choice of where they could live and, in cases where they did have a choice, it was very limited. People complained that they were located in the interior and amongst neighbours with whom they could not associate. In Aranya, for instance, one person who ran a shop to earn part of his livelihood was given a plot in the interior of a cluster, where few customers would venture, and he could not sell his goods.

To develop an allocation system which is equitable is difficult without seeming to favour one group over another. Therefore development authorities are not too keen to get involved in any allocation process that leaves any room for choice. However, decentralizing allocation is necessary if an equitable environment is to be developed.

People who are going to live in a residential environment must be given a choice of location. In small projects allocation can be easily undertaken by the community itself. In large projects, as in the case of Aranya, the development authority along with an NGO must develop a system by which an equitable choice in plot selection is guaranteed.

Any allocation system that is undertaken must be initiated at the project planning and design stage, and not after it is completed. A short list of selected beneficiaries drawn by lottery could then be used as the basis for developing an equitable and open allocation system. Under this system the development authority would undertake a preliminary lottery to identify and select the beneficiaries. Plots would not be allocated at this time. Once the lottery had been established and beneficiaries selected, a second, more refined round could be undertaken among the beneficiaries, based on family ties, family life-style and occupation. In the second round the selected beneficiaries would be asked to complete a form which would ask for (a) family ties, kinship and language; (b) family status – that is whether they have young children, are elderly, are single parents, single workers, etc.; and (c) whether they need to work out of their house and, if so, the kind of work they intend to undertake.

This survey would also assist the designers in filling the needs of the group that will be living in their project. To date, in most projects, needs have been determined by extrapolating from already existing settlements. Using the proposed system a more accurate picture will emerge, and this will result in efficient planning for the level of facilities needed. The designers and the NGO would be able to assess community needs. The number of plots for the elderly, families with children, families needing work space and others with special needs could be determined. A new lottery taking all this into consideration could then be held to determine the allocation of plots in each neighbourhood or sector. It would be important to bear in mind that the neighbourhood size should remain small and not exceed more than a hundred households, in order to keep the process manageable. Once the list of allottees with their sectors and plots had been established, plots could be exchanged to accommodate those who would like to live next to particular groups of people or who would prefer another location. An NGO could be given the responsibility of looking after the allocation process and plot exchanges. The development authority is likely to be dragged into the internal politics if it takes on this responsibility, and this situation is bound to become worse once the process of exchanging plots is under way.

Using this system, equity would be maintained. Needs – economic and social – would be recognized. Areas for every group would be designated within each sector, so that no one sector was developed only for the elderly or families with children, or ethnic groups, or a particular religion. Different ethnic, religious and other groups would be mixed, but income groups would not.

In an equitable and transparent system, exchange and transfer of plots would be controlled to ensure that the process did not get out of hand. Exchanging plots could involve a fee levied by the NGO which would then be used to establish the community cooperative. A fixed fee would be levied if the exchange were made in the same neighbourhood or block, but if households wanted to exchange plots between blocks or to move into different house types, then the cooperative would receive a fee amounting to a certain percentage of the difference in the price of the plots. Care would have to be taken that beneficiaries were satisfied with the process. If conflicts arose they would have to be resolved impartially and quickly; otherwise those dissatisfied with the process might refuse to cooperate, making it difficult to undertake other community development work. In smaller projects the community could undertake its own allocation process and decide who was given which plot.

The equitable and transparent system proposed above would allow the development authority, NGOs and the beneficiaries to make decisions regarding the allocation of plots and houses in an equitable yet controlled manner. Using these techniques of allocation after agreement has been given by the community, rather than selective rules enforced either by the development agency or the NGO, might lead individuals to veto the process and weaken the powers of the development agency and the NGO to enforce solutions that stress the common over the individual good.

Supporting egalitarian housing developments

The amount of urban space that an individual controls today is assumed to be directly proportional to their status and/or income.[16] It is always assumed that the higher the income the larger the plot demanded and conversely the lower the income the smaller the plot. Rybczynski et al., in their studies of squatter settlements in Indore, show that there is actually no particular correlation between family income and plot size.[17] They found that size rather than income was the decisive factor: larger families had larger plots, suggesting that variety in terms of both plot sizes and income must be provided if a community that is representative of society is to develop. What is not clear from their studies is whether larger families had larger incomes and were therefore able to afford the larger plots, because in reality, with the high cost of serviced urban land, there has to be some direct correlation between affordability and plot size.

In Orangi, for example, the plot sizes vary from 80 square yards to 420 square yards. In the late 1970s, when the settlement was being developed, the rate was Rs 1 per square yard and the slightly better off and the astute paid Rs 80 to Rs 420 and bought up to four plots for speculation. Today these same plots are worth 50 times more: an 80 square-yard plot with services costs anywhere from Rs 60,000 to Rs 100,000, depending on location. Therefore, the provision of plots according to family size or family needs, without taking affordability into consideration, could only be done if there were no cost to serviced land, and if land were not part of the economic system. That is hard to imagine, given present political and socio-economic conditions.

The problems faced because of high cost of serviced land are further compounded when new development projects are undertaken primarily for one income group. It may be difficult to change the land market, but a move towards a more egalitarian approach may be needed if we are to stop predetermining social and economic mix in neighbourhoods across cities. This is not to say that income levels should be mixed indiscriminately, but a judicious approach, such as that taken by the designers of the Aranya township, has both social and economic benefits, including cross-subsidy possibilities. In Aranya township the lower-income group is located along the periphery of the poorest clusters. The middle-income and low-income groups have much in common and can assist each other in the development of the settlement. Further mixing of income groups is bound to take place, and is already taking place, as houses are sold and resold. In Aranya for example, several low-income houses have been sold for over Rs 80,000 to 100,000. At that rate, a poor person cannot afford to buy a built house even if it is only 35 m². If houses are being sold for over Rs 100,000, they can only be bought by those who can afford to pay this amount. In Orangi, too, family incomes of those living next to each other vary considerably and range from Rs 500 a month to Rs 25,000 a month in the same neighbourhood.

In the design and development of mixed-income projects our attention should be directed toward that segment of the population that needs housing the most. The argument by Bhatt et al.[18] that, even when several income groups are accommodated in a project, they should still be segregated into different clusters in the project, is contrary to what happens in traditional settlements where, regardless of income level, families from the same clan or religious group live next to one another.[19] Mixing of plots to replicate a traditional system of either squatter settlement or historical neighbourhoods (where groups of people with the same socio-religious affiliations live together with their own religious and community spaces) may not be totally possible. That level of community participation is probably unattainable in both state and private housing schemes. The expectations of the upper-middle and high-income groups are different and so are their life-styles.

Income mixing in housing developments may be more successful if housing cooperatives manage it before the housing is designed. A greater degree of compatibility is likely to occur if residents are allowed to live in developments of their own choosing. They may choose to live somewhere and with particular people for economic gains rather than socio-religious ties or other cultural affinities. In housing that is more or less forced upon residents it is unwise to count on neighbourliness for the project's success.[20] Mixed-income housing need not repeat traditional systems of socio-religious grouping to create equitable and sustainable environments. A well-managed community-based organization that is formed by the residents with assistance from either NGOs or other social organizations with clear aims can achieve the same goals, as was done in the Citra Niaga project.

Integrating site design for urban development

It has been argued that urban development is not a sector like other traditional sectors involved in the development of urban areas. The merit of urban development is the opportunity it affords to coordinate and integrate – based on priorities and plans – various components on an area basis.[21] An issue is whether or not such coordination and integration is possible and practical, and whether there is a limit to such endeavours. In the formulation of a programme and a project, along with functional linkages, institutional arrangements, legal framework and the efficiency of implementation also matter. In the context of this analysis functional linkages are being discussed.[22]

Most new housing developments undertaken by government agencies are narrowly focused and do not take into account larger city or urban area development. The site and urban design parameters are set by local site-specific decisions. This study also shows that both large and small-scale urban projects are designed to be self-sufficient. Cultural and commercial facilities are provided only for project use. Their relationship to neighbouring developments is not taken into consideration. When projects such as Citra Niaga respond to city scale and local conditions, clear connections between city functions and relationships to adjacent sites can be established. Design and site-planning practice ought to recognize, incorporate and integrate conditions in the immediate vicinity.

A successful urban layout manages to incorporate in its design the requirements of various activities and functions and to respond at both the public and private level. The scale of the solid and void, the size of the blocks, the street networks, both vehicular and pedestrian, the relationship between the residential and commercial areas, the provision of open spaces and the manipulation of various zones are important for the creation of a successful fabric.

Circulation patterns and modern vehicular systems have to be accommodated. Cars and other vehicles are important in today's society. In most developing countries they are also a prized possession that is protected and cherished. Conflict between cars and pedestrians has so far been dealt with by separating them into zoned vehicular and pedestrian systems, but vehicular roads are often too wide and act as barriers, and pedestrian paths are often unsafe. It is not what is possible but what is desirable that must guide our design efforts. Vehicular and pedestrian traffic can stay mixed if the speed of the vehicular traffic is controlled and through traffic is prohibited. The Aranya township has carefully worked out its circulation pattern, mixing the two where required and separating them only in the interior of the project.

Movement patterns need not be organic to be successful: there is nothing inherently wrong with the grid system. Jaipur is based on a rectilinear capillary system, yet it is a successful traditional Indian city with all the vibrancy and qualities that traditional settlements are supposed to have.[23] The Vieux Carré, the French quarter in New Orleans, is another example of a city planned on a rectilinear frame, in which each street has a different character and its own vibrancy. Its most important character-istics are that it has a square faced on to a river frontage and that it has a hierarchy of street widths, not a regular grid. A judicious mixture and overlapping of systems, such as that planned in Aranya, is required to develop a system that will suit the needs of everyone.

Most land-use plans continue to separate commercial and residential activities, although many have criticized this practice.[24] However, most low-income and economically weak sections of the society depend for their livelihood on having commercial activity near their houses. The site plan of Aranya township recognizes this need and has provided spaces that allow multiple activities to flourish. Unless such spaces are clearly identified and maintained by the people who will use them, however, the chances that these spaces will be appropriated or misused is high.

Aranya and Khuda-ki-basti were both designed to focus inward on themselves, instead of using open and public spaces to tie them to the rest of the city. Drawing boundaries around a site and not looking beyond it is one shortcoming of our design and planning as it is practised today. This approach overlooks the fact that historically each part of the town developed in relation to the others.

Even when the shape the city will take is controlled at the city-wide level by development authorities, housing projects must be designed in terms of what happens adjacent to them if we are to create public spaces that relate to the city. In Citra Niaga, the project was designed so that it provided not only a focus for public activities but also spaces that linked with the adjacent sites so the development did not become insulated. As a result Citra Niaga has become a catalyst for other developments and has created an urban structure that responds to the city. In order to integrate uses and activities, commercial and communal activities need not only to be dispersed within a development, but some of the larger areas need to be located where the township or neighbourhood meets the rest of the city.

Conclusion

Given the weak capacity of governments to meet the growing requirements for developing equitable and economically sustainable urban housing, development authorities need to draw on the full complement of human energy in the cities by encouraging the participation of the private sector, the community and the NGOs. The above assessment highlights some of the problems encountered in planning and designing housing for the poor and some of the strategies used to reduce inequity and optimize community choice through community involvement. Until now community involvement has not been seen as a routine part of building new projects in developing countries, though its importance and effectiveness in upgrading projects have been recognized for the last two decades. Several projects in various developing countries have successfully undertaken both small and large projects involving the community. In most new projects, however, it has been secondary. It is hoped that community involvement will become an integral part of all new projects. Several international agencies are recognizing its importance in new urban development projects for the poor and are recommending that NGOs and the private sector play a much greater role in their development.[25]

A new agenda for urban equity and sustainability

- *Ensure sustainability of shelter and the environment through affordability over time.* From the onset, development should include community control and providers must be receptive to community priorities.
- *Create and execute policies in flexible ways.* The process of shelter and urban systems delivery is not simple, nor does it happen in a vacuum.
- *Create new partnerships to coordinate the role of the various actors in development.* Partners may vary within various shelter delivery systems, but they must include some of the following groups: national governments, local governments, private sector enterprises, NGOs and community groups.
- *Acknowledge and promote the existence of formal and informal systems of development.* Economic sustainability can only be achieved through community training, skills transfer and the development of democratic organizational structures which respect community priorities.
- *Establish credibility with grassroots organizations and people through training and consumer education.* The introduction of policy reforms should be accomplished through the presentation of strategic plans which demonstrate the projects goals to the public. This must occur at the beginning of the process, not as an afterthought. The interactions with the community must be an ongoing process, not a one-time exercise.
- *Change thinking patterns.* Room must be made to adapt projects to the participants' ability to implement them.

- *Share, adapt and replicate successful approaches that work.* Projects must be designed and implemented so that they can be transferred and adapted in other communities. The lessons of successful implementation must be documented, and effective training material has to be created, without which replication is difficult, if not impossible.

The above action-steps show what project planners, designers, managers and development authorities need to do in order to promote community involvement and to improve both process and product. Designers and planners have a particularly significant role to play in building housing developments for the poor. Leaving all choices to the community is not the answer; instead the designers and planners should concentrate on developing and designing housing environments that present clear choices to the community and are adaptable and understood by them. *Ad hoc* choice tends to be misused, as the community does not comprehend uncontrolled alternatives. Total community involvement is also not possible since the community is made up of individuals, each of whom has his or her own set of requirements. Individuals tend to want the most for themselves, but individual gain may not necessarily mean communal gain, and therefore controls have to be established.

Controls, as we have seen, are best established at the overall planning level by the development agency, and at the community level by NGOs, who can play an intermediary role. Besides establishing controls and guidelines, designers, planners and organizers of the development should also strive to inform the community about these controls and about what has been designed and developed, and where the boundaries between personal and collective spaces lie. They should also teach the community how its involvement can assist in making neighbourhoods into equitable and economically sustainable environments in the long run. Finally, reducing inequity and increasing choice should not be viewed as ends in themselves but as important steps in creating conditions that foster, nurture and develop equitable urban environments.

CHAPTER 8

Our Urban Future: Opportunities and Challenges

During the past three decades, the number of the urban poor and, consequently, deficiencies in urban housing and services in developing countries have increased rapidly. Governments in developing countries have used four interrelated approaches to provide shelter and services to the urban poor: on-site upgrading, site-and-services schemes, granting security of tenure to residents of squatter settlements and providing subsidized low-income housing. The success rate of each of these approaches has not had as wide an impact as was expected; nevertheless important lessons have been learned from the experience. These lessons, however, are in danger of being lost because most developing country governments are only willing to support these efforts when international assistance has backed these projects. The result is that most projects have remained as demonstrations, and have never been adapted or replicated. It is now time to reassess the situation and move on to incorporate the lessons learned into national and local urban management strategies.

This study has shown that rapid urbanization is not productively seen as either a crisis or a tragedy. Since there is no way it will be halted, it is better seen as a challenge for the present and the future. This book has highlighted that controlling rapid urbanization and reaping its benefits are not easy and will require fundamental changes in approach by those involved in urban development. In spite of a proliferation of innovative approaches to urban challenges, the seriousness of urban problems is accelerating and threatening all societies. Conventional approaches to information sharing within and between cities choke the potential to replicate solutions and incorporate them into public policy. Given the magnitude of the urban problems, it is necessary that new methods are developed so that the time it takes for a solution to be implemented and be incorporated into public policy is reduced.

In the preceding chapter, I have made recommendations towards a better understanding of how innovative programmes are implemented and how they could be replicated and adapted in different social and cultural conditions. These recommendations are meant to be strategic rather than project-oriented; however, for any of the recommendations to succeed the locus of the responsibility must rest within the cities themselves. The recommendations that lead to sustainable and equitable developments, however, run the risk of becoming ends in themselves and placed among a list of things to accomplish. But they are really building blocks to be used as part of a comprehensive approach that will develop conditions where inequity is reduced, choices are increased and participation of various actors in the development process optimized.

The importance of international cooperation

Citizens of Berlin, Bombay, Boston and Bogota all face problems of severely stressed urban infrastructure, poverty, political disillusionment and social and cultural alienation. The world's largest metropolises, the mega-cities, are experiencing even more critical environmental degradation, economic stress and cultural alienation, and without innovative solutions face a bleak future.

Amidst all the gloom in cities there are rays of hope, most visibly through an outpouring of promising new development programmes. This new generation of urban innovation is taking place in cities all over the world. Community-based organizations, government agencies at the local and national levels and private sector entrepreneurs are trying new approaches leading to several successful innovative projects. The majority of these new programmes have been initiated by the people who live in the most severe conditions. They are taking the lead in making significant impacts on their physical, economic and social environment. These innovative solutions have to be supported and multiplied, because only through replication and adaptation can these solutions have a significant and sustainable impact on our cities.

It is through cross-cultural learning, replication and adaptation that effective urban practices can have a significant and sustainable impact on our cities. Even if they are small in scale, through replication, tested solutions multiply their effect by changing broader practice. Micro-level change matters in several ways: first, through transfers and adaptation, they have a ripple effect; second, by facilitating system-challenging transfers, the impact of small-scale success becomes great; and third, micro-revolutions can promote macro-level institutional innovation when they get incorporated into public policy.[1]

Over the past three decades time and resources have been wasted as governments, foundations or non-profit organizations reinvented the wheel and recreated past failures. But in time of severe resource constraints we need to discover a way to learn from each other's success and to multiply the impact of approaches that work. According to Janice Perlman:

> there seems to be a market imperfection in the area of urban and social policy. In other fields, this type of copying is the norm. In the computer industry, for

example, companies go to great lengths to glean intelligence about information their counterparts have devised. In popular culture, such 'innovations' as Teenage Mutant Ninja Turtles or fashion trends such as wearing baseball caps are copied by people in the most remote corners of the world. But urban innovations appear to be the best-kept secrets in the world – not only between cities, but also within the same city.[2]

Successful solutions addressing pressing urban problems such as poverty alleviation, economic development and environmental regeneration, are undocumented and inaccessible to others who could benefit from the experience.

Sharing approaches that work

Today's social, environmental and economic challenges are great. They are also common to many cities. In a recent study by the United Nations Development Programme, the mayors of 135 cities world-wide rated a range of problems in urban areas as 'most severe'. The findigs were as follows.

Most severe problems in urban areas[3]	%
Unemployment	63
Inadequate housing	43
Garbage disposal	38
Violence/crime	36
Poverty	34
Inadequate sanitation /sewerage	33
Air pollution	32
Inadequate transportation	29
Inadequate water	24
Inadequate social services	22
Civil apathy	22
Discrimination (ethnic, women, poor)	14

The idea that successful local approaches to urban problems can be and should be adapted and replicated is finally being incorporated into the policies of international agencies. The vast majority of these efforts, however, have been initiated on an *ad hoc* basis, with little attempt to synthesize the knowledge accumulated about how sharing approaches works or to build a methodology.

Synthesizing the knowledge gained from undertaking transfers allows urban leaders to develop cross-sectoral partnerships, utilize tested solutions to inform policy and promote exchange among equals replacing the current model where so-called 'experts' provide the solution.

Peer-to-peer learning promotes the kind of technical cooperation, as opposed to technical assistance, that leads to appropriate adaptation, new problem solving and longer-term relationships between innovators. The teaching and mentoring is done by those who have first-hand experience of the problem, and who have invented and implemented the solution. A critical obstacle to this type of exchange is that innovative problem-solvers in the social sector are usually too beleaguered fighting for survival and handling crises to be concerned with replication. Without a mechanism for recording and exchanging successes and failures, innovations often die out when funding agencies move on to other projects, and the chance for reaching scale and having a major impact is lost. This is unacceptable in today's climate of exacerbated social needs and extreme budgetary constraints.[4]

It is now conspicuously clear that the innovation diffusion process is not self-propelling. It is time to take a strategic look at how the process can be supported and stimulated so that urban leaders and practitioners can develop more effective cross-sectoral partnerships and participate more efficiently in technical cooperation. Without sharing, according to Robert Davies, 'these innovations will remain islands of excellence in a sea of poverty'.[5]

A catalyst for change

Adaptation or replication of any programme or project is not simple. It requires a comprehensive approach that includes identifying, distilling and disseminating the positive approaches; strengthening the leaders and groups who are evolving them; and finding sources of support to multiply their efforts.

A four-part strategy for sharing approaches that work has been developed by the Mega-Cities Project,[6] and has important lessons to offer for those interested in adapting and replicating projects. As illustrated in Figure 8.1, the process begins with matching the innovation to the need. In this stage, successful solutions are identified and documented; the information disseminated through a wide variety of methods; and a product champion identified who would be willing to oversee the adaptation, and be willing to go through the stages that the project may take before final implementation.

The transfer procedure also involves building a transfer task force, adapting the innovation to the local context and implementing the transfer. This process also depends on a network of committed individuals, that will eventually evolve into a strong and flexible long-term partnership. Once established, a single partnership may be re-utilized in the transfer of additional innovations and in the ongoing impacting of public policy. Manuel Castells has stated that 'in the changing global economy the governance and management of large cities will require new transnational

Steps	Match innovation to need	Build transfer task force	Adaptation	Implement transfer
	• Document solutions • Disseminate through a detailed dissemina-tion plan • Identify problem • Match solution to problem	• Introduce concept to stake holders • Negotiate preliminary transfer commitment • Secure commitment from stake holders and decision-makers	• Conduct site visits • Survey local conditions • Develop transfer implementa-tion plan • Mobilize resources • Publicize transfer plan	• Pilot demonstration project • Implement full-scale transfer • Trace and evaluate results
Mega-Cities role	'catalyst'	'broker'	'facilitator'	'supporter'

Note: The transfer procedure not only depends on the 'network of networks', it is also becomes a mechanism for strengthening the flexible, long-term partnerships which comprise that network.

Figure 8.1 Methodology for innovation transfer and adaptation

networked organizations'.[7] Through this transfer approach, a 'network of networks' can be developed as an independent transnational voice for urban civil society. Paralleling that of the private and public sectors, this global effort is intended to fill an important function in global organization and local decision-making.

This 'network of networks' develops the links between local innovation and global impact. While its members act as catalysts to transfer in-novations to other urban communities, they also access decision-makers and policy forums, thereby changing official mind-sets and decentralizing the process of problem-solving.

The transfer of urban innovations and lessons learned

The successful adaptation of innovations to new environments follows certain *patterns*, requires particular *pre-conditions*, involves a range of *players* and follows a common *process*. The lessons learned from some of these adaptations and transfers are illustrated below.

Patterns

There is increasing evidence to show that transfers may be successfully facilitated across cities with diverse political systems, cultures and economic bases. The transfer of Bangkok's *Magic Eyes* Anti-littering Programme to Rio de Janeiro illustrates how diverse cultures can benefit from the same innovative idea.[8] A unique anti-littering campaign targeted at children, the programme utilizes green cartoon eyes derived from traditional Thai mythology and songs and rhymes to remind children and their parents not to drop litter. After reducing littering in Bangkok by an estimated 85 per cent, it is now being replicated in Rio de Janeiro as part of the Clean Rio campaign through the Department of Sanitation and the School System. The enigmatic green eyes of the Thai version, however, have been reinterpreted as a playful cartoon extraterrestrial more appropriate to Brazilian culture.[9]

The transfer process will differ according to public, private, or voluntary sector, especially in terms of the timing and importance of consensus, resource allocation and implementation. In Cairo, members of the Zabbaleen community have been given the training, equipment and start-up funds necessary to organize small micro-enterprises where they convert trash into marketable products such as shoes, textiles, or pots and pans. In this way, the Zabbaleen receive the benefits of adding value to the recyclable waste and channel their profits into improving their community through the creation of better housing, schools and health care centres. The Zabbaleen initiative is now being replicated in Bombay through the Municipal Corporation of Greater Bombay, and in Manila through a network of NGOs and People's Organizations. The two processes are unfolding very differently. The Cairo–Bombay transfer is taking an institutional and research-oriented approach while the Cairo–Manila approach is more participatory and activist.[10]

While both transfers are benefiting from seed funding from the UNDP–LIFE Programme, the Manila team has raised additional funds from UN Volunteers and is further along in the process. Recently the Bombay team has secured a two-year commitment of funds from the British Council, and a feasibility study is now being completed.

Preconditions

When adapting a solution to a new location, the political environment and readiness of the general public are crucial factors in ensuring the success. The more closely the imported idea relates to changes in public policy, the more important it will be to have government support. The opportune time for transfer is when a 'window of opportunity' opens in the political process or when the general public is ready to take action on an issue. A forthcoming election, or a change in government regulations coupled with public pressure, sets the ideal environment in which to introduce new ideas into a city.

In Metro-Manila, the government's solution of building incinerators to handle the city's solid waste has been opposed by environmentalists who allege that incinerators let off toxic steam and produce hazardous ash. Development NGOs also oppose the government plan since the shutting down of dump sites would mean the loss of livelihood for thousands of urban poor residents. These groups are naturally supportive of the Zabbaleen transfer as it represents an economically sustainable and environmentally suitable solution to Manila's solid waste dilemma. Recent elections provided the incentive for government officials to support this initiative. Scavengers as well as other concerned citizens form a significant number of the electorate.

In Pakistan, the Orangi Pilot Project has been able to replicate its project to other sites in Karachi and in other cities in Pakistan after the Karachi Municipal Corporation accepted the OPP method of providing urban infrastructure services to poor communities. This validation of their work provided the OPP with a 'window of opportunity' to undertake work in others' sites and cities.

Players

A transfer is more likely to succeed when a transfer 'broker' links the solution with the stakeholders in the 'window of opportunity' and continues to serve as the transfer agent. In the case of the Orangi Pilot Project, once the external and internal components of the project were accepted by the Karachi Municipal Corporation, the OPP was able to work as an intermediary and consultant to replicate its approach in other cities.

While maximum participation increases the sense of ownership, it also provides the opportunity for representatives from participating sectors in the importing community to be matched by their peers in the community where the innovation originated. The peer-to-peer transfer ensures the appropriate language, subculture and legitimacy. The whole concept of the OPP was based on the premise that multiplying the impact of local programmes is most effectively done among peers.

Process

In order for the transfer to be successful, stakeholders need to identify obstacles to be overcome, and dimensions in which they are willing to act. Experiential education through site visits and face-to-face interaction is the best way to pinpoint these essential components.

Valuable learnings from the site visit often alter the original transfer plan. It is critical, therefore, to ensure flexibility in the adaptation of an innovation to a new context. Before the site visit to Cairo, the members of the Manila Transfer Task Force anticipated that the innovation transfer would focus primarily on technologies and systems, but after the trip the team members concluded that what was actually to be transferred was the 'enterprise approach'. This enterprise approach observed in the Zabbaleen community convinced the Manila team that the scavengers should not be viewed as beneficiaries of development projects, but as garbage industry workers with a vital role in the development of their community. Since its members come from an NGO/non-profit perspective, adjustment from the traditional approach of conflict-confrontation or demand-making for government action is required.

Though site visits are important, they have to be managed carefully because they could very easily turn into recreational trips instead of educational. In one of the OPP's efforts to replicate the project in another community in Karachi, a number of site visits were organized and in the end they became recreational trips. Since the community was not empowered to make decisions about the project, they used the opportunity to get out of their environment and visit others parts of the city.[11]

Finally, the power of transfer lies not only in its tangible outcomes but also in its symbolic and psychological value. The transfer of the Zabbaleen Environment and Development Project to Manila is proceeding extremely well and in many ways can already be judged a success. Not only has cooperation between urban leaders in Manila and Cairo been stimulated, but the exposure trip by the Manila team was one concrete application of both the Mega-Cities Project's strategy behind innovation transfers and its sponsor, the UNDP–LIFE Programme: technical and personal cooperation between developing countries. Furthermore, South-North and South-South transfers have a great symbolic impact. They change the status of citizens in developing nations from beneficiaries to innovators.

For adaptation and transfers to be used effectively, the conditions under which urban development projects are to be undertaken must change. The role of government agencies, private developers, financing agencies, NGOs and the community must evolve from a situation in which these groups are used as cheap implementers to achieve a short-term goal to one in which each group becomes an integral part of the process of development which all civil societies undertake.

Increasing local control

Central governments in developing countries continue to control most urban development administrative and financial policies. One can point to a growing number of instances where there has been participation of the community, NGOs and representatives of the private economic sector in decisions about their lives and livelihoods. But the sad fact is that these are nearly always exceptions to the normal decision-making process, and there are few institutionalized mechanisms in place to guarantee that such involvement does occur. Urban policy for the present is made at best through representative democracy, with few opportunities for direct involvement, particularly for the poor.

Local control over administrative, financial and redevelopment decisions is of high priority to ensure broad participation. Central government agencies are too far removed from conditions in particular cities where urban development takes place to perform that function. They are also unable to distinguish between regions, subregions, cities and areas within cities. By increasing local control, local groups might stand a better chance of making appropriate decisions and taking quick action.

Another reason why local control is important is that urban management policy seems to be developing in the direction of broader participation. If local communities are expected to deliver, maintain and implement their own facilities then they must be permitted to help decide when, where, how and at what level of service this will be done.

Increasing local control is not easy. Political forces and institutionalized behaviour of public bureaucracies are major impediments, as are the many small and insulated decision-making structures that will have to be opened up. This is demonstrated by the fact that, although a number of countries have an official policy of cooperation with NGOs, their true involvement in urban management and development decisions in those countries is minimal and their role is mainly that of a cheap provider of services.[12]

Training urban professionals

Increasing local control over urban development programmes requires adequately trained government leaders and civil service officers from national and local governments; programme managers and field officers; staff of NGOs and non-profit groups; community leaders; and planners and designers. All of these will have different roles and functions, and the content and method of their training must therefore be different.

Most urban development officials do not have the necessary skills to work effectively with NGOs and community-based organizations. They need to be retrained and their approach reoriented from rigid decision-making to a more flexible approach. In addition, they need to learn to be more conciliatory, so they can work effectively with poor communities. Staff from NGOs, leaders from formal or informal community organizations and non-profit groups have to be trained in the process of planning, implementing, monitoring and evaluating projects that use community involvement approaches.

Planners and designers have to be trained to understand the implications of design and planning for community involvement. As this study has shown, planning and design decisions play an important role in enabling or deterring community involvement.[13] In addition, planners also have to be trained to understand that actual community requirements and preferences might differ from their own perceptions of them.[14] Flexibility at all stages of planning and design has to be built in to allow for changes to be made by the community itself.

Besides technical training, a programme to improve the understanding of each group's ultimate goal – achieving local control over decision-making – needs to be instituted. In most cases, even with good intentions, most government officials, NGOs, planners and designers and leaders of community organizations adopt prescriptive measures for local control.[15] In most instances where, how and at what stages the community is involved are predetermined, and limits to their participation are set. This determination is necessary. However, what is also needed is a process by which the community itself arrives at these limits. This is difficult to achieve and the process may not be the same in all cases. Nevertheless, it is only through repeated awareness reorientations that prescriptive measures for local control can be avoided and a process for local control developed.

Improving interagency and inter-city cooperation

Policies and programmes aimed at providing urban services and housing require several organizations with different resources, skills, objectives and procedures.[16] Effective implementation therefore depends partly upon the effectiveness of inter-agency coordination. Besides inter-agency coordination inter-city coordination is also required. Inter-city coordination might also allow for exchanges and sharing of approaches that work. Coordination between programmes instituted in neighbouring cities or parts of the same city is useful for determining what has worked and what has not.[17]

Actions needed to facilitate such interagency and inter-city cooperation include the creation and maintenance of open systems of communication and exchange of information. Approaches to ensure such cooperation include clear delineation of responsibilities, standardization of rules and procedures for implementation, and delegation of adequate authority.[18] However, most of these necessitate the formation of another coordinating agency, and this may mean one more bureaucratic bottle-neck. Frequent exchange of information between personnel from various programmes including government officials, NGOs and community programme leaders is a better solution. Each will then be aware of the steps the others are taking so that they may support one another in addressing common issues.

Improving local dialogue

To ensure that all segments of society are represented in urban development decision-making, regular and frequent communications between local authorities, NGOs, community organizations and other non-profit organizations are required. These discussions have to go beyond representative democracy to direct involvement of all groups.[19]

City building involves careful planning, programming and the ability to resolve problems on the spot. In the complex situation of today this calls for a different kind of organization and level of communication, one that is non-hierarchical, more collegial, open to a variety of participants and less burdened by regulation. It also calls for different technical and managerial skills. It is a question not just of replacing bureaucratic organizations in order to improve efficiency, but of allowing equal and non-hierarchical representation. Improving and facilitating discussion on a regular basis might be one such approach, but it will be difficult since it assumes a common base where power is shared equally by all participants. In reality, power is controlled by a few and those in power may not want to relinquish it. Those who gain power may not understand the responsibility that comes with it and may misuse it.[20] Nevertheless, this risk must be taken. If some controls and regular local-to-local dialogue are implemented, the risk willbe substantially reduced.

Can reducing inequity and increasing choice lead to sustainable and equitable environments?

The interest in developing policies that seek to reduce inequity and increase community choice in urban development programmes is certainly lukewarm, but it is clear that reducing inequity, increasing choice and developing conditions where local control can be established increase the probability of developing sustainable and equitable environments. As the case-studies show, investigation in community involvement in housing is now directed at specific problems from within a particular frame of reference, which is acceptable and realistic to those who commission it.[21] The need for research that is relatively unfettered by institutional constraints and does not make the formulation of policy paramount is also needed.[22] However, unfettered research is not a definitive answer, since problems seem to arise because local organizations involved in urban development programmes for the poor are unaware of research even when it has been done.[23]

Even though this book advocates increased participation of three groups – the community, the private sector and NGOs – in urban development programmes, it does not see this as a panacea. By having each of these groups participate, sustainable and equitable environments do not by definition result. It is precisely this notion – that success will be guaranteed if the community, the private sector and the NGOs participate – that this study has tried to dispel.

The roles of the government and of the private sector raise separate theoretical propositions. The political right eschews subsidy and sees state intervention as being less effective and less efficient than the operation of market forces. The political left sees the private sector as exploitative and only driven by capital accumulation. Between these extreme positions lies a large middle ground where research and practice offer solutions. It is within this middle ground that new approaches have been undertaken with good results, and it is precisely this middle ground that this study advocates.

However, to arrive at this middle ground, government agencies, private sector organizations and the community have to change their notions about how urban development is undertaken. To practise in the middle ground, this study has identified three strategies: government agencies have to develop selective control mechanisms; private sector organizations have to play a more productive role and work with the government agencies; and the community has to start accepting responsibility for undertaking and managing aspects of the programme.

A diversity of approaches, systems and policies is being advocated. But in order to achieve this diversity, a series of conditions have first to be established. The conditions identified in the first half of this chapter are not easily achieved, and there is no guarantee that once they have been achieved a level playing field where effective power-sharing is possible will have been established. Conditions under which each community, city, subregion and region develop are distinct. Increased local control may produce ideas and allow more voices to be heard, but unless the best of these opinions are translated into development programmes they will have no meaning in the long run.

Problems that arise with private sector, community and NGO involvement

Private sector, community and NGO involvement and the problems they bring have already been discussed, but it must once again be emphasized that none of these groups can be viewed as monolithic organizations.[24] Within each there are numerous subdivisions, and what may be good for one may not be good for another. Each have their own agendas that drive them to participate, and they are all different.

The case-studies show that private developers rarely function purely in the interests of the community. Profit is what generally guides their participation. Profit need not be the only motive, however. Some private developers, if given the opportunity, work amicably with the government and the community to achieve common goals.

Within the community, too, there are subgroups with needs that may conflict with the others. In Citra Niaga, for example, a choice was made as to who could participate in the project and who could not. Those whose activities did not match the purposes of the project were left out. Coercion and money had to be used to get these groups to revoke their claims. As a result not all subgroups were happy with the project.

NGO involvement can develop overdependency. Even though the Orangi project has been successful, OPP's fundamental approach stems from the fact that the problems are still identified by them. A true measure of success will be when the services of non-government organizations are no longer needed. At that stage the community's own organization would be able to identify and solve most problems. Unfortunately OPP has so far not worked very hard at developing the idea of self-sufficiency. Instead, it has identified problems and arrived at solutions using the community. To this extent it is no better than agencies that use NGOs as cheap implementors.

The involvement of communities, NGOs and private sector organizations must not be viewed as a foolproof solution. Instead, what this study has identified are development factors that involve each of these groups, their potential contributions and their shortcomings.

A new vision for equity and sustainability

Let me close with a vision. A vision that sees development nurtured by empowering people so that they can create their own identities and their own institutions. This vision of sustainable urban development is people-centred and gender-conscious, and seeks equity for all and the empowerment of the poor, the disenfranchised, the vulnerable and the weak.

This vision sees all development having cultural rootedness, and recognizes that governance, institution building and enhancing human capacities are central to the development process and may in fact be the key that unleashes economic well-being.

It is a vision that places short-term actions within a long-term framework. A vision that predicts that by encouraging peer-to-peer exchanges, i.e., transferring an idea from one community to another, does more than simply expand the reach of a particular solution (scaling out horizontally); it also broadens the focus of inovators from their immediate geographical vicinity to their entire city or society.[25]

Today, a coherent understanding of planning, design and participation is emerging – one which recognizes planning and design as a process rather than as a product. The process can go on only if it is helped along. It will cease if efforts are not continually made to sustain it. The planning and design process can be an effective means of ensuring community involvement if it is used to improve efficiency of practice, make projects an integral part of urban development and promote cooperation.[26]

The evidence set forth in the preceding chapters argues for the recognition of fundamental changes in our approaches to providing housing, especially for the poor. Many of the suggestions and proposals offered are seen as feasible ways of improving society's chances of solving its urban development problems. They are not blueprints, however, but simply ideas for strategies that might generate new approaches, help deal more adequately with the immediate, increasingly severe housing shortage and provide actions for preventing difficulties that may otherwise arise in the future.

As the government's role in addressing social needs and planning for the future is debated very publicly and perhaps divisively, there is an explicit opportunity for intermediary groups, foundations and international development agencies to help shape the public conversation by fostering the necessary constituencies, engaging policy, business and opinion leaders and promoting dialogue and collaboration among diverse groups.

Finally it is important to note that issues of rebuilding civic life, while dependent on increasing synergy and coordination between existing organizations and institutions, are not necessarily amenable to familiar programmes and solutions carried out in familiar ways. Success in this work may not be measurable in traditional ways, for example, by the construction of new housing units or creation of new programmes and organizations or leveraging sums of money. Rather, it may be measurable only by reference to more subtle and yet powerful evidence of growing civic life – increases in the quality of and depth of discourse, and enhanced level of collective engagement, or an increasing well-being among the city's residents. The challenge for governments will be learning to recognize, value and proclaim these critically important indicators of success.

In the light of this new thinking, governments and international development agencies in the region have two options for the future development of cities. They can join the chorus in the praise of structural adjustment, macro-policy reforms and urban management as a way of assisting the urban poor; or they can stand apart from the rest, not necessarily in opposition, and take the position that structural adjustment and macro-policy reforms, however necessary, do not have a uniformly positive impact on the quality of life of the urban poor. This book recommends a move away from the preoccupation with structural adjustment and macro-policy reforms, and identifies other ways to enhance the quality of life of the people. Our challenge is to support specific projects, programmes and policies that reduce the vulnerability of the poorest and promote urban development with a human face. Several innovative steps undertaken within countries in the developing world, by governments, NGOs, community-based groups and the private sector, constitute a basis for hope and optimism – that sustainable and equitable urban development is possible with coordinated national, regional and international action.

As we approach the third millennium, we are faced with the challenge of coping with our urban future, but we also have the opportunity to change the way humanity relates to the urban environment. It is a challenge that all of us – governments, the private sector, the NGO community and the people – have to meet, by working collaboratively to overcome the obstacles that we face in our everyday attempts to create a better urban future. We have to rise to this challenge and must not let this opportunity escape us. We must think of better ways of promoting development and convince policy-makers and the world at large to change.

Ultimately, the responsibility for making cities habitable rests with their governments and their people. If governments can learn again how to serve the public, they can regain their power – the power that comes from harnessing the combined imaginations and enterprise of millions of human beings.

Notes

1. The challenges of a changing urban world

1. UNCHS, *On the Road to Istanbul*, Signpost No. 1 (December 1994).
2. Kenneth E. F. Watt et al., *The Unsteady State: Environmental Problems, Growth and Culture* (Honolulu: East West Center, 1977), p. 5.
3. United Nations, *World Urbanization Prospects* (New York, 1993).
4. Ibid.
5. Ibid.
6. UNDP, *Cities, People and Poverty, Urban Development Cooperation for the 1990s*, a UNDP Strategy Paper (New York, 1991).
7. Jorge E. Hardoy, Sandy Cairncross and David Satterthwaite (eds), *The Poor Die Young: Housing and Health in Third World Cities* (London, 1990).
8. World Bank, *Urban Policy and Economic Development: an Agenda for the 1990s* (Washington, DC, 1991)
9. Hardoy, Cairncross and Satterthwaite (eds), *The Poor Die Young*.
10. UNDP, *The Urban Environment in Developing Countries* (New York, 1992).
11. Kenneth J. Davey, *Elements of Urban Management* (Urban Management Programme, Washington, DC, 1993).
12. World Bank, *Urban Policy and Economic Development*.
13. Janice Perlman, 'Global urbanization: challenges and opportunities', in *Urban Management: Policies and Innovations in Developing Countries*, ed. G. Shabbir Cheema (Westport, CT, 1993), pp. 31–5, has identified the first five of the obstacles.
14. World Bank, *Urban Policy and Economic Development*.
15. John Habraken, 'Reconciling variety and efficiency in large-scale projects', *Large Housing Projects: Design, Technology and Logistics*, Proceedings of the 5th seminar in a series (Cambridge, MA: Aga Khan Program for Islamic Architecture, 1985), pp. 46–53.
16. Nabeel Hamdi, *Housing Without Houses* (New York: Van Nostrand Reinhold, 1991), pp. 26–9.
17. Bishwapriya Sanyal, 'Does development trickle up?', in Lim Gill-Chin (ed.), *Korean Economic Development* (Urbana: Consortium on Development Studies, University of Illinois, 1988), pp. 63–76.
18. Babar Mumtaz, 'The housing question (and some answers)', *Mimar*, 28 (1988), p. 19.
19. Sanyal, 'Does development trickle up?', pp. 63–76.
20. Ibid.
21. David R. Goldfield, 'Neighborhood preservation and community values', in I. Altman and A. Wandersman (eds), *Neighborhood and Community Environments*, Vol. 9 (New York: Plenum Press, 1987), p. 254.
22. Saad Eddin Ibrahim, commenting in Robert Powell (ed.), *The Architecture of Housing* (Geneva: the Aga Khan Award for Architecture, 1990), p. 158.
23. Ibid.
24. Bong Koo Lee, 'Major urban development issues: an overview', *Urban Policy Issues*, Proceedings of the Regional Seminar on Major National Policy Issues (Manila: Asian Development Bank, 1987), pp. 36–7.

25. Ibid., p. 37. Also see D. W. Drakakish-Smith and Yen-man Yeung, 'Public housing in the city states of Hong Kong and Singapore', Occasional Paper No. 8 (Canberra: Development Studies Centre, Australian National University, 1977).

26. Ibid.

27. In India it is estimated that national housing savings average about 20 per cent of income.

28. M. J. Pherwani, 'The future prospects of housing finance in India', *Housing Finance International* (June 1991), p. 33.

29. 'Chairman's statement', *Thirteenth Annual Report 1989–90*, HDFC (Bombay, 1990), p. 9.

30. Ibid.

31. Ibid., p. 10.

32. Pherwani, 'The future prospects of housing finance in India', p. 32.

33. William Mangin, 'Latin American squatter settlements: a problem and a solution', *Latin American Research Review* (1967), was perhaps the first person actually to call these settlements a 'solution' even with their problems.

34. Tony Schuman, 'The agony and the equity: a critique of self-help housing', in Rachel Bratt, Chester Hartman and Ann Meyerson (eds), *Critical Perspective on Housing* (Philadelphia: Temple University Press, 1986), p. 467.

35. Bishwapriya Sanyal, 'Does development trickle up?', pp. 63–76.

36. Ibid., p. 68.

37. Arif Hasan, in *The Human Face of the Urban Environment*, a report to the Development Community, Environmentally Sustainable Development Proceedings, Series No. 5 (World Bank, 1995), p. 15.

38. Ibid., pp. 68–70.

39. Horacio Caminos and Reinhard Goethert, *Urbanization Primer* (Cambridge, Mass: MIT Press, 1978).

40. For further details, see Marie-Agnes Bertaud, *A Model for the Preparation of Physical Development of Alternatives for Urban Settlement Projects* (the Bertaud Model), Economic Development Institute (EDI) (Washington, DC: World Bank, 1985), pp. 2–3.

41. Schuman, 'The agony and the equity: a critique of self-help housing', pp. 463–73.

42. Lisa Peattie, 'Some second thoughts on site-and-services', *Habitat International*, 6, 1/2 (1982), pp. 134.

43. Ibid., p. 135.

44. Geoffrey Payne, *Urban Housing in the Third World* (London: Leonard Hill, 1977), p. 186.

45. Solomon Benjamin, an architect and planner from India, takes a look at the transformation of raw farmland into a bustling colony of homes, factories, commerce and services on the outskirts of Delhi. His study provides an example of how urban development and economic activities are intricately tied and concludes that if new housing areas are to survive, incentives for economic development are crucial. *Jobs, Land and Urban Development: the Economic Success of Small-Scale Manufacturers in East Delhi, India* (Cambridge, MA: Lincoln Institute of Land Policy, 1991).

46. United Nations Centre for Human Settlements, *Report of Habitat: United Nations Conference on Human Settlements*, E. 76. IV. 7 (Vancouver: UNCHS, 1976), Chapter II.

47. Akhtar Badshah and Richard Ludwig, 'Regional Program for urban management in Asia and the Pacific Region', report prepared for the Regional Program

Division, Regional Bureau for Asia and the Pacific, United Nations Development Programme (1992), pp. 44.

48. Ismail Serageldin, in *The Human Face of the Urban Environment*, a report to the Development Community, Environmentally Sustainable Development Proceedings, Series No. 5 (World Bank, 1995), p. 4.

2. Responding to changing needs

1. G. Shabbir Cheema and Dennis A. Rondinelli (eds), *Decentralization and Development: Policy Implementation in Developing Countries* (Beverly Hills, CA: Sage Publications, 1983), p. 11.

2. Ibid., p. 13.

3. Keith Griffin, 'Economic development in a changing world', *World Development*, Vol. 9, No. 3 (1981), pp. 221–6.

4. Bishwapriya Sanyal, 'Does development trickle up?', in Lim Gill-Chin (ed.), *Korean Economic Development* (Urbana: Consortium on Development Studies, University of Illinois, 1988), pp. 63–76.

5. Jan Pronk and Mahbub ul Haq, 'Sustainable development must be fair to all people and all resources', *Earth Summit Times* (13 May 1992), p. 18.

6. Kenneth E. F. Watt *et al.*, *The Unsteady State: Environmental Problems, Growth and Culture*, (Honolulu: East–West Center, 1977), pp. 7–9.

7. Dudley Weeks, 'Learning alternative futures: the dominant conceptual, behavioural, and structural patterns of contemporary human society and the design of polsocioeconomics alternatives', doctoral dissertation, University of Hawaii, 1976.

8. See UNDP, *Human Development Report 1990*, pp. 85–90; see also Bong Koo Lee, 'Major urban development issues: an overview', *Urban Policy Issues*, Proceedings of a Regional Seminar on Major National Policy Issues (Manila: Asian Development Bank, 1987), pp. 26–7, and Sivaramakrishnan, 'Regional review of the urban policy issues – Asia' (New York, UNDP, 1990).

9. Romila Prasad, Afzal Raza Khan and Vindhya Wasant Pandey, 'Role of women in improving environmental quality in slums', *Human Settlements for Sustainable Development* (New Delhi: Indian Environmental Society, 1992), p. 171.

10. Ibid.

11. Ibid., p. 172.

12. Bertha Turner and Andrew Maskrey, 'Women's Construction Collective', in Bertha Turner (ed.), *Building Community* (London, 1988), pp. 162–6.

13. Orapin Sopchokchai, 'Magic Eyes: environmental awareness in Bangkok', a case-study produced by the Mega-Cities project and Thailand Development Research Institute, 1990.

14. Alka Karande, 'City of Bombay, health scenario and child-to-child programme implementation', an unpublished case-study.

15. Madhu Jain and Ramesh Menon, 'The greying of India', *India Today* (30 September, 1991), p. 25.

16. Cheema and Rondinelli (eds), *Decentralization and Development: Policy Implementation in Developing Countries*, p. 297.

17. Sugiarso Padmopranoto, 'Indonesia country paper', in Asian Development Bank, *Urban Policy Issues* (Manila: Asian Development Bank, 1987), pp. 431–76.

18. Om Prakash Mathur, 'Urban Services and the Private Sector: Realities and Issues' (New Delhi, India: National Institute of Urban Affairs, 1989).

19. Dennis A. Rondinelli and John D. Kasarda, 'Privatization of urban services,

shelter and infrastructure in developing countries: an overview of experience', Presented at UNDP Regional Seminar on Private Sector Initiatives in Urban Housing and Services in Asia and the Pacific (Bali, January 1992), p. 16.

20. G. Shabbir Cheema, 'The role of voluntary organisations', in G. Shabbir Cheema and Dennis Rondinelli, (eds), *Decentralization and Development* (Beverly Hills: Sage Publications, 1983), pp. 203–29.

21. Ibid.

22. Akhtar Badshah and Richard Ludwig, 'Regional program for urban management in Asia and the Pacific Region', Report prepared for the Regional Programme Division, Regional Bureau for Asia and the Pacific, United Nations Development Programme (1992), p. 17.

23. Ibid., p. 18.

24. Rondinelli and Kasarda, 'Privatization of urban services, shelter and infrastructure in developing countries: an overview of experience', p. 1.

25. Ibid.

26. PADCO Inc., *India: Public-Private Partnerships in Land Development* (New Delhi, India: US Agency for International Development, 1991), pp. 16–18.

27. Ibid.

28. L. Ralston, J. Anderson and E. Colson, 'Voluntary efforts in decentralized management', Working paper (Berkeley: University of California, Institute of International Studies, 1981).

29. PADCO Inc., *India: Public-Private Partnerships in Land Development*, pp. 16–18.

30. Rondinelli and Kasarda, 'Concept paper: privatization of urban services', p. 31.

31. Ibid., pp. 31–3.

32. Dennis A. Rondinelli, 'Extending urban services in developing countries: policy options and organizational choices', *Public Administration and Development*, Vol. 6, No. 1 (1986), pp. 1–21.

33. Rondinelli and Kasarda, 'Concept paper: privatization of urban services,' pp. 35–7.

34. Lloyd Rodwin and Bishwapriya Sanyal, 'Shelter, settlement, and development: an overview', in Lloyd Rodwin (ed.), *Shelter, Settlement and Development* (Winchester, MA: Allen and Unwin, 1987), p. 4.

35. Ibid., p. 7.

36. G. Shabbir Cheema, *Urban Shelter and Services: Public Policies and Management Approaches* (New York: Praeger, 1987), p. 81.

37. Ibid.

38. Rod Burgess, 'Petty commodity housing or dweller control? A critique of John Turner's views on housing policy', in *The Urban Informal Sector: Critical Perspectives on Employment and Housing Policies*, ed. R. Bromley, Oxford: Pergamon Press, 1979, pp. 1105–35.

39. Alan Gilbert and Peter Ward, 'Community participation in upgrading irregular settlements: the community response', *World Development*, 12:9 (September 1984), p. 913.

40. This is the major focus of the book by John Turner, *Housing by People: Towards Autonomy in Building Environments* (London: Marion Boyars, 1976).

41. J. O'Connor, *The Fiscal Crisis of the State* (New York: St Martin's Press, 1973), p. 6.

42. Rod Burgess, 'Petty commodity or dweller control?, pp. 1105–33.

43. Ibid., p. 1126.

44. Ibid., p. 1130.

45. Shlomo Angel and Stan Benjamin, 'Seventeen reasons why the squatter problem can't be solved', *Ekistics*, 242 (January 1976).

46. Ibid.

47. The opportunities and constraints in community participation have been summarized from G. Shabbir Cheema, *Urban Shelter and Services*, pp. 82–5. For a more detailed discussion of the significance of community participation see, among others, Yue-man Yeung, 'Provision of basic urban services in Asia: the role of people-based mechanisms', paper presented to the Expert Group Meeting on Policy Issues in Urban Services for the Poor, Nagoya, Japan, 13–17 August 1985; J. Turner, *Housing by People*; and Gilbert and Ward, 'Community participation'.

48. Caroline Moser, 'Community participation in urban projects in the Third World', *Progress in Planning*, Vol. 32 (New York: Pergamon Press, 1989), pp. 105–6.

49. Ibid., p. 127.

50. His Highness the Aga Khan commented in Robert Powell (ed), *The Architecture of Housing* (Geneva: the Aga Khan Award for Architecture, 1990), pp. 163–5.

51. Madhu Jain and Ramesh Menon, 'The greying of India', *India Today* (30 September 1991), p. 25.

52. K. McCamart and C. Durrett, 'Cohousing in Denmark', in K. Frank and S. Ahrentzen (eds), *New Households New Housing* (New York: Van Nostrand Reinhold, 1989), p. 100.

53. Shlomo Angel *et al.*, *Land for Housing the Poor* (Singapore: Select Books, 1988), in their work on land-sharing projects in Bangkok have shown that even in upgrading slum houses, the residents tend to some extent to opt for contractor-built houses, as was the case in the Soi-Sengki and Managkasila land-sharing projects. But in Klong Toey, another project in Bangkok, the residents built their own homes.

54. Shlomo Angel, 'Instead of focusing on housing, focus on urban land development', *Open House International*, 11, 4 (1986).

55. William Doebele, 'Land policy', in Lloyd Rodwin (ed.), *Shelter, Settlement and Development* (Winchester, MA.: Allen and Unwin, 1987), pp. 110–32.

56. Responding to a state-wide need for affordable housing, the MHP provides state support and coordinates other public and private resources for local housing. SHARP is a shallow rental subsidy which promotes mixed-income housing and HOP combines low-interest mortgage rate financing with various state and local contributions in order to produce sufficient incentives to for-profit and non-profit developers to construct mixed-income home ownership developments. For a detailed study, see Rachel Bratt, *Rebuilding a Low-Income Housing Policy* (Philadelphia: Temple University Press, 1989).

57. Roger Zetter, 'Land issues in low-income housing', in Geoffrey Payne (ed.), *Low-Income Housing in the Developing World* (New York, 1984), pp. 221–31, provides a quick survey of the various methods of land assembly and supply used.

3. NGOs and the community: participation for integrated area development

1. Arif Hasan, *Profiles of Five Pakistani Cities*, report for the Swiss development Corporation (Karachi, May 1990).

2. Ibid.

3. *Pakistan's Low Cost Housing Project Report*, Asian Development Bank, 1989.

4. For a comprehensive analysis of the development of the *katchi abadis* in Karachi, see Arif Hasan, 'The informal sector: assessment and review of existing conditions' (Karachi, 1990).

5. Arif Hasan, Government, International Agencies, and OPP Collaboration for the Replication of OPP's Low Cost Sanitation Program, a paper from the Second Annual World Bank Conference on Environmentally Sustainable Development, September 1994, Washington, DC, p. 7.

6. In March of 1986 the Prime Minister announced that all *katchi abadis* in Pakistan were to be given legal status and could not be demolished.

7. Perween Rahman and Hafeez Arain, *The Role of Thalla in Housing* (Karachi: Orangi Pilot Project, 1986), p. 1.

8. Akhter Hameed Khan, *Orangi Pilot Project Programs* (Karachi: OPP-RTI, 1994), p. 3.

9. The exchange rate in 1995 is $1 = Rs 25.45.

10. Arif Hasan, 'Urban services through community participation: a study of the Low-Cost Sanitation Program of the Orangi Pilot Project', *OPP's Low Cost Sanitation and Housing Program – An Overview* (Karachi, 1986), p. 6.

11. Ibid.

12. Arif Hasan, 'Orangi Pilot Project, Karachi, a low-cost sewer system by low-income Pakistanis', in Bertha Turner (ed.), *Building Community* (London, 1988), p. 85.

13. Arif Hasan, 'The housing programme of the Orangi Pilot Project', in *OPP's Low Cost Sanitation and Housing Program – An Overview* (Karachi, 1986), p. 65.

14. The BCCI scandal has not affected the work of OPP. Aga Hasan Abidi is revered in Pakistan as a generous philanthropist and as someone who challenged the Western banking supremacy. To date no BCCI banks in Pakistan have been closed nor are they expected to close. The BCCI foundation is a separate organization and not directly connected to the bank.

15. Orangi Pilot Report, *46th Quarterly Progress Report* (Karachi, April–May–June 1991), p. 2.

16. Hasan, 'Urban services through community participation' (Karachi, 1986), p. 6.

17. Ibid.

18. Hasan, 'Orangi Pilot Project, Karachi, a low-cost sewer system by low-income Pakistanis'.

19. For a comprehensive analyses of Dr Akhter Hameed Khan's life and development of his philosophy for community work, see A. F. Robertson, *People and the State* (Cambridge: Cambridge University Press, 1984), pp. 44–5; and Adele Freedman, 'Dr Akhtar Hameed Khan', *Mimar*, 34 (March 1990), p. 27.

20. Hasan, 'Urban services through community participation', pp. 2–5.

21. Akhter Hameed Khan, *Orangi Pilot Project Program*s (Karachi: OPP-RTI, 1994), p. 7.

22. Khan, *Orangi Pilot Project Programs*s (Karachi: Orangi Pilot Project, 1991), p. 9.

23. Ibid.

24. Ibid.

25. Hasan, 'Urban services through community participation,' pp. 6–7.

26. Ibid., p. 7.

27. Ibid., p. 8.

28. Ibid., p. 9.

29. Arif Hasan, Government, International Agencies, and OPP Collaboration for the Replication of OPP's Low Cost Sanitation Program, a paper from the Second Annual World Bank Conference on Environmentally Sustainable Development, September 1994, Washington, DC, USA.

30. Akhter Hameed Khan, *Orangi Pilot Project Programs* (Karachi: OPP–RTI, 1994), p. 10.

31. *Low Cost Sanitation Program of the Orangi Pilot Project – Statistical Data* (Karachi: Orangi Pilot Project, November 1989).

32. Ibid.

33. Ibid.

34. Akhter Hameed Khan, *Orangi Pilot Project Programs* (Karachi: OPP–RTI, 1994), p. 24.

35. Hasan, Government, International Agencies, and OPP Collaboration for the Replication of OPP's Low Cost Sanitation Program, p. 6.

36. Akhter Hameed Khan, *Orangi Pilot Project Programs* (Karachi: OPP–RTI, 1994), p. 24.

37. Ibid., p. 27.

38. Ibid., p. 28.

39. Ibid., p. 29.

40. Perween Rahman and Hafeez Arain, in *The Role of Thalla in Housing* (Karachi: Orangi Pilot Project, 1986), provide an interesting and detailed account of how the thallawala operates, how he is able to provide credit to home owners, where he gets his building material from and his actual costs of doing business.

41. Ibid.

42. Ibid.

43. Hasan, 'The housing programme of the Orangi Pilot Project', pp. 65–6.

44. Khan, *House Building by Low-Income Families in Orangi* (Karachi: OPP, 1990), p. 9.

45. Based on interview with Mr Raza, a thallawala, in Orangi, August 1991.

46. Rahman and Arain, *The Role of Thalla in Housing*, p. 13.

47. Ibid., p. 24.

48. Ibid., p. 23.

49. Khan, *Orangi Pilot Programs*, (Karachi, OPP-RTI, 1994), p. 19.

50. Another independent supplier of batten and tile has been functioning in Korangi, which is another settlement in southern Karachi. However, the size of slabs used there is thinner, i.e., one and a half inches thick. Slabs designed by OPP have a recess on their underside which forms a pleasant pattern when viewed from inside the house.

51. Rahman and Arain, *The Role of Thalla in Housing*, p. 13.

52. Arif Hasan, Government, International Agencies, and OPP Collaboration for the Replication of OPP's Low Cost Sanitation Program, p. 7.

53. Ibid., p. 8.

54. For a detailed evaluation of OPP's replication of the Orangi Project, see Arif Hasan, *Scaling-Up of the OPP's Low-Cost Sanitation Programme* (OPP-RTI Publication, 1993).

55. Khan, *Orangi Pilot Project Programs* (Karachi: OPP-RTI, 1994), p. 12.

56 Hasan, Government, International Agencies, and OPP Collaboration for the Replication of OPP's Low Cost Sanitation Program.

57. Akhter Hameed Khan, *Orangi Pilot Project Programs* (Karachi: OPP-RTI, 1994), p. 13.

58. See, Hasan, *Scaling-Up of the OPP's Low-Cost Sanitation Programme* (OPP-RTI Publication, 1993), pp. 59–65.

4. Multi-sectoral partnerships for environmental micro-enterprise development

1. Nemat Guenena, *The Zabbaleen Environmental and Development Program* (EQI, 1995).

2. It is worth mentioning that most buildings serviced are in wealthy neighbourhoods where in addition to the fee contracted with the owner of the building, a monthly fee from the residential unit was charged. In the early 1980s a monthly sum of LE 0.50–1.50 per residential unit was charged. Today, fees range from LE 1–5 depending on the area. Prices in low-income districts range from LE 1–1.5, from LE 1.3 to 2.5 in middle-income districts and from LE 2.5 to 5 in more affluent districts. It is also important to note that most poor residents cannot afford to pay for this service and for Zabbaleen, the value of household waste in poor areas is minimal, therefore many poor neighbourhoods remain unserviced or rely on the municipal services.

3. Environmental Quality International, *People of the Gabbal: Life and Work among the Zabbaleen of Manshiet Nasser*, Report No. 3, Solid Waste Component: The First Egypt Urban Development Project (Cairo, 1981), pp. 11–12. Also, Marie Assad and Nadra Garas, 'Experiments in community development in a Zabbaleen settlement', *Cairo Papers in Social Science*, Vol. 16: 4 (Cairo: The American University in Cairo, 1994).

4. The Zabbaleen Environmental and Development Programme has been adapted from the case-study prepared by the Mega-Cities Project and included in the monograph *Environmental Justice; Promising Solutions at the Intersection of Environment and Poverty* (Mega-Cities Project Inc., 1994).

5. Several reports prepared by EQI and others have been referred to extensively for this section. They include: Mounir S. Neamatalla, Ragui Assaad, Linda Oldham, Amr Soueni and Fatma El Gohry, *Solid Waste Collection and Recycling in Cairo: a System in Transition* (Cairo, 1985). Sabbour Associates, *Manshiet Nasser Upgrading: Final Report Part I and II Urban Planning*, presented to Cairo Governorate (Cairo 1982), and Tecke Belgin, Linda Oldham and Frederic C. Shorter, *A Place to Live: Families and Child Health in a Cairo Neighborhood* (Cairo: The American University in Cairo Press, 1994).

6. Mounir S. Neamatalla, Ragui Assaad, Linda Oldham, Amr Soueni and Fatma El Gohry, *Solid Waste Collection and Recycling in Cairo: a System in Transition* (Cairo, 1985).

7. The demand for soil conditioners is large and rapidly increasing. Market studies indicate that there is a general shortage of such conditioners. The demand to supply ratios for organic soil conditioners ranges from 5:1 to 7:1 depending on the nature of the soil and on the availability of alternatives. The input material at Moqattam plant is very fine and rich in organic content; accordingly, the plant produces only fine compost at a maximum capacity of 25,500 tons/year. Nemat Guenena, *The Zabbaleen Environmental and Development Program* (EQI, 1995).

8. Mounir S. Neamatalla, Ragui Assaad, Linda Oldham, Amr Soueni and Fatma El Gohry, *Solid Waste Collection and Recycling in Cairo: a System in Transition*, Cairo, 1985.

9. Nemat Guenena, *The Zabbaleen Environmental and Development Program* (EQI, 1995).

10. Ibid.

11. Ibid.

12. Ibid.

13. In Chapter 8, I have discussed some aspects of the Zabbaleen transfer to Bombay and Manila; see also Akhtar Badshah and Reena Lazar, 'Sharing approaches that work: transfer and adaptation of urban innovations', *Special Issue Cooperation South – New Directions* (TCDC, New York, May 1995).

14. Nemat Guenena, *The Zabbaleen Environmental and Development Program* (EQI, 1995).

5. Local government and private sector partnerships for land-sharing and incremental development

1. United Nations Centre for Human Settlements (UNCHS), 'Pressure on the supply of land for the poor' (1984), p. 25.

2. Banashree Mitra, 'Delhi's unauthorized colonies', *Architecture + Design* (Jan–Feb 1988), p. 31.

3. Ibid., p. 34.

4. Shlomo Angel and Somsook Boonyabancha, 'Land-sharing as an alternative to eviction', *Third World Planning Review*, 10, 2 (May 1988), p. 108.

5. Yasmeen Lari, 'The Lines Area Resettlement Project, Karachi', *Urban Housing*, Proceedings of the 2nd seminar in the series, Designing in Islamic Cultures (Cambridge, Mass: the Aga Khan Program for Islamic Architecture, 1982), pp. 56–64.

6. Somsook Boonyabancha, 'A slum community's thirty-year struggle in Thailand', in Bertha Turner (ed.), *Building Community* (London, 1988), pp. 75–80.

7. H. A. Waris Husain, *Establishment of Pavement Traders (Informal Sector) in Samarinda City* (Samarinda, Indonesia, n.d.), p. 7.

8. The exact number of original occupants that were given either kiosks or stalls was not made available to the author, even though a full inventory of the settlement was done before the project was started.

9. All figures and technical data have been used courtesy of the Aga Khan Award for Architecture. Romi Khosla, 'Technical Report, Citra Niaga, Samarinda, Indonesia', 1989.

10. The analysis of the present values of the shops and their earning capabilities were determined by the author on a visit to the project in January 1990. The analysis of the project is based on my survey and interviews with the mayor, officials from the city authority, the management board, the shopkeepers and the architects involved.

11. For a comprehensive report, see Akhtar Badshah, 'Land sharing: an innovative approach to the squatter problem', *Housing, Squatter Settlements and the Informal Sector* (Berkeley: Center for Environmental Design Research, 1991), pp. 1–25.

12. Adnan Hameed Aliani and Yap Kioe Sheng, 'The incremental development scheme in Hyderabad: an innovative approach to low-income housing', *Cities* (May, 1990), p. 138.

13. The Pakistani rupee was valued at Rs 24.60 to a US $1 in August 1991. The rate of exchange in 1986 was Rs 17 to $1.

14. Tasneem Siddiqui, 'Innovation and success in sheltering the urban poor', in Robert Powell, (ed.), *The Architecture of Housing* (Geneva: Aga Khan Trust for Culture, 1990), p. 76.

15. Aliani and Kioe Sheng, 'The incremental development scheme in Hyderabad', p. 140.

16. Jan J. van der Linden, *Successful Supply of Plots for the Poor: the Case of Hyderabad*, Urban Research Working Papers (Amsterdam: Free University, 1989), p. 16.

17. Ibid., p. 18.

18. Ibid., p. 19.

19. Ibid.

20. Arif Hasan, *Evaluation of the HDA's Khuda-ki-basti Incremental Housing Scheme* (Karachi: House Building Finance Corporation, 1990), pp. 27–39.

21. Aliani and Kioe Sheng, 'The incremental development scheme in Hyderabad', p. 144.

22. Octroi is a tax levied in Pakistan on any goods manufactured in one city and transported to another city. In the case of Khuda-ki-basti the octroi tax on building materials manufactured in Hyderabad added another level of hardship for the residents.

23. Ibid., p. 143.

24. Hasan, *Evaluation of HDA's Khuda-ki-basti Incremental Housing Scheme*, pp. 41–2.

25. Aliani and Kioe Sheng, 'The incremental development scheme in Hyderabad', p. 143.

26. Hasan, *Evaluation of HDA's Khuda-ki-basti Incremental Housing Scheme*, p. 41.

27. Ibid.

28. Ibid., p. 40.

29. Jan J. van der Linden, 'Successful supply of plots for the poor: the case of Hyderabad', p. 60.

30. '180-sq. ft. subsidized houses planned', *The Times of India* (28 July 1991), pp. 1–3.

6. Local government and private sector partnerships for low-cost housing design

1. The statistics were compiled by the foundation from the 1971 census. See Vastu Shilpa Foundation, *Aranya: An Approach to Settlement Design* (Ahmedabad, HUDCO, 1990), p. 9.

2. According to an interview with M. L. Bhatt, chief engineer and head of planning, IDA, on 16 July 1991.

3. Since there was no school of architecture in Indore and no well-known architects had practised there, he organized in 1982 an exhibition of work by architects from the surrounding states to which the public, developers and government officials were all invited. Architects who showed works included B. V. Doshi, Anant Raje, Suryakant Patel, Hasmukh Patel, Uttam Jain and Kanvinde. As part of this exercise, IDA also felt that some of its projects should be designed by these architects. When Doshi visited Indore he was taken around the city and shown the areas to be developed as part of the master plan. They asked him to design either a housing project or a bus terminal, but when Doshi saw a large open area near Dewas, along the national highway, and inquired as to what was being planned for it he was told it was for a site-and-services project. He saw that to the south of this site, Sector 54 was already under development, and asked whether he could do this project. He was told that a project was already being developed by IDA with the government in Bhopal and the World Bank and that the project had already had initial approval.

4. The current rate of exchange is Rs 30 =US$1.

5. Vastu Shilpa Foundation, *Aranya: an Approach to Settlement Design*, p. 11.

6. Ibid., p. 12.

7. Vastu Shilpa Foundation, 'Residential open spaces – a behavioral analysis', (Ahmedabad, May 1988), pp. 147–57.

8. Ibid.

9. Caminos developed a model and tools for determining and calculating the services needed for housing projects. Caminos's method can be described as a reduction of any housing environment to a set of quantifiable and comparable data. See Horacio Caminos and Reinhard Goethert, *Urbanization Primer* (Cambridge, Mass: MIT Press, 1978), pp. 104–15.

10. Interview with B. V. Doshi on 2 August 1991.

11. Vastu Shilpa Foundation, *Aranya: an Approach to Settlement Design*, pp. 25–6.

12. Ibid., p. 22.

13. Ibid., pp. 9–10.

14. Airoli, a sites-and services scheme in New Bombay, financed by the World Bank and at that time one of the largest site-and-services projects, is typical of sites-and services projects in India.

15. Vikram Bhatt and his students from McGill were in Indore doing studies of the slums there. They were critical of Doshi's approach and questioned its viability. Doshi asked IDA to let the McGill group try and develop an alternate design.

16. Interview with M. L. Bhatt on 19 July 1991.

17. In India there is a reservation system to help the so-called 'backward classes' which includes the 'Harijans' or untouchables, tribal and other groups that need special assistance. In October 1990 there were major riots in India when the government increased the quota for these classes in all government jobs and education.

18. In India generally, in housing projects property changes 'owners' on what is called a power of attorney. A legal document transferring the power from one individual to another is prepared. This allows the new 'owner' to use and *de facto* own the place. The title is, however, retained in the name of the previous owner. To ensure that the previous owner does not come back to claim the property, a rental agreement for 30 or more years is also signed, making it practically impossible for the original owner to reclaim possession. Rental laws in India make it very difficult for a landlord to evict a tenant and such an agreement ensures against eviction. Recent survey of Bodella housing in New Delhi shows that over a seven-year period, of the 630 families that live there, only 10 to 12 original families to whom the plot were allotted are still living there. It is also interesting to note that this transfer took place in the first two years of the scheme.

19. Two cooperative housing schemes in Delhi, one developed by the private sector and the other by the government, show that the primary aim of such cooperatives is for financing the scheme. Some restrictions for transfer of property have also been implemented here.

20. Mulk Raj, the ex-Director of Finance, HUDCO, suggests putting the house title in the name of the wife, as she is much less likely to sell out than a husband.

21. Interview with M. L. Bhatt on 19 July 1991.

22. In the Khuda-ki-basti project local suppliers were encouraged to set up shop around the township. In principle no octroi tax was to be levied for building materials bought by Khuda-ki-basti residents. However, in practice this has not worked. The three octroi posts between Hyderabad and Khuda-ki-basti invariably levy a tax. Here police, leaders or the court have been of no help.

23. Narmada is a major river in Central India. There is a river redevelopment project that has been undertaken with financing from the IMF and the World Bank. The Narmada Valley Project is expected to inundate an area of hundreds of miles, drowning out several thousand villages. A major controversy has erupted between environment protection groups who are looking after the resettlement of the villages and government officials in charge of the project.

24. Studies of Indore slums by Rybczynski et al., *How the Other Half Builds* (Montreal: Center for Minimum Cost Housing, McGill University, 1984 and 1986), pp. 3–14; they describe common spaces being shared by residents; however, they do not throw light on why and how that sharing of spaces comes about.

25. Manuel Castells, *The Urban Question* (Cambridge, MA: MIT Press, 1977), p. 108.

26. In Indore one of these projects involves 20,000 families located in river beds or in major access areas in the development plan. The National Housing Bank has about Rs 1,000 million for the purpose. Even though a relocation plan has been drawn up and these families will be relocated on IDA schemes or housing board schemes, Aranya township is not being considered as one possible site. Also no plans that relate to community and family groupings have been worked out.

7. A new agenda for urban equity and sustainability

1. UNCHS, *Global Report on Human Settlements* (Nairobi, 1988).

2. Jan Pronk and Mahbub ul Haq, 'Sustainable developments must be fair to all people and all resources', *Earth Summit Times* (13 May 1992), pp. 18–19.

3. G. Shabbir Cheema and Dennis Rondinelli (eds), *Decentralization and Development: Policy Implementation in Developing Countries* (Beverly Hills, CA: Sage Publications, 1983), p. 11.

4. George Peterson, 'Urban economy and productivity', in *State of Urbanization in Asia and the Pacific* (Bangkok: UNESCAP, 1993).

5. Caroline Moser, 'Community participation in urban projects in the Third World', *Progress in Planning*, 32 (1989), pp. 71–133.

6. Perween Rahman and Hafeez Arain, *The Role of Thalla in Housing* (Karachi: the Orangi Pilot Project, 1986), p. 10.

7. Mike Douglass, 'The political economy of urban poverty and environmental management in Asia: access, empowerment and community-based alternatives', *Environment and Urbanization* 4 (October 1992), pp. 9–32.

8. See Government of India, *Report of the National Commission on Urbanization*, Vol. 2 (New Delhi, August 1988). Also see Charles Correa, *The New Landscape* (Bombay, 1985), p. 54.

9. Jamel Akbar, *Crisis in the Built Environment: the Case of the Muslim City* (Singapore: Concept Media, 1988), pp. 17–22.

10. The World Bank, *World Development Report 1992: Development and the Environment* (New York: Oxford University Press, 1992), Box 5.5, p. 107.

11. Arif Hasan, *Evaluation of the HDA's Khuda ki basti Incremental Housing Scheme* (Karachi: House Building Finance Corporation of Pakistan, 1990), suggested, based on his evaluation of the block sizes there, that 100 families represents a workable block size.

12. Vikram Bhatt et al., *How the Other Half Builds*, Vol. 3 (Montreal: Center for Minimum Cost Housing, McGill University, 1990), p. 7.

13. Yatin Pandya, 'Slum houses as a user responsive product: a case study, Indore, India', M. Arch. thesis, McGill University, Montreal, 1988.

14. Madhu Jain and Ramesh Menon, 'The greying of India', *India Today* (September 1991), p. 25.

15. Villa Victoria, designed in the late sixties in Boston, is one example. The elderly are located in a high-rise tower while the rest of the community live in townhouses. More recent projects have tried a more integrated approach.

16. Charles Correa, *The New Landscape* (Bombay: Book Society of India, 1985), p. 54.

17. Witold Rybczynski et al., *How the Other Half Builds*, Vol. 2 (Montreal: Center for Minimum Cost Housing, McGill University, 1986), pp. 24–36.

18. Bhatt et al., *How the Other Half Builds*, Vol. 3, p. 5.

19. For examples of traditional patterns of how clans occupy particular areas in towns, see Douglas Goodfriend, 'Old Delhi: modern lessons from traditional architecture and urban form', *Design* (January/March 1981), and Akbar, *Crisis in the Built Environment*, pp. 71–92.

20. Clare Cooper-Marcus and Wendy Sarkissian, *Housing as if People Mattered* (Berkeley: University of California Press, 1986), p. 42.

21. Bong Koo Lee, 'Major urban development issues: an overview', *Urban Policy Issues*, Regional Seminar on Major National Urban Policy Issues, Manila, 3–7 February 1987, Asian Development Bank, pp. 31–3.

22. Institutional arrangements and efficiency of implementation have already been touched upon in Chapter 2 and will also be discussed in the concluding chapter.

23. Kulbushan Jain, 'Morphostructure of a planned city, Jaipur, India', *Architecture Plus Urbanism* (August 1978), pp. 107–20.

24. Christopher Alexander and Kevin Lynch are among the scholars that have studied city form and shown why areas of cities are vibrant and full of variety. See Kevin Lynch, *A Theory of Good City Form* (Cambridge, MA: MIT Press, 1981) and Christopher Alexander, *A Pattern Language* (New York: Oxford University Press, 1977).

25. See UNDP, *Cities, People and Poverty: Urban Development Cooperation for 1990s* (New York, United Nations Development Programme, 1991).

8. Our urban future: opportunities and challenges

1. Akhtar Badshah and Reena Lazar, 'Sharing approaches that work: transfer and adaptation of urban innovations', *Special Issue Cooperation South – New Directions*, (New York: TCDC, May 1995), pp. 29–33.

2. Janice Perlman and Elwood Hopkins, 'From city to city,' *Healthcare Forum Journal* (May–June 1994), p. 40.

3. UNDP, *Proceedings of the International Colloquium of Mayors on Social Development*, 18–19 August, 1994, p. 65.

4. Akhtar Badshah and Reena Lazar, 'Sharing approaches that work: transfer and adaptation of urban innovations'.

5. Robert Davies, keynote address at the conference on 'Action in Partnership', organized by the Prince of Wales Business Leaders Forum, Rio de Janeiro, Brazil, May 1995.

6. The Mega-Cities Project is an international network of NGOs working in 18 of the world's largest urban areas. The project is dedicated to building and

maintaining a network of transnational urban leaders through which the transfer of successful solutions can take place.

7. Manuel Castells, 'The governance of Mega-Cities in the New World Order', keynote address at the Mega-Cities Seventh Annual Meeting, Jakarta, August 1993.

8. The Mega-Cities teams involved in the 'Magic Eyes' transfer are: in Bangkok, Orapin Sopchokchai, Thailand Development Research Institute (TDRI); in Rio de Janeiro, Marlene Fernandes at the Instituto Brasileiro de Administracao (IBAM).

9. This transfer has been initiated by the Mega-Cities Project, Inc.

10. The Mega-Cities teams involved in the Zabbaleen transfers are: in Cairo, Mounir Neamatalla at Environmental Quality International; in Manila, Maria-Anna Ignacio at the Partnership of Philippine Support Service Agencies; in Bombay, Sneha Palnitkar at the All India Institute for Local Self-Government (AIILSG); in Los Angeles, Gene Grigsby at the University of California, Los Angeles, with Charlotte Bullock at Concerned Citizens of South Central.

11. Arif Hasan, *Scaling-Up of the OPP's Low-Cost Sanitation Programme* (OPP-RTI Publication, 1993), p. 23.

12. Akhtar Badshah and Richard Ludwig, 'Regional Program for urban management in Asia and The Pacific Region', report prepared for the Regional Programme Division, Regional Bureau for Asia and the Pacific (United Nations Development Programme, 1992), p. 17.

13. Khuda-ki-basti is a clear example of where design decisions have had an obvious influence on community involvement.

14. Aranya is an example.

15. In Aranya and Khuda-ki-basti development agency officials, planners and good designers had intentions, but problems arose in these projects because the process for self-control was prescriptive.

16. Aranya and Khuda-ki-basti both highlight the complexity of developing new housing programmes. The level of interagency coordination required is complex, and the managerial and persuasion skills needed are intricate.

17. In Indore, the settlement-improvement programme which is city-wide and undertaken by the same agency, has problems in coordination between different parts of the city. The importance of information exchange between various sub-programmes is equally important if such programmes are to be successful.

18. See G. Shabbir Cheema, *Urban Shelter and Services* (New York: Praeger, 1987), p. 200.

19. Citra Niaga and Orangi are two examples where dialogue between the various groups was the key to achieving an open relationship which allowed the project to be implemented and successful.

20. The misuse of power by the local *dalals* in Khuda-ki-basti is a clear example of how such new-found power can cause another set of problems.

21. Khuda-ki-basti and Citra Niaga are two examples where community involvement was directed and limited to particular aspects of the project. For a theoretical discussion, see International Research Workshop Seminar (IRWS), 'Land value changes and the impact of urban policy upon land valorization processes in developing countries', *International Journal of Urban and Regional Research*, 15, 4 (1991), pp. 623–8.

22. Peter M. Ward and Chris Macoloo, 'Articulation theory and self-help housing practice in the 1990s', *International Journal of Urban and Regional Research*, 16, 1 (1992), p. 60, have also proposed a similar level of research be undertaken.

23. In Indore, officials from the Indore Development Authority that were

undertaking squatter settlement upgrading were unaware of the Orangi approach. However, they were aware that a successful project had been undertaken by the Hyderabad Development Authority.

24. In Chapter 2 the advantages and risks of private sector, NGO and community involvement have been discussed. The case-studies have also highlighted what the advantages and risks are.

25. The Mega-Cities Project work on 34 transfers, 8 international and 26 within and between New York City and Los Angeles, shows some evidence that transferring an idea from one community to another does more than simply expand the reach of a particular solution, it also broadens the focus of urban leaders from their immediate geographical vicinity to their entire city or society.

26. Nabeel Hamdi, *Housing Without Houses* (New York: Van Nostrand Reinhold, 1991), p. 86. Also see John Habraken, 'The control of complexity', *Places*, 4, 2 (1987), pp. 3–15, and Cheema, *Urban Shelter and Services*.

Bibliography

Abrams, Charles, *Man's Struggle for Shelter in an Urbanizing World*, Cambridge, MA: MIT Press, 1964.

Abt, Clark C., *Serious Games*, New York: Viking, 1970.

Achtenburg, Emily and Peter Marcuse, 'Towards the decommodification of housing', in *Critical Perspective on Housing*, ed. Bratt, Hartman and Meyerson, Philadelphia: Temple University Press, 1986, pp. 474–83.

Akbar, Jamel, *Crisis in the Built Environment: the Case of the Muslim City*, Singapore: Concept Media, 1988.

Alexander, Christopher et al., *A Timeless Way of Building*, New York: Oxford University Press, 1979.

— *A Pattern Language*, New York: Oxford University Press, 1977.

Aliani, Adnan Hameed and Yap Kioe Sheng, 'The incremental development scheme in Hyderabad: an innovative approach to low-income housing', *Cities*, May 1990, pp. 133–48.

Alimuddin, Salim, 'Dynamics of housing in low income urban settlement: case study', B. Arch. thesis, Dawood College of Engineering and Technology, Karachi, 1989.

Altman, I. and A. Wandersman (eds), 'Home Environments', *Human Behavior and Environment*, 8, New York: Plenum Press, 1985.

— 'Neighborhood and Community Environments', *Human Behavior and Environment*, 9, New York: Plenum Press, 1987.

Anderson, Stanford (ed.), *On Streets*, Cambridge, MA: MIT Press, 1986.

— 'The fiction of function', *Assemblage*, 2, 1988, pp. 19–31.

Angel, Shlomo, 'Instead of focusing on housing, focus on urban land development', *Open House International*, Special Issue Biennial International Shelter Workshop, 11: 4 (1986).

— and Somsook Boonyabancha, 'Land-sharing as an alternative to eviction', *Third World Planning Review*, 10: 2 (May 1988), pp. 107–22.

— and Stan Benjamin, 'Seventeen reasons why the squatter problem can't be solved', *Ekistics*, 242 (January 1976).

— et al., *Land for Housing the Poor*, Singapore: Select Books, 1988.

Appleyard, Donald, *Planning a Pluralist City*, Cambridge, MA: MIT Press, 1976.

Argyris, C., R. Putman and D. McCain, *Action Science – Concepts, Methods, and Skills for Research and Intervention*, London and San Francisco: Josey-Bass, 1985.

Arnold, Peri E., 'Herbert Hoover and the continuity of American policy', *Public Policy*, 20: 4 (Fall 1972), pp. 525–44.

Arnstein, Sherry A., 'A ladder of citizen participation', *Journal of the American Institute of Planners*, 45: 4 (12 July 1969).

Assad, Marie and Nadra Garas, 'Experiments in community development in a Zabbaleen settlement', *Cairo Papers in Social Science*, 16: 4, Cairo: American University Press, 1994.

Atterbury, Grosvenor, 'How to get low cost houses', *Proceedings of the Fifth National Conference on Housing*, Providence, 1916.

Bacon, Edmund, 'Language of cities', *Design and Conservation in the City*, ed. Gerald Dix and John Nelson Tarn, Town Planning Review, 1985, pp. 174–96.

— *Design of Cities*, New York: Viking Press, 1967.

Badshah, Akhtar, 'Land sharing: an innovative approach to the squatter problem', *Housing, Squatter Settlements and the Informal Sector*, 27, Berkeley, CA: Center for Environmental Design Research, 1991, pp. 1–25.

— and Alka G. Badshah, 'An approach to designing residential quarters', in *Preservation of Islamic Architectural Heritage*, Riyadh: Arab Urban Development Institute, 1988, pp. 291–7.

— and Reena Lazar, 'Sharing approaches that work: transfer and adaptation of urban innovations', *Cooperation South*, UNDP-TCDC, May 1995, pp. 29–33.

— and Richard Ludwig, 'Regional Program for urban management in Asia and the Pacific Region', report prepared for the Regional Program Division, Regional Bureau for Asia and the Pacific, United Nations Development Programme, 1992.

Bamberger, Michael and Albert Harth Deneke, 'Can shelter programs meet low-income needs? The experience of El Salvador', in *Low-Income Housing in the Developing World*, ed. Geoffrey Payne, New York: John Wiley and Sons, 1984, pp. 37–54.

Bauer, Catherine, *Modern Housing*, Boston and New York: Houghton Mifflin Company, 1934, reprinted New York: Arno Press, 1974.

— 'The dreary deadlock of public housing', *Architectural Forum*, 106, May 1957, pp. 140–2.

Belgin, Tecke, Linda Oldham and Frederic Shorter, *A Place to Live: Families and Child Health in a Cairo Neighborhood*, Cairo: American University Press, 1994.

Bender, R. and J. Parman, 'A framework for industrialization', in *The Form of Housing*, ed. Sam Davis, New York: Van Nostrand Reinhold, 1977, pp. 173–90.

Benjamin, Solomon, *Jobs, Land and Urban Development: the Economic Success of Small Scale Manufacturers in East Delhi, India*, Cambridge, MA: Lincoln Institute of Land Policy, 1991.

Bentz, Bruce, 'User design and construction of housing', in *Conference on People and Physical Environment Research*, ed. D. Joiner et al., Wellington, NZ: P.D. Hasselberg Government Printer, 1983, pp. 392–400.

Berger, Peter and Richard Neuhaus, *To Empower People: the Role of Mediating Structures in Public Policy*, Washington, DC: American Enterprise Institute for Public Policy, 1971.

Bertaud, Marie-Agnes, *A Model for the Preparation of Physical Development of Alternatives for Urban Settlement Projects (The Bertaud Model)*, Economic Development Institute (EDI), Washington DC: World Bank, 1985.

Bhatt, Vikram, et al., *How the Other Half Builds*, Vol. 3. Montreal: Center for Minimum Cost Housing, McGill University, Research Paper 11, 1990.

Boonyabancha, Somsook, 'A slum community's thirty-year struggle in Thailand', in *Building Community*, ed. Bertha Turner, London, 1988, pp. 75–80.

Bottomley, T., *An Introduction to Co-operatives*, London: Intermediate Technology Publications, 1979.

Boudon, Philippe, *Lived-in Architecture: Le Corbusier's Pessac Revisited*, Cambridge, MA: MIT Press, 1979.

Boyer, Christine M., *Dreaming the Rational City: the Myth of American City Planning*, Cambridge, MA: MIT Press, 1983.

Bratt, Rachel, *Rebuilding a Low-Income Housing Policy*, Philadelphia: Temple University Press, 1989.

Broadbent, Geoffrey, *Emerging Concepts in Urban Space Design*, London: Van Nostrand Reinhold, 1990.

Bromley, R. (ed.), *The Urban Informal Sector: Critical Perspectives on Employment and Housing Policies*, Oxford: Pergamon Press, 1979.

Bullock, Nicholas and James Reed, *The Movement for Housing Reform in Germany and France 1840–1914*, Cambridge: Cambridge University Press, 1985.

Burgess, Rod, 'Petty commodity housing or dweller control? a critique of John Turner's views on housing policy', in *The Urban Informal Sector: Critical Perspectives on Employment and Housing Policies*, ed. R. Bromley, Oxford: Pergamon Press, 1979, pp. 1105–35.

Burnett, John, *A Social History of Housing 1815–1985*, London: Methuen, 1986.

Burns, L. S. and B. Ferguson, 'Criteria for future shelter and settlement policies in developing countries', in *Shelter, Settlement and Development*, ed. Lloyd Rodwin, United Nations Publication, Winchester, MA: Allen and Unwin, 1987, pp. 281–303.

Cabannes, Yves, 'Architects: social catalysts or alchemists of forms?', *The Architect as Enabler*, special issue of *Architecture and Competitions*, 1985, pp. 103–4.

Caminos, Horacio and Reinhard Goethert, *Urbanization Primer*, Cambridge, MA: MIT Press, 1978.

Casciato, Maristella, 'Housing in Europe 1900–1940' (notes from class taught at MIT, 1988).

Castells, Manuel, 'The governance of mega-cities in the New World Order', keynote address at the Mega-Cities Seventh Annual Meeting, Jakarta, August 1993.

— *The Urban Question*, Cambridge, MA: MIT Press, 1977.

Chana, T. S., 'Nairobi: Dandora and other projects', in *Low-Income Housing in the Developing World*, ed. G. Payne, New York: John Wiley and Sons, 1984, pp. 17–36.

Chauhan, Akhtar, 'Housing the people', *Architecture + Design*, November–December, 1991, pp. 71–9.

Cheema, G. Shabbir (ed.), *Urban Management: Policies and Innovations in Developing Countries*, Westport, CT: Praeger, 1993.

— *Urban Shelter and Services: Public Policies and Management Approaches*, New York: Praeger, 1987.

— and Dennis A. Rondinelli (eds), *Decentralization and Development: Policy Implementation in Developing Countries*, Beverly Hills, CA: Sage Publications, 1983.

Chen, M., 'Development projects for women: Oxfam America's Program in India and Bangladesh', paper presented at the Conference on International Women's Decade and Beyond, New York: American Association of University Women, 1984.

CIDCO, *New Bombay: an Outline of Progress*, Bombay: July 1989.

Cockburn, Charles and Sultan Barakat, 'Community prosperity through reconstruction management', *Architecture + Design*, January–February 1991, p. 61.

Cohen, Michael A., 'The challenge of replicability: towards a new paradigm for urban shelter in developing countries', *Open House International*, 8: 4 (1983), pp. 15–21.

Coleman, Alice, *Utopia on Trial*, London: Hilary Shipman, 1985.

Collier, David, *Squatters and Oligarchs*, Baltimore, MD: Johns Hopkins University Press, 1976.

Cooper-Marcus, Clare, 'User needs research in housing', in *The Form of Housing*, ed. Sam Davis, New York: Van Nostrand Reinhold, 1977, pp. 139–70.

— and W. Sarkissian, *Housing as if People Mattered: Site Design Guidelines for Medium-Density Family Housing*, Berkeley: University of California Press, 1986.

Correa, Charles, 'An essay for JAE', *Journal of Architecture Education*, 40: 2 (1987), 12.

— *The New Landscape*, Bombay: Book Society of India, 1985.

— 'Transfers and transformations', *Design for High-Intensity Development*, proceedings of an International Conference on Urban Design. Cambridge, MA: Aga Khan Program for Islamic Architecture, 1986, pp. 11–14.

Cromley, Elizabeth, 'Apartments and collective life in nineteenth-century New York', in *New Household New Housing*, ed. Karen Franck and Sherry Ahrentzen, New York: Van Nostrand Reinhold, 1989, pp. 20–46.

Curtis, William, 'Towards an authentic regionalism', *Mimar*, 19 (January–March 1986).

Davey, Kenneth, *Elements of Urban Management*, Washington, DC: Urban Management Programme, 1993.

Davies, Robert, 'Keynote Address' at the conference on *Action in Partnership*, organized by the Prince of Wales Business Leaders Forum, Rio de Janeiro, Brazil, May 1995.

Davis, Otto, 'Shall we encourage or discourage the apartment house?', *Housing Problems in America*, proceedings of the National Conference on Housing, Providence, 9–11 October 1916, pp. 333–9.

Davis, S. (ed.), *The Form of Housing*, New York: Van Nostrand Reinhold, 1977.

Dear, Michael and Allen J. Scott (eds), *Urbanization and Urban Planning in Capitalist Society*, London and New York: Methuen, 1981.

Diba, Kamran, 'Shushtar New Town', *Lotus International*, 36 (1982), pp. 118–24.

Dixon, Michael, 'The Canadian guru of bottom-up theory', *Boston Globe*, 10 August 1986.

Doebele, W. A., 'Land policy', in *Shelter, Settlement and Development*, ed. Lloyd Rodwin, United Nations Publication, Winchester, MA: Allen and Unwin, 1987, pp. 110–32.

Doshi, B. V. et al., 'Aranya Township, Indore', *Mimar*, 28 (June 1988).

Douglass, Mike, 'The political economy of urban poverty and environmental management in Asia: access, empowerment and community-based alternatives', *Environment and Urbanization*, 4 (October 1992).

Dowd, Douglas, 'Accumulation and crisis in US. capitalism', *Socialist Revolution*, 5: 2 (June 1975), pp. 7–44.

Doxiadis, Konstantinos, *Between Dystopia and Utopia*, London: Faber and Faber, 1966.

Drakakish-Smith, D. W. and Yen-man Yeung, 'Public housing in the city states of Hong Kong and Singapore', Occasional Paper no. 8, Canberra: Development Studies Centre, Australian National University, 1977.

Dube, S. C., *Modernization and Development: the Search for Alternative Paradigms*, London: Zed Books, 1988.

Dumarcy, Jacques, *The House in Southeast Asia*, Singapore: Oxford University Press, 1987.

Engels, F., *The Housing Question*, New York: International Publisher, 1935.

Environmental Quality International, *People of the Gabbal: Life and Work Among the Zabbaleen of Manshiet Nasser*, Report no. 3, Solid Waste Component: the First Egypt Urban Development Project, Cairo: 1981.

Fathy, Hasan, *Architecture for the Poor*, Chicago: University of Chicago Press, 1973.

Fishman, Robert, *Urban Utopias in the Twentieth Century: Ebenezer Howard, Frank Lloyd Wright, Le Corbusier*, Cambridge, MA: MIT Press, 1982.

Fonseca, Rory, 'The walled city of Delhi: urban renewal and an indigenous community', *Landscape*, 17 (Fall 1969), pp. 13–25.

Frampton, Kenneth, 'The evolution of housing concepts 1870–1970', *Lotus International*, 10 (1975), pp. 24–33.

Franck, Karen, 'Overview of collective and shared housing', in *New Household New Housing*, ed. K. Franck and S. Ahrentzen, New York: Van Nostrand Reinhold, 1989, pp. 3–19.

Freedman, Adele, 'Dr Akhtar Hameed Khan', *Mimar*, 34 (March 1990), p. 27.

Friend, John and Allen Hickling, *Planning Under Pressure: the Strategic Choice Approach*, Oxford: Pergamon Press, 1987.

Gans, Herbert, *Urban Villagers*, New York: Free Press, 1962.

Gibson, Tony, 'Sooner done than said', *Architects Journal*, 30 (1980), pp. 204–5.

Gilbert, Alan, 'The tenants of self-help housing: choice and constraint in the housing market', *Development and Change*, 14 (1983), pp. 449–77.

— and Peter Ward, 'Community participation in upgrading irregular settlements: the community response', *World Development*, 12: 9 (September 1984).

Glazer, Nathan and Mark Lilla (eds), *The Public Face of Architecture, Civic Culture and Public Spaces*, New York: The Free Press, 1987.

Global Report on Human Settlements, Oxford: Oxford University Press for the United Nations Center for Human Settlements (HABITAT), 1987.

Goldfield, David R., 'Neighborhood preservation and community values', *Neighborhood and Community Environments*, 9, ed. I. Altman and A. Wandersman, New York: Plenum Press, 1987, pp. 223–56.

Goodfriend, Douglas, 'Old Delhi: modern lessons from traditional architecture and urban form', *Design* (January/March 1981).

Government of India, *Report of the National Commission on Urbanization*, Vol. 2, New Delhi: August 1988.

Griffin, Keith, 'Economic development in a changing world', *World Development*, 9: 3, 1981. pp. 221–6.

Grigsby, William, *Housing Markets and Public Policy*, Philadelphia: University of Pennsylvania Press, 1963.

Guenena, Nemat, *The Zabbaleen Environmental Development Project*, Cairo: Environmetal Quality International, 1995.

Gutman, Robert, *Architectural Practice: a Critical View*, Princeton, NJ: Princeton Architectural Press, 1988.

— *The Design of American Housing. A Reappraisal of the Architect's Role*, New York: Publishing Center for Cultural Resources, 1985.

— 'Educating architects: pedagogy and the pendulum', in *The Public Face of Architecture*, ed. Nathan Glazer, and Mark Lilla, New York: The Free Press, 1987, pp. 443–71.

Habraken, John, 'The control of complexity', *Places*, 4: 2 (1987), pp. 3–15.

— 'Design for adaptability, change and user participation', *Housing Process and Physical*

Form, proceedings of Seminar Three in the series Architectural Transformations in the Islamic World, Aga Khan Award for Architecture, 1979, pp. 23–9.

— 'Reconciling variety and efficiency in large-scale projects', *Large Housing Projects: Design, Technology and Logistics*, proceedings of the 5th seminar in a series, Designing in Islamic Cultures, Cambridge, MA: Aga Khan Program for Islamic Architecture, 1985, pp. 46–53.

— *Supports: an Alternative to Mass Housing*, New York: Praeger Publishers, 1972.

Hall, P., 'Metropolitan settlement strategies', in *Shelter, Settlement and Development*, ed. Lloyd Rodwin, United Nations Publication, Winchester, MA: Allen and Unwin, 1987, pp. 236–62.

Hamdi, Nabeel, *Housing Without Houses: Participation, Flexibility, Enablement*, New York: Van Nostrand Reinhold, 1991.

— 'Training and education: inventing a program and getting it to work', *Habitat International*, 10: 3 (1986), pp. 131–9.

— et al., 'Planning Assistance Kit: a planning guide for community based organizations', unpublished manual, Cambridge, MA: MIT, Department of Architecture, 1989.

Hardoy, J. and D. Satterthwaite, *Squatter Citizen: Life in the Urban Third World*, London: Earthscan Publications, 1989.

— Sandy Cairncross and D. Satterthwaite (eds), *The Poor Die Young: Housing and Health in Third World Cities*, London: Earthscan Publications, 1990.

Harlean, James, 'Lessons from government experience in housing', *National Municipal Review*, 10: 8 (August 1921), pp. 427–33.

Harvey, David, *Social Justice and the City*, Baltimore, MD: Johns Hopkins University Press, 1973.

— *The Urbanization of the City*, Baltimore, MD: Johns Hopkins University Press, 1985.

Hasan, Arif, 'The Orangi Pilot Project, Karachi', in *The Human Face of Urban Development*, ed. Ismail Serageldin and Michael A. Cohen, report to the Development Community, Environmentally Sustainable Development Proceedings, Series no. 5, New York: World Bank, 1995.

— 'Government international agencies and OPP collaboration for the replication of OPP's Low Cost Sanitation Program', paper from the Second Annual World Bank Conference on Environmentally Sustainable Development, Washington, DC, September 1994.

— *Scaling-Up of the OPP's Low-Cost Sanitation Programme*, Karachi: OPP-RTI Publication, 1993.

— 'Squatter settlements in Karachi', *Mimar*, 38 (March 1991), pp. 45–7.

— *Evaluation of the HDA's Khuda-ki-basti Incremental Housing Scheme*, Karachi: House Building Finance Corporation of Pakistan, 1990.

— *Profiles of Five Pakistani Cities*, report for the Swiss Development Corporation, Karachi, 1990.

— 'The Informal Sector: Assessment and Review of Existing Conditions', unpublished report, 1990.

— 'Orangi Pilot Project, Karachi. A low-cost sewer system by low-income Pakistanis', in *Building Community*, ed. Bertha Turner London, 1988, pp. 82–8.

— *A Study on Metropolitan Fringe Development in Karachi, Focusing on Informal Land Subdivision*, report for UNESCAP, Karachi, 1987.

— *OPP'S Low Cost Sanitation and Housing Program – An Overview*, Karachi, 1986.

Hatch, Richard, Foreword, in *New Household New Housing*, ed. K. Franck, and S. Ahrentzen, New York: Van Nostrand Reinhold, 1989, pp. ix–x.

Hayden, Dolores, *Redesigning the American Dream*, New York: Norton, 1984.

Hayter, Teresa, *The Creation of World Poverty: an Alternative View to the Brandt Report*, London: Pluto Press in association with Third World First, 1981.

Heath, Thomas, *Method in Architecture*, London: John Wiley and Sons, 1984.

Hester, Randolph T., 'Participatory design and environmental justice: *pas de deux* or time to change partners', *Journal of Architectural and Planning Research*, 4: 4 (1987), pp. 289–300.

Hillier, Bill, 'Against enclosure', in *Rehumanizing Housing*, ed. N. Teymur, T. Markus and T. Woolley, London: Butterworths, 1988, pp. 63–88.

— 'The city of Alice's dreams', *Architects' Journal*, 184: 28, pp. 39–41.

— and J. Hanson, *The Social Logic of Space*, Cambridge: Cambridge University Press, 1984.

Hirschman, Albert, *Development Projects Observed*, Washington, DC: Brookings Institution, 1967.

Housing Development Finance Corporation, *Thirteenth Annual Report 1989–90*, Bombay: 1990.

Housing and Urban Development Corporation, *Twenty Years of HUDCO*, New Delhi: 1990.

Housing in the Islamic City, proceedings of a symposium held in Ankara, Turkey, July 1984.

Housing Process and Physical Form, proceedings of Seminar 3 in the series Architectural Transformations in the Islamic World, Aga Khan Award for Architecture, 1979.

Howard, Ebenezer, *Garden Cities of Tomorrow*, ed. F. J. Osborn, London: Faber and Faber, 1965.

Illich, Ivan, *Tools for Conviviality*, London: Calder and Boyers, 1973.

Ingberman, Sima, 'Normative and evolutionary housing prototypes in Germany and Austria: the viennese superblocks, 1919–1934', *Oppositions*, 13 (1978), pp. 77–82.

International Research Workshop Seminar (IRWS), 'Land value changes and the impact of urban policy upon land valorization processes in developing countries', *International Journal of Urban and Regional Research*, 15: 4 (1991), pp. 623–8.

Jackson, Antony, *A Place Called Home: a History of Low-Cost Housing in Manhattan*, Cambridge, MA: MIT Press, 1976.

Jacobs, Jane, 'The uses of city neighborhoods', in *Neighborhood, City and Metropolis, An Integrated Reader in Urban Sociology*, ed. Robert Gutman and David Popenoe, New York: Random House, 1970, pp. 819–37.

— *The Death and Life of Great American Cities: The Failure of Town Planning*, New York: Random House, 1961.

Jain, Kulbushan, 'Morphostructure of a planned city, Jaipur, India', *Architecture Plus Urbanism* (August 1978), pp. 107–20.

Jain, Madhu and Ramesh Menon, 'The Greying of India', *India Today* (September 1991), pp. 24–33.

Jakobsen, L., *Regional Planning for Urbanization in Eastern India, Improvement Programme for Metropolitan Calcutta: 1964–1971*, Calcutta: Calcutta Metropolitan Planning Organization, 1965.

Jencks, Charles, *The Language of Post-Modern Architecture*, New York: Rizzoli, 1977.

Jere, Harrington, 'Lusaka: local participation in planning and decision making', in *Low-Income Housing in the Developing World*, ed. Geoffrey Payne, New York: John Wiley and Sons, 1984, pp. 55–68.

Joglekar, M. N., 'Multi-institutional cooperation', *Architecture + Design*, January–February 1991, pp. 78–84.

— 'Indian guide for requirements of cluster planning', n.p., n.d.

Judge, Tony, 'The political and administrative setting', *Participation in Housing*, Working Paper 57, ed. Nabeel Hamdi and Robert Greenstreet, Oxford: Oxford Polytechnic Department of Town Planning, 1981, pp. 41–58.

Karande, Alka, 'City of Bombay, health scenario and child-to-child programme implementation', unpublished case-study, n.d.

Karwe, Irawati, *Kingship Organization in India*, Poona: Deccan College, 1953.

Khan, Akhter Hameed, *Orangi Pilot Project Programs*, Karachi: Orangi Pilot Project–RTI, 1994.

— *House Building by Low Income Families in Orangi*, Karachi: Orangi Pilot Project, 1990.

— *Orangi Pilot Project Programs*, Karachi: Orangi Pilot Project, 1991.

Khan, Hasan-Uddin, 'Tradition and modernity: on the development of an "authentic" domestic architecture', keynote address at the First World-Third World Symposium, University of California, Berkeley, October 1990.

Khosla, Romi, 'Technical Report, Citra Niaga, Samarinda, Indonesia', Aga Khan Award for Architecture, Geneva, 1989.

King, Anthony (ed.), *Buildings and Society: Essays on the Social Development of the Built Environment*, London: Routledge and Kegan Paul, 1980.

Kirke, John, 'The provision of infrastructure and utility services', in *Low-Income Housing in the Developing World*, ed. Geoffrey Payne, New York: John Wiley and Sons, 1984, pp. 233–48.

Koenigsberger, Otto, 'The interventions of housing policy alternatives, their development and impact in the Third World since the 1950s', paper presented at the International Symposium on Implications of a Support Policy for Housing Provision, 9–11 Dec. 1987, at the Development Planning Unit, University College London.

Krier, Leon, 'Developing the traditional city', *Design for High-Intensity Development*, proceedings of an international conference on urban design held in Kuala Lumpur, Cambridge, MA: Aga Khan Program for Islamic Architecture, 1986, pp. 1–9.

Kuhn, Thomas S., *The Structure of Scientific Revolutions*, Chicago: Chicago University Press, 1962, rept. 1970.

Kumar, Sanjay, 'Understanding urban housing transformations: case studies of Belapur, Bodela and Aranya, India', Aga Khan Summer Travel Grant report, 1991.

Large Housing Projects: Design, Technology and Logistics, proceedings of the 5th seminar in the series Designing in Islamic Cultures, Cambridge, MA.: The Aga Khan Program for Islamic Architecture, 1985.

Lari, Yasmeen, 'The Lines Area Resettlement Project, Karachi', *Urban Housing*, proceedings of the 2nd seminar in the series Designing in Islamic Cultures, Cambridge, MA: Aga Khan Program for Islamic Architecture, 1988, pp. 56–64.

Lawrence, Roderick, *Housing, Dwellings and Homes, Design Theory, Research and Practice*, Chichester, UK: John Wiley and Sons, 1987.

Lee, Bong Koo, 'Major urban development issues: an overview', *Urban Policy Issues*, Regional Seminar on Major National Policy Issues, Manila: Asian Development Bank, 1987, pp. 18–59.

Leonard, H. Jeffrey and Patti Petesch, 'The ecology of urban poverty', in *Cities*, Butterworth (Februrary, 1990), pp. 37–40.

Lerup, Lars, 'Building the Unfinished', *Architecture and Human Action*, 53, Sage Library of Social Research, 1977.

Lewcock, Ronald, 'Working with the past', proceedings of the conference Theories and Principles of Design in the Architecture of Islamic Societies, Cambridge, MA: Aga Khan Program for Islamic Architecture, 1988, pp. 87–96.

Lewin, A. C., *Housing Co-operatives in Developing Countries*, Chichester and New York: John Wiley and Sons, 1981.

Lim, William, *Cities for People: Reflections of a Southeast Asian Architect*, Singapore: Select Books, 1990.

— 'Public housing and community development', *Mimar*, 7 (January–March 1983), pp. 20–34.

Lloyd, Michael, 'Schools: the challenge of change', *The Architect as Enabler*, special issue of *Architecture and Competitions* (1985), pp. 80–3.

Lotus International, nos 33, 34 and 36, Venice: Gruppo Editoriale Electa, 1982.

Low Cost Sanitation Program of the Orangi Pilot Project – Statistical Data, Karachi: Orangi Pilot Project, November 1989.

Lynch, Kevin, *A Theory of Good City Form*, Cambridge, MA: MIT Press, 1981.

— *The Image of the City*, Cambridge, MA: MIT Press, 1979.

McCamant, K. and C. Durrett, 'Cohousing in Denmark', in *New Households New Housing*, ed. K. Franck and S. Ahrentzen, New York: Van Nostrand Reinhold, 1989, pp. 95–126.

McGill, M. E. and M. E. Hornton, *Action Research Designs For Training and Development*, Washington, DC: National Training and Development Press, 1973.

McLeod, Mary, 'Architecture or revolution: Taylorism, technocracy, and social change', *Art Journal*, 2 (1983), pp. 132–47.

Mangin, William, 'Latin American squatter settlements: a problem and a solution', *Latin American Research Review* (1967).

Mathur, Om Prakash, 'Urban services and the private sector: realities and issues', New Delhi, India: National Institute of Urban Affairs, 1989.

— and Caroline Moser, 'The urban informal sector: an agenda for future research', *Regional Development Dialogue*, 5: 2 (1984), pp. ix–xxi.

Mehta, Meera and Dinesh Mehta, 'Metropolitan housing markets: a case study of Ahmedabad', *Economic and Political Weekly* (October 1987), pp. 1701–9.

Mega-Cities Project, *Environmental Justice: Promising Solutions at the Intersection of Environment and Poverty*, case-study, New York, 1994.,

Mitra, Banashree, 'Delhi's unauthorized colonies', *Architecture + Design*, (January– February 1988), p. 30–4.

Mongold, Neil, 'Community architecture: myth and reality', master's thesis, MIT, 1988.

Montgomery, Roger, 'High density, low-rise housing and changes in the American housing economy', in *The Form of Housing*, ed. Sam Davis, New York: Van Nostrand Reinhold, 1977, pp. 83–112.

Moore, C., G. Allen and D. Lyndon, *The Place of Houses*, New York: Holt, Rinehart, Winston, 1984.

Moser, Caroline, 'Community participation in urban projects in the Third World', *Progress in Planning*, 32 (1989), pp. 71–133.

Moudon, Anne Vernez, *Built for Change: Neighborhood Architecture in San Francisco*, Cambridge, MA: MIT Press, 1986.

— (ed.), *Public Streets for Public Use*, New York: Van Nostrand Reinhold, 1987.

Mueller, W., 'Translation of user requirements into house designs: a multi-dimensional scaling analysis', *Journal of Environmental Psychology*, 1: 2 (1981), pp. 97–116.

Mulkh Raj, 'Housing to urban infrastructure finance in India: a review of corporate experience' (n.d.).

— and Kiran Wadhva, 'Distributional aspects of urban land in India', paper presented at the IASHS 19th World Congress, September 1991.

Mumford, Lewis, 'The Garden City idea and modern planning', in *Garden Cities of Tomorrow*, ed. F. J. Odsborn, London: Faber and Faber, 1965.

Mumtaz, Babar, 'The housing question and some answers', *Mimar*, 28 (June 1988), pp. 17–22.

Neamatalla, Mounir, Ragui Assaad, Linda Oldham, Amr Soueni and Fatma El Gohry, *Solid Waste Collection and Recycling in Cairo: a System in Transition*, Cairo: EQI, 1985.

Newman, Bernard, 'The apartment house', *Housing Problems in America*, Providence: Proceedings of the National Conference on Housing, 9–11 October 1916.

Newman, Oscar, *Community of Interest*, New York: Anchor Press, Doubleday, 1981.

— *Defensible Space: People and Design in the Violent City*, New York: Macmillan, 1972; London: Architectural Press, 1973.

Nientied, P. and J. Van der Linden, 'Approaches to low-income housing in the Third World', *International Journal of Urban and Regional Research*, 9: 3 (1985), pp. 311–29.

O'Connor, J., *The Fiscal Crisis of the State*, New York: St Martin's Press, 1973.

Orangi Pilot Project, 46th Quarterly Progress Report, Karachi: April–May–June, 1991.

Ozkan, Suha, 'The architecture of mass housing', in *The Architecture of Housing*, ed. Robert Powell, Geneva: Aga Khan Award for Architecture, 1990, pp. 120–30.

PADCO, *India: Public–Private Partnerships in Land Development*, US Agency for International Development, New Delhi, India, 1991.

— *Site and Unit Design Handbook*, Office of Housing and Urban Programs, Washington, DC, 1984.

Padmopranoto, Sugiarso, 'Indonesia country paper', *Urban Policy Issues*, Manila: Asian Development Bank, 1987.

Pakistan's Low Cost Housing Project Report, Manila: Asian Development Bank, 1989.

Pandya, Yatin, 'Slum houses as a user responsive product: a case study, Indore, India', M. Arch. thesis, McGill University, Montreal, 1988.

Pasteur, David, *The Management of Squatter Upgrading*, Westmead: Saxon House, 1979.

Payne, Geoffrey (ed.), *Low-Income Housing in the Developing World*, New York: John Wiley and Sons, 1984.

— *Urban Housing in the Third World*, London: Leonard Hill, 1977.

Peattie, Lisa, 'Anthropological perspective on the concepts of dualism, the informal sector and marginality in developing urban economies', *International Regional Science Review*, 5: 1 (1982), pp. 1–31.

— 'Some second thoughts on site-and-services', *Habitat International*, 6: 1/2 (1982), pp. 131–9.

Perlman, Janice, *The Myth of Marginality: Urban Poverty and Politics in Rio de Janeiro*, Berkeley: University of California Press, 1976.

— 'Global urbanization: challenges and opportunities', in *Urban Management: Policies and Innovations in Developing Countries*, ed. G. Shabbir Cheema, Wesport, CT: Praeger, 1993.

— 'A dual strategy for delibrate social change', *Cities*, Butterworth, February 1990, pp. 3–15.

— and Elwood Hopkins, 'From city to city', *Healthcare Forum Journal*, May–June 1994.

Peterson, George, 'Urban economy and productivity', *State of Urbanization in Asia and the Pacific*, Bangkok: UNESCAP, 1993.

Pherwani, M. J., 'The future prospects for housing finance in India', *Housing Finance International* (June 1991), pp. 31–7.

Pihlak, Madis (ed.), *The City of the 21st Century*, proceedings of the City of 21st Century Conference, Tempe: Arizona State University, Department of Planning, College of Architecture and Environmental Design, April 1988.

Pommer, Richard, 'The flat roof: a modernist controversy in Germany', *Art Journal*, 43 (1983), pp. 158–69.

Porter, William, 'Changing Perspectives on Residential Area Design', in *The Experience of the Guyana Program of Venezuela*, ed. L. Rodwin, Cambridge, MA: Joint Center for Urban Studies of MIT and Harvard University, 1969, pp. 252–69.

— 'Technology, form and culture in architecture: misconception and myth', *Architecture Education in the Islamic World*, Geneva: proceedings of the Aga Khan Award Seminar, 1986, pp. 49–59.

Powell, Robert (ed.), *The Architecture of Housing*, Geneva: Aga Khan Trust for Culture, 1990.

Prakash, Ved, *New Towns In India*, Durham, NC: Duke University Program in Comparative Studies on Southern Asia, 1969.

Prasad, Romila, Afzal Raza Khan and Vindhya Wasant Pandey, 'Role of women in improving environmental quality in slums', *Human Settlements for Sustainable Development*, New Delhi: Indian Environmental Society, 1992.

Pronk, Jan and Mahbub ul Haq, 'Sustainable development must be fair to all people and all resources', *Earth Summit Times*, 13 May 1992.

Prussin, Labelle, 'The conceptual environment', *Mimar*, 27 (1988), pp. 54–9.

Rabeneck, Andrew, David Sheppard and Peter Town, 'Housing flexibility/adaptability?', *Architectural Design*, 49 (February 1974), pp. 76–81.

Rahman, Perween and Hafeez Arain, *The Role of Thalla in Housing*, Karachi: Orangi Pilot Project, 1986.

Rainwater, Lee, *Behind Ghetto Walls: Black Families in a Federal Slum*, Chicago: Aldine, 1970.

Ralston, L., J. Anderson and E. Colson, 'Voluntary Efforts in Decentralized Management', working paper, Berkeley: University of California, Institute of International Studies, 1981.

Rapoport, Amos, *History and Precedent in Environmental Design*, New York: Plenum Press, 1990.

— 'The personal element in housing: an argument for open-ended design', *Royal Institute of British Architects Journal*, 75: 7, pp. 300–7.

Ravetz, Alison, 'Malaise, design and history: scholarship and experience on trial', in *Rehumanizing Housing*, ed. N. Teymur, T. Markus and T. Woolley, London: Butterworths, 1988, pp. 155–65.

Renaud, B., *National Urbanization Policy in Developing Countries*, New York: Oxford University Press, 1981.

Robertson, A. F., *People and the State*, Cambridge: Cambridge University Press, 1984.

Robertson, Jaquelin Taylor, 'The current crisis of disorder', in *The Public Face of Architecture*, ed. N. Glazer and M. Lilla. New York: Free Press, 1987, pp. 472–98,

Rodwin, L. and B. Sanyal, 'Shelter, settlement, and development: an overview', in *Shelter, Settlement, and Development*, ed. Lloyd Rodwin, United Nations Publication, Winchester, MA: Allen and Unwin, 1987, pp. 3–31.

Rondinelli, Dennis, *Secondary Cities in Developing Countries: Policies for Diffusing Urbanization*, Beverly Hills, California: Sage Publications, 1983.

— and John D. Kasarda, 'Privatization of urban services, shelter and infrastructure in developing countries: an overview of experience', Regional Seminar on Private Sector Initiatives in Urban Housing and Services in Asia and the Pacific, Bali: UNDP, 1992.

Roweis, Shoukry and Allen Scott, 'The urban land question', in *Urbanization and Urban Planning in Capitalist Society*, ed. Michael Dear and Allen Scott, New York: Methuen, 1981, pp. 123–158.

Rybczynski, Witold et al., *How the Other Half Builds*, Vols 1 and 2, Montreal: Center for Minimum Cost Housing, McGill University, Research Papers 9 and 10, 1984 and 1986.

Saarinen, Eliel, *The City: its Growth, its Decay, its Future*, New York: Reinhold Publishing, 1943.

Sabbour Associates, *Manshiet Nasser Upgrading: Final Report Part I and II: Urban Planning*, Cairo: Cairo Governate, 1982.

Saini, Balvant, 'Manandher's dilemma – architect or activist: a professional predicament', *Architecture and Design*, 4: 2 (1988).

Salas, Julian, 'An analysis of Latin American auto-construction: a plural and mass phenomenon', *Open House International*, 13: 4 (1988), pp. 2–11.

Sanoff, Henry, *Design Games: Playing for Keeps with Personal and Environmental Design*, Los Altos: William Kaufman, 1979.

— *Designing with Community Participation*, Hutchinson Ross, 1978.

Sanyal, Bishwapriya, 'Does development trickle up?', in *Korean Economic Development*, ed. Lim Gill-Chin, Urbana: Consortium on Development Studies, University of Illinois, 1988, pp. 63–76.

— 'The urban informal sector revisited', *Third World Planning Review*, 10: 1 (1988), pp. 64–82.

Schlandt, J., 'Economic and social aspects of council housing in Vienna between 1922 and 1934', trans. Sima Ingberman, *Oppositions*, 13 (Summer 1978) pp. 84–7.

Schoenauer, N., 'Early European collective habitation', in *New Household New Housing*, ed. K. Franck and S. Ahrentzen, New York: Van Nostrand Reinhold, 1989, pp. 47–70.

Schuman, Tony, 'The agony and the equity: a critique of self-help housing', in

Critical Perspectives on Housing, ed. Rachel Bratt, Chester Hartman and Ann Meyerson, Philadelphia: Temple University Press, 1986, pp. 463–473.

Searing, H., 'With red flags flying: housing in Amsterdam', *Art and Architecture in the Service of Politics*, Cambridge, MA: MIT Press, 1978.

Sen, G., 'Space: concept and meaning', *Mimar*, 27 (1988), pp. 60–3.

Serageldin, Ismail, 'Housing the poor: the role of the public sector', *Urban Housing*, proceedings of the 2nd seminar in the series Designing In Islamic Cultures, Cambridge, MA: Aga Khan Program for Islamic Architecture, 1982, pp. 74–84.

— *The Human Face of the Urban Environment*, report to the Development Community, Environmentally Sustainable Development Proceedings, Series no. 5, World Bank, 1995.

— *Nurturing Development*, World Bank, 1995

Serageldin, Mona and Francois Vigier, 'Changing roles and procedures in the design of public buildings', *Architecture and Community*, New York: Aperture Books, 1983, pp. 46–52.

Shafi, Syed, 'New towns the answer to urban congestion – future pattern of growth for communities', *The Statesman*, Calcutta, 22 September 1964, p. 6.

Shah, Kirtee, 'People participating in housing action: meaning, scope and strategy', in *Low-Income Housing in the Developing World*, ed. G. Payne, New York: John Wiley and Sons, 1984, pp. 199–208.

Siddiqui, Tasneem, 'Innovation and success in sheltering the urban poor', in *The Architecture of Housing*, ed. Robert Powell, Geneva: Aga Khan Award for Architecture, 1990, pp. 74–81.

Silverman, Jerry M., 'Technical assistance and aid agency staff – alternative techniques for greater effectiveness', *Technical Paper* 28, Washington, DC: World Bank, 1984.

Singh, A. M. and A. Kellas-Viitaren, *Invisible Hands: Women in Home Based Productions*, Sage Publications, 1987.

Sivaramakrishnan, K. C., 'Regional review of the urban policy issues – Asia', New York: UNDP, 1990.

Sopchokchai, Orapin, 'Magic eyes: environmental awareness in Bangkok', case-study produced by the Mega-Cities Project and the Thailand Development Research Institute, 1990.

Spence, R. and D. J. Cook, *Building Materials in Developing Countries*, New York: John Wiley and Sons, 1983.

Stedman Jones, Gareth, *Outcast London*, Oxford: Clarendon Press, 1981,

Stein, C. S., *Towards New Towns for America*, New York: Van Nostrand Reinhold, 1957.

Stern, Robert, 'La ville bourgeoisie', *Architectural Design*, 51: 10/11 (1981), pp. 4–12.

Stewart, W. F. R., *Children in Flats: a Family Study*, London: National Society for the Prevention of Cruelty to Children, 1970.

Strassmann W. P., *The Transformation of Urban Housing*, World Bank Research Publication, Baltimore, MD: Johns Hopkins University Press, 1982.

Stretton, Hugh, *Urban Planning in Rich and Poor Countries*, Oxford: Oxford University Press, 1978.

Tafuri, M. and F. Dal Co, *Modern Architecture*, trans. Robert Erich Wolf, New York: Harry N. Abrams, 1979.

Tay Kheng Soon, 'Cheras and Setapak Jaya: Two experimental housing projects in Kuala Lumpur', *Large Housing Projects*, Design, Technology, and Logistics, Proceedings of the 5th seminar in the series Designing In Islamic Cultures, Cambridge, MA: Aga Khan Program for Islamic Architecture, 1985, pp. 12–20.

— *Mega-Cities in the Tropics: Towards an Architectural Agenda for the Future*, Singapore: Institute of Southeast Asian Studies, 1989.

Taylor, Brian Brace, 'Rethinking colonial architecture', *Mimar*, 13 (1984), pp. 16–25.

— 'Step by step: enabling Pakistan's urban poor to build', *Mimar*, 35 (June 1990), pp. 47–52.

Teicher, Jonathan L., 'Enabling housing', master's thesis, MIT, 1989.

Teymur, Necdet, Thomas Markus and Tom Woolley (eds), *Rehumanizing Housing*, London: Butterworth, 1988.

Turner, Bertha (ed.), *Building Community: a Third World Case Book*, Habitat International Coalition, London: Building Community Books, 1988.

— and Andrew Maskrey, 'Women's construction collective', in *Building Community*, ed. Bertha Turner, London: Building Community Books, 1988, pp. 162–6.

Turner, John, *Housing by People: Towards Autonomy in Building Environments*, London: Marion Boyars, 1976.

— Introduction, *Building Community: a Third World Case Book*, ed. Bertha Turner, Habitat International Coalition, London: Building Community Books, 1988, pp. 13–15.

— 'Barriers and channels for housing development in modernizing countries', *American Institute of Planners Journal*, 33: 3 (May 1967).

— and R. Fichter, *Freedom to Build*, New York: Macmillan, 1972.

Unger, D. G. and A. Wandersman, 'The importance of neighboring: the social, cognitive and affective aspects of neighboring', *American Journal of Community Psychology*, 13 (1985), pp. 138–69.

Ungers, Matthias, 'The Vienna superblocks', trans. Sima Ingberman, *Oppositions*, 13 (Summer 1978), p. 83.

United Nations, *World Urbanization Prospects*, New York: UN, 1993.

United Nations Centre for Human Settlements, *Pressure on the Supply of Land for the Poor*, Nairobi: UNCHS, 1984.

— *Report of Habitat: United Nations Conference on Human Settlements*, E. 76. IV. 7, Vancouver: UNCHS, 1976.

— Global Report on Human Settlements, Nairobi, 1988.

— *On the Road to Istanbul*, Signpost no. 1, December 1994.

United Nations Development Programme, *Cities, People and Poverty: Urban Development Cooperation for the 1990s*, New York: UNDP, 1991.

— *The Urban Environment in Developing Countries*, New York: UNDP, 1992.

— *Human Development Report 1990*, New York: Oxford University Press, 1990.

— *Human Development Report 1992*, New York: Oxford University Press, 1992.

— *Human Development Report 1993*, New York: Oxford University Press, 1993.

— *Human Development Report 1994*, New York: Oxford University Press, 1994.

— *Proceedings of the International Colloquium of Mayors on Social Development*, New York, 1994.

— 'Public/private partnerships in expanding access to housing finance', project document prepared for the Regional Bureau for Asia and the Pacific, 1990.

Urban Housing, proceedings of the 2nd seminar in the series Designing in Islamic Cultures, Cambridge, MA: Aga Khan Program for Islamic Architecture, 1982.

Van der Linden, Jan J., *Successful Supply of Plots for the Poor: the Case of Hyderabad*, Urban Research Working Papers, Amsterdam: Free University, 1989.

— E. Meijer and P. Nientied, 'Informal housing in Karachi', *Habitat International Journal*, 9: 3/4 (1985).

Vastu Shilpa Foundation for Studies and Research in Environmental Design, *Aranya: an Approach to Settlement Design, Planning and Design of Low-Cost Housing Project at Indore*, New Delhi: HUDCO, 1990.

— *Residential Open Spaces: A Behavioural Analysis*, Ahmedabad, 1988.

— *Report on Low-Cost Housing Township at Indore*, Indore: Indore Development Authority, 1983.

Venturi, Robert, *Complexity and Contradiction in Architecture*, New York: Museum of Modern Art, 1966.

Vigier, Francois, *Housing in Tunis*, Cambridge, MA: Aga Khan Program for Islamic Architecture, 1987.

Walter, Eugene V., *Placeways*, Chapel Hill: University of North Carolina Press, 1988.

Ward, Colin, 'Community architecture: what a time it took for the penny to drop', *Built Environment*, 13: 1 (1987), pp. 22–32.

— *Housing, an Anarchist Approach*, London: Freedom Press, 1983.

— 'Self-help and mutual aid in housing: the development of an ideal', in *Participation in Housing*, ed. Nabeel Hamdi and Robert Greenstreet, Working Paper 57, Oxford: Oxford Polytechnic Department of Town Planning, 1981, pp. 1–15.

Ward, Peter (ed.), *Self-help Housing: a Critique*, London: Mansell, 1982.

— and Chris Macoloo, 'Articulation theory and self-help housing practice in the 1990s', *International Journal of Urban and Regional Affairs*, 16: 1 (1992), pp. 60–80.

Waris Husain, H. A., *Establishment of Pavement Traders (Informal Sector in Samarinda City)*, Samarinda, Indonesia, n.d.

Watt, Kenneth et al., *The Unsteady State: Environmental Problems, Growth and Culture*, Honolulu: East West Center, 1977.

Webber, M. M. (ed.), *Explorations into Urban Structure*, Philadelphia: University of Pennsylvania Press, 1964.

Weeks, Dudley, 'Learning alternative futures: the dominanat conceptual, behavioural, and structural patterns of contemporary human society and the design of polsocioeconomics alternatives', doctoral dissertation, University of Hawaii, 1976.

Wiesinger, Rita, 'Housing the Third World's poor', *International Journal for Housing Science and its Applications*, 8: 4 (1984), pp. 349–60.

Wooley, Thomas A., *Community Architecture: an Evaluation of the Case for User Participation in Architectural Design*, Ph.D. dissertation, Department of Architecture, Oxford Polytechnic, 1985.

World Bank, *World Development Report 1992: Development and the Environment*, New York: Oxford University Press, 1992.

— *Urban Policy and Economic Development: an Agenda for the 1990s*, Urban Development Division, Infrastructure and Urban Development Department, February 1991.

Wright, Gwendolyn, *Building the Dream: A Social History of Housing in America*, Cambridge, MA: MIT Press, 1983.

Yeang, Ken, *The Tropical Veranda City*, Malaysia: Longman, 1987.

Yeung, Yue-man, 'Provision of basic urban services in Asia: the role of people-based mechanisms', paper presented to the Expert Group Meeting on Policy Issues in Urban Services for the Poor, Nagoya, Japan, 13–17 August 1985.

Young, Michael and Peter Willmott, *Family and Kinship in East London*, London: Routledge and Kegan Paul, 1957; rept. 1986.

Zetter, Roger, 'Land issues in low-income housing', in *Low-Income Housing in the Developing World*, ed. G. Payne. New York: John Wiley and Sons, 1984. pp. 221–31.

Index

Abidi, Aga Hasan, 43, 143
Abrams, Charles, 11
accountability, 154
Aga Khan Foundation, 43
Aga Khan Medical University, 49
Aga Khan Rural Support Programme, 43
Ahmedabad Urban Development Authority, 28
aid: bilateral agencies, 150; international, 15
AIDS, 15
Akbar, Jamel, 156
Angel, Shlomo, 31
Animal Health Project, Cairo, 73
Aranya township, India, 39, 112–15, 117, 119, 121–2, 124–8, 130–7, 142, 151, 153–5, 159–62, 164, 166
architects, 8, 98, 155
architectural design, 123
asbestos, 55
Asian Development Bank, 28, 41, 60, 110
Association for the Care of Garbage Collectors, *see* Zabbaleen Gameya
Association for the Protection of the Environment, Egypt, 69, 151–2
Athavlay, P. S., 119

Balochis, 41
Bangkok, land-sharing agreements, 90
Bangladesh, creation, 40–1
Bank of Credit and Commercial International (BCCI), 43, 143
batten-and-tile roofing, 55–6, 58–9
behaviour patterns, and physical space, 39
Benjamin, Solomon, 31
Bertaud Model, 13
Bertaud, Alain, 12
Bertaud, Marie-Agnes, 12
Bhatt, M. L., 124, 127–8, 164
Biharis, 41
block committees, 103

block-making, mechanized, 53–4, 56–8
Bombay, 24, 84, 111, 128, 140; –Dehli National Highway, 112, 114; Municipal Corporation, 174; slum communities, 25
Boston, USA: Fanniul Hall Marketplace, 97; urban planning, 38
bricks, 147
building industry, 10; mason training, 57–8, 64; waterproofing, 55
building materials, 52, 55–6, 58, 60; industry, 10; local, 63; manufacture, 51; recycling, 90
bureaucracies, 6, 27, 33
Burgess, Rod, 31

Cairo, 65, 174, 176; municipal dump, 71; municipality, 144; solid waste crisis, 68; waste collection, 66–9, 73–4, 77–8, 84–5
Cairo Cleaning and Beautification Authority (CCBA), 65–6, 80
Caminos, Horacio, 12, 115
capital, flows, 5
Castells, Manuel, 135, 172
Catholic Relief Services, Egypt, 73
central planning, 18
centrally planned economies, breakdown, 6
Centre for Minimum Cost Housing, McGill University, 122
cesspools, 61
Chao Praya River, pollution, 24
'child-friendly environments', 36
Child-to-Child Health Programme, Bombay, 24–5
children, 160; health, 45; labour force, 23–4, project, 96
Citra Niaga Urban Development Project, Indonesia, 38, 88, 91, 94, 98–9, 110–11, 142–4, 146, 151–5, 165, 181; shopping centre, 93
client groups, 159
cluster planning, 154–6

'co-housing', 36
commercial spaces, 135
communes, religious, 37
community management, 155
community organization, formation, 89
community participation/involvement,
     7, 30, 34–5, 82, 164, 167–8;
     advantages, 32; constraints, 33;
concrete: curing, 53; footings, 54; pre-
     casting, 121; reinforced, 52, 58
construction standards, 149
cooking, 23
Coptic Orthodox Church, 68–9, 77
corruption, 103–4
cost recovery, 107
courtyards, 115–16, 134–6
credit groups, Egypt, 72
crime, 8, 92, 94
cross-subsidy, 120

Dakhla, Egypt, 66
dalals (land middlemen, Pakistan), 42,
     101–2, 108, 144, 149, 151
Danish collective housing model, 36
Davies, Robert, 172
debt crisis, 5–6
decentralization, 18, 26
decision-making, limits to national, 15
deference, traditions of, 35
deforestation, 92
Delhi, 128
demography, trends, 2, 36
designers, urban, 168
developers; private, 110–11, 145, 147,
     149, 180; illegally occupied land, 87;
     time pressure, 159
development agencies, 8
development programmes, urban, 22,
     27; human-centred, 17
diarrhoea, 48
disabled people, 22; building codes, 25;
     ramps, 26
Dispensary of the Order of St Mary, 77
donkey carts, 56
Doshi, B. V., 112–13, 115, 121, 134–5,
     153
drainage, 26; secondary drains, 47–8
'dynamic steady state', 1
dysentery, 48

economic recession, world, 14
'economical weaker sector' (EWS), 134;
     areas, 125; groups, 121; house plans,
     135; housing, 112–13, 116, 118–19;
     land plots, 117, 120, 128, 134
Egypt, government, 69–70
elderly people, 22, 25–6, 36–7, 159–60
electricity: cables, 125; illegal con-
     nections, 132
elites, 5; attitudes to poor, 31
empowerment: community, 17–18
Environmental Protection Company,
     Cairo, 74
Environmental Quality International
     (EQI), 67–9, 74, 81–2; 151–2
epidemics, 3
equity, 141; conceptualization, 20;
     development strategies, 21
European Community, 75
export development model, 15

families: changing life-styles, 36–7, 159
fertilizer, from organic waste, 75
Ford Foundation, 68–9, 71–2, 75
fossil fuels, 3
fundamentalists, religious, 60

Gindy, Ezzet Naim, 76
Girgis, Yacoub, 72
Goethert, Reinhard, 12
government role, 180, 182; in Asia, 27
Grameen Bank, Bangladesh, 23
'grassroots', 11
grazing encroachment, 119
grid plans, 105
Gulshan-e-Shahbaz, Pakistan, 100, 107

Habitat I Conference, 14
Habitat II, 'The World City Summit',
     14
Haq, Mahbub ul, 141
Hasan, Arif, 11, 42, 60, 110
haudi (septic tank), 47–8
health visitors, 77
Home Ownership Opportunity
     Program, USA, 38
Hong Kong, housing, 9
hopelessness, 5
hospitals, 107
House Building Finance Corporation,
     India, 103, 105

house ownership, 19
households, female headed, 35
houses, ventilation, 54–5, 58–9
Housing and Urban Development Corporation, India, 28–9, 113–14, 138
Housing Development Finance Corporation (HDFC), India, 10
housing: allocation processes, 123, 126, 138, 161–4; design, 34, 121; finance, 10; ownership patterns, 127; private construction, 29; target group incomes, 35
Hyderabad, 104, 106; municipal corporation, 62
Hyderabad Development Authority (HDA), 100–10, 144, 149, 152, 154
hygiene, 75, 78

Ibrahim, Saad Eddin, 8
identity cards, 102
illegal subdivisions, 108
incinerators, 175
incomes: distribution, 18; urban, 3
income groups, mixing, 164–5
incremental development schemes, 107–9
India, 9–10, 28–9, 37
Indonesia, 10, 26; timber exports, 92
Indore Development Authority (IDA), 112, 117, 122–7, 129–30, 132–3, 137–8, 152, 163
inequity, 179; global resources, 20
informal sector, 3, 29, 40, 92, 95, 118, 146
infrastructure, urban, 12
innovation transfers, urban, 170–3, 175
Institute for Development Studies, Samarinda, 93, 151
inter-city coordination, 178
Ismael, Antonio, 93, 152
Ismailabad, Pakistan, 100

Japan, 38
jhuggis (shacks), 52
Jombang, East Java, 98

Kamel, Leila, 152
Kampung Improvement Programme, Jakarta, 7, 93

Karachi, 41, 48, 50, 60–1, 106, 140, 176; Development Authority, 45, 143; growth, 40; –Hyderabad highway, 100; Municipal Corporation, 63, 175
katchi abadi (illegal subdivison/ISD), 40–1, 45, 48, 60–1, 101
Katchi Abadi Improvement and Regularization Program, 41, 60
Khan, Akhter Hameed, 42–3, 143, 152
Kharga Oases, Egypt, 66
Khuda-ki-basti (Settlement of God), Pakistan, 100; Incremental Development Scheme, 39, 88, 101–4, 106–10, 142–5, 149, 151–4, 157–8, 160, 166
kindergartens, 130
kiosks, 91, 93, 95–6
kitchen gardening, 23

Lahore Development Authority (LDA), 60
land: development, 38; illegally occupied, 87; informal ownership, 7, 88, 90, 109; informal supply, 88; management, 2; market, 7; ownership regulation, 4; 'readjustment ventures', 38; speculation, 128; tenure, 70; titles, 103
land-sharing, 16, 38, 88, 97–8, 111; negotiation, 89–90; success rates, 91
land-use plans, 166
landscaping, 23
lane organization, 157
Lima, Peru, 11
Linden, Jan Van der, 108, 110
'linear cluster' model, 115–16
Lines Area project, Karachi, 90
lintels, 56; design, 54; pre-cast, 53
littering, 174
'local enablements', 11
local government, 27–8
looting, 140
Los Angeles, 140
low-income settlements, 13; development projects, 156

Madhya Pradesh Electricity Board (MPEB), 125
Madhya Pradesh Housing Board (MPHB), 112

'Magic Eyes' campaign, Bangkok, 24, 174
Mahakam River, 92
malaria, 48
management, urban, 16
Mangin, William, 11
manholes, 46–7, 116, 118, 125
Manila, 84, 174; Transfer Task Force, 176
Massachusetts Housing Partnership, 38
Maternal Health Care Programme, Cairo, 76
McGill University, 122
mega-cities, 170
Mega-Cities Project, 84, 172, 176
Metro-Manila, 175
middlemen, land, 102, 109
migrants, 36; migration patterns, 2
minibus services, Asia, 29
Misr Service, 80
Mohajirs, 41, 104
Moqattam settlement, Cairo, 65–7, 69–76, 81, 84
mortality rates, 49; infant, 59
municipalities: finance, 2; institutional weakness, 4; role, 21
munshi (accountant), 56
muspidah (local authority), 94

Nagar, Arjun Singh, 129
Narmada River canal, 133
National Housing Authority, Thailand, 90
National Housing Bank (NHB), India, 10, 29, 132
Neamatalla, Mounir, 152
New Delhi region, 26
non-governmental organizations (NGOs), 12, 19, 21, 27, 29, 33, 38, 40, 61–5, 68, 70, 94, 97–8, 110–11, 142, 144, 150, 154, 162–3, 167–8, 174, 177–80, 183; competition for funds, 18; overdependency, 181
nullah (creeks), 46–7

O'Connor, James, 31
open markets, 120
open spaces, 134, 156
Orangi, Karachi, 40, 87, 107, 146, 153, 155, 157, 160, 163–4

Orangi Pilot Project (OPP), 39–41, 43, 52–6, 59, 62, 64, 132, 142–4, 147–8, 150–1, 154, 158, 175–6, 181; health and family planning programme, 49; housing programme, 52, 57–8; lane organization, 46; Low Cost Sanitation Programme, 60–1; sanitation programme, 42, 44, 48; Women Work Centres, 50, 51
Order of St Mary's Dispensary, 76
Order of the Daughters of St Mary, Cairo, 77
Oxfam, 71, 73

paper recycling, 75–6
Parikh, Himanshu, 123
Parshwanath Group, India, 28
partnerships, public–private, 8
Pathan migrants, 41
patronage, brokers, 103
pavement traders (*Kaki lima*), 91–3, 95–6
Peattie, Lisa, 11
pedestrian networks/systems, 117, 118, 165–6
peer-to-peer exchange, 181–2
peripheral locations, urban, 13
Perlman, Janice, 11, 170
pigpens, 79–80
planners, urban, 4–5, 9, 168, 177–8, 181
plastic-granulating machines, 71, 76, 79
play areas, 117–18
plaza performances, 98
plots of land: sizes, 160, 163; titles, 99–101
pollution, 16; air, 3
population growth, urban, 1–4
Port Authority, Thailand, 90
postal services, lack, 131
poverty, 3, 6
pre-casting, 121
private sector, 150, 180
privatization, 28; opposition to, 29–30
product champions, 152, 172
productivity, urban, 2
Pronk, Jan, 141
property values, 87
prostitution, 92, 94
'provider' approach, 7
PT Grivantara Architects, 93; PT. AFDOL, 99

public sector management, 4
public spaces, 166
public transport, 13, 99, 104; cost
   recovery rates, 26
Punjabi migrants, 41

rags, recycling, 71
Rao, Shanker, 133
'reception areas', 101, 108
Republic of Korea, 10, 38; housing, 9
Rio de Janeiro, 140
riots, 140
roofing, 52–3, 58–9, 148; design, 55;
   reinforced concrete, 56
rug weaving, 75–6
Rybczynski, Witold, 163

Samarinda Development Authority,
   Borneo, 92, 144, 146
Samuel, Bishop, 68, 152
San Francisco, urban planning, 38
sanitation, 3, 61–3, 78
Sanyal, Bishwapriya, 11–12
Sasono, Adi, 93
scabies, 48
School of Architecture and Planning,
   India, 115
schools, 117, 131
screeding, 55
'self-build', 116, 121
Self-Employed Women's Association,
   Ahmedabad, 23
'self-help', 7, 11, 13, 19, 22, 42; housing,
   31; projects, 35
Serageldin, Ismail, 15
sewage disposal, 4, 99, 106, 115, 133,
   147, 158; lines, 63; pipe diameter,
   47; underground, 59
shop-houses, 95–6
shopping centres, 97
Siddiqui, Tasneem, 152
Sikanderabad, squatter settlement, 100
Sind Industrial and Trading Estate
   (SITE), 100
Sind Regional Transport Corporation,
   104
Sindhis, 41, 104
Singapore, housing, 9–10
single parents, 36–37
'site-and services' developments, 6, 8,

12–13, 16, 19, 35, 38–9, 99, 105,
   108, 110, 112, 121, 133, 136, 156,
   169; problems, 14
site-planning practices, 165
slums, 14, 27, 29, 92; 'clearance' projects, 8; improvement projects, 129;
   transformation, 97; upgrading, 6
Small Industries Project, Cairo, 71–2, 79
small-scale enterprises, 83
soakpits, 44, 106; one chamber, 158
social justice, 14
Soeur Emmanuelle Fund, 71, 74–5
solid waste, 65; management, 26;
   recycling, 16
speculators, 127
squatters, 38, 87–8, 92, 97–8, 142;
   settlements, 3, 7, 11, 14, 19, 27, 29,
   31, 41, 99–100 115, 133, 143, 169
staircases, 135–6, 148; design, 54
State Housing Assistance for Rental
   Production Program, 38
state, role of, 8
structural adjustment programmes, 5–6,
   28, 183
Sukkur, Pakistan, 61
Sumarijanto, Michael, 93
supermarket type project, 92–3
'support' approach, 8
sustainability, 15, 141; ecolgical, 5
Swiss Development Corporation, 43

Taiwan, 38
Taylor, Brian Brace, 110
technology transfer, 15
textiles: factories, 130; stitchers, 50–1,
   95
Thai Environmental and Community
   Development Association, 24
Thaliand, 128
thalla (building material yard), 51, 53–4,
   56, 60, 147–8
thallawalas, (building suppliers), 42,
   57–8, 60, 64, 147–8, role, 51
title deeds, 102
trade patterns, 15
tree planting, 119
'trickle-down' theories, 6, 9
trucks, 74
Turner, Bertha, 11
Turner, John, 30–1

typhoid, 48

'unauthorized colonies', 87–8
United Nations, 1–2; Conference on
   Environment and Development
   (UNCED), 19, 140–1; Development
   Programme, 171; UNDP-LIFE
   Programme, 174, 176; UNICEF, 24,
   43; Urban Basic Services Programme, 61
United States, public housing, 8
urban development, private sector
   involvement, 28
urban planners, 1, 61, 141
urban policies, developing world, 21
urban services, imbalance, 26
urbanization, 3; rapid, 169
'user' approach, 12

vaccines, 77
Vatsu Shilpa Foundation for Environmental Design (VSF), 112–14,
   118–20, 122–5, 135, 138
vehicles: speed, 118; systems for, 165–6
Vieux Carré, New Orleans, 166

waderas (feudal landlords), 103
Wadie, Samia, 76
wages, urban, 2
Wahi people, 65–6, 74, 85
waste: collection, 74, 158; management,
   3; recycling, 4, 78–9, 83, 86, 174

water supply, 48, 78, 99, 106, 115,
   132–3; contamination, 3; cost
   recovery rates, 26; drinking, 59
Watt, Kenneth E. F., 1, 20
Weeks, Dudley, 20
William, Sawsan, 77
women: Egyptian low-income, 72;
   empowerment of poor, 80; house-
   hold heads, 35; labour force, 22
Women Headed Household Project,
   Cairo, 72
Women's Construction Collective,
   Jamaica, 23
World Bank, 12, 28, 41, 60, 108, 110,
   113, 129, 153; Shelter Project, 62;
   International Development
   Association, 69–70

Zabbaleen people, 65, 68, 70, 72, 75–6,
   81, 86, 143, 152, 174; livelihood, 66;
   informal information system, 85;
   women, 77
Zabbaleen Environmental and
   Development Project, 39, 65, 67, 69,
   72, 76–80, 82–5, 142, 144, 146, 176;
   dependency creation, 82; uneven
   distribution of benefit, 83;
Zabbaleen Gameya/Association of
   Garbage Collectors, 68–9, 71, 73–4,
   79, 151
Zamalek, Cairo, 80